The Biblical Seminar

24

THE OLD TESTAMENT
IN FICTION AND FILM

THE OLD TESTAMENT IN FICTION AND FILM

ON REVERSING THE HERMENEUTICAL FLOW

LARRY J. KREITZER

Sheffield Academic Press

PN
56
.B5
K7340
1994

Published by Sheffield Academic Press Ltd
Mansion House
19 Kingfield Road
Sheffield, S11 9AS
England

Typeset by Sheffield Academic Press
and
Printed on acid-free paper in Great Britain
by Cromwell Press
Melksham, Wiltshire

British Library Cataloguing in Publication Data

A catalogue record for this book is available
from the British Library

ISBN 1-85075-487-X

CONTENTS

Larry Kreitzer's previous volume, *The New Testament in Fiction and Film* (1993), opened up unmapped interdisciplinary territory. Theology, literature and film-studies were Dr Kreitzer's chosen fields, his aim being to demonstrate that 'standard works of modern fiction' dealing with biblical passages and themes, and the films, mini-series and even children's cartoons based on them, are eminently capable of 'reversing the hermeneutical flow'—that is, helping us to appreciate the truths of Scripture more fully in the light of their reworkings at the hands of authors, screenwriters, cinema directors and producers. This companion volume offers material for a fresh set of interpretative seminars, this time tracing the imaginative projection of texts and themes drawn from the Old Testament.

Like all academic critics of film, Larry Kreitzer confesses himself addicted to the cinema. He makes no apology for starting his first chapter among the big-budget biblical epics of the 1950s and 60s, a wide-angle technicolor world whose images seem as stylized as those of a Veronese canvas. Cecil B. De Mille's *The Ten Commandments* (1956), with its resonant dialogue and glitteringly literal-minded miracles, is perhaps only the best-known of the cohort of blockbusters Kreitzer roll-calls, but as he points out (how effortlessly popular culture performs its hermeneutics!) most of us find it hard to visualize the parting of the Red Sea without recalling De Mille's image of a thousand extras and two 'harmless Niagaras'. Kreitzer's study is full of insights like this, for he delights in showing that what Hollywood thieves from theology (Indiana Jones's quest for the Lost Ark) or literature (the debt of *Jaws* to Melville's—or Huston's—*Moby-Dick*) it restores refreshed to the common myth-kitty. Not that *The Old Testament in Fiction and Film* is exclusively concerned with high-profile cinema: there is an extended critical summary of Krzysztof Kieslowski's sequence of television films *Decalogue* (1990), where the Ten Commandments which have under-pinned corporate morality for six thousand years (routinely transgressed, routinely ignored) provide a refuge for the lives of quiet desperation in a Warsaw tower block during the crisis of Communism.

The central section of Kreitzer's book concentrates on some of the most mythologically potent works of modern literature. The (whale-sized) chapter on *Moby-Dick* invites us to 'dive deep' for all the dualisms which Melville's novel contains, linking the White Whale with the two inscrutable sea-beasts of Jon. 1.17 and Job 41. Mary Shelley's *Frankenstein*, perhaps the most potent modern fable of creation, is shown to be a refraction of Genesis via Milton, while John Steinbeck's *East of Eden* emerges as a midrash of the Cain and Abel story in the American frontier cult: a study of guilt, brutality, free will and heroic resentment carried down the generations and from sea to shining sea. All three works have been the subject of multiple film treatments (in the case of *Frankenstein* of over two hundred of them), and Kreitzer is able to use these productions to shed fresh light on their various sustaining myths. Hollywood has granted *Moby-Dick* its share of happy endings (kill the fish, get the girl). Incongruous, certainly, but no less challengingly incongruous, in Kreitzer's view, than the unexpected endorsement of divine providence in the epilogue to Melville's base text, the book of Job. Elia Kazan's film of *East of Eden* (1955) unleashed the young James Dean: a Cain-like archetype of fatality, frustration and remorse. And film-makers continue to expand the *Frankenstein* myth, very often in feminist directions. Rather as the Priestly source of Genesis insists that 'male and female created he them', so screenwriters refuse to subordinate woman-monster to her mate: James Whale's *The Bride of Frankenstein* (1935) gives the Bride a kind of moral and aesthetic priority (she finds Karloff brutal and ugly); while *Frankenstein Created Woman* (1966), one of the later offerings from the House of Hammer, combines two dead lovers in a single (female) body.

Kreitzer spins his most complex 'intertextual web' in the book's final chapter, which juxtaposes the fatalism of Qoheleth with what seems the somewhat adolescent nihilism of Hemingway's *A Farewell to Arms*. Kreitzer finds similarities between the attempts of recent commentators to brighten up Qoheleth's message, and the efforts of the screenwriters for the 1932 and 1957 films of the Hemingway novel to let a little sunshine in on Catherine Barclay's death—as, it seems, the author did himself in an earlier manuscript ending. At first glance both Qoheleth and Hemingway may take a grim view of mortality; yet at a deeper level, Kreitzer demonstrates, they are optimists in spite of themselves, rejoicing in the certainty of death partly because it yields life such sumptuous meaning, that though there may be no 'Farewell to Arms', no 'discharge' in life's war, the boots of one's comrades make comforting music on the march to the grave.

Larry Kreitzer is more anxious than he needs to be that his efforts will expose him to devastating raids from the disciplines whose frontiers he crosses; his work combines appreciation of and deference towards his predecessors in all three fields with a rigorous determination to put their insights to constructive use, and a sly talent for turning over the profitable details of their researches (his footnotes are a delight). Too modestly Kreitzer refers to the 'playfulness' with which he has built and stocked his treasure house. *The Old Testament in Fiction and Film* was probably fun to research and write: it is certainly fun to read. But it is also a work of weight and value: not least because it provides a blueprint for similar discussions the readers may wish to initiate themselves, as they ponder the way in which the Scriptures continue to supply synopses, sub-texts and (surprisingly often) moral authority for the films and books of our fallen world.

Julian Thompson
Hertford College, Oxford
Summer 1994

ABBREVIATIONS

AB	Anchor Bible
AL	*American Literature*
AQ	*American Quarterly*
Bib	*Biblica*
BJRL	*Bulletin of the John Rylands Library*
BLS	Bible and Literature Series
BSS	Biblical Seminar Series
CBQ	*Catholic Biblical Quarterly*
CW	*Catholic World*
CWCPS	Contemporary Writers in Christian Perspective Series
DR	*Dalhousie Review*
EC	Epworth Commentaries
EIC	*Essays in Criticism*
ELH	*English Literary History*
Exp	*The Explicator*
ExpTim	*Expository Times*
HistRel	*History of Religions*
HR	*Hemingway Review*
HSL	*Hartford Studies in Literature*
HTR	*Harvard Theological Review*
HUCA	*Hebrew Union College Annual*
IC	Interpretation Commentary
ICC	International Critical Commentary
IDB	G. A. Buttrick (ed.), *Interpreter's Dictionary of the Bible*
Int	*Interpretation*
IR	*Iliff Review*
JBL	*Journal of Biblical Literature*
JPC	*Journal of Popular Culture*
JSL	*Journal of the School of Languages*
JSOT	*Journal for the Study of the Old Testament*
JSOTSup	*Journal for the Study of the Old Testament*, Supplement Series
JSS	*Journal of Semitic Studies*
K-SJ	*Keats-Shelley Journal*
LCL	Loeb Classical Library
LFQ	*Literature and Film Quarterly*
MFS	*Modern Fiction Studies*

NCB	New Century Bible
NCL	Nineteenth-Century Literature
NEB	New English Bible
NEQ	*New English Quarterly*
NCF	*Nineteenth-Century Fiction*
NLH	*New Literary History*
OTG	Old Testament Guides
OTL	Old Testament Library
PMLA	*Proceedings of the Modern Language Association*
RES	*Review of English Studies*
SAQ	*South Atlantic Quarterly*
SQ	*Steinbeck Quarterly*
SR	*Sewanee Review*
StudRom	*Studies in Romanticism*
TSLL	*Texas Studies in Literature and Language*
VT	*Vetus Testamentum*
WBC	Word Biblical Commentary
WTJ	*Westminster Theological Journal*
ZAW	*Zeitschrift für die alttestamentliche Wissenschaft*

INTRODUCTION

Within the essays contained in this book I would like to continue an experiment in the hermeneutical task which I began in *The New Testament in Fiction and Film* (1993). In the Introduction to that volume I defined the attempt as one in which

> the aim is to reverse the flow of influence within the hermeneutical process and examine select NT passages or themes in light of some of the enduring expressions of our own culture, namely great literary works and their film adaptations.[1]

This book is intended as a companion to that earlier effort, only this time it deals with some Old Testament passages and themes. Nevertheless, the intention remains the same even if the particular subject matter is slightly different. The suggestion is that by examining more closely how modern literature deals with the Old Testament we can often discover something fresh and new about the Scriptures themselves. At the same time, by noting how cinematic versions of those works of literature interpret the texts upon which they are based, we can watch the hermeneutical process in action and also gain valuable insight into the Old Testament texts. For this reason I have once again deliberately chosen standard works of modern fiction which not only build upon biblical passages or ideas, but which also have enjoyed cinematic expression as one of their avenues of popular awareness.

1. *The Old Testament on Film*

For many people film is one of the major means whereby biblical stories are known and by means of which images of biblical characters are formed. I have little doubt that for a great many more people than we

---

1. *The New Testament in Fiction and Film: On Reversing the Hermeneutical Flow* (BSS, 17; Sheffield: JSOT Press, 1993), p. 19.

might care to admit, Charlton Heston is the dominant mental picture of Moses and that many people believe the Red Sea parted precisely as Cecil B. De Mille directed it to in *The Ten Commandments* in allowing the children of Israel to escape from Egypt.[1] Probably a great many people have their understanding of Old Testament characters framed as much by Saturday afternoon viewings of biblical epics as through any close contact with the particular stories they depict as they are recorded in Scripture itself. Films such as Michael Curtiz's *Noah's Ark* (1929), De Mille's *Samson and Delilah* (1949), Henry King's *David and Bathsheba* (1951), Alberto Gout's *Adam and Eve* (1956), King Vidor's *Solomon and Sheba* (1959), Raoul Walsh's *Esther and the King* (1960), Henry Koster's *The Story of Ruth* (1960), Richard Pottier's *David and Goliath* (1961), Irving Rapper's *Joseph and his Brethren* (1962), Robert Aldrich's *Sodom and Gomorrah* (1963), and John Huston's *The Bible* (1966) function in this regard. While the bulk of biblical epic films were made in the 1950s and 1960s we should not think that Hollywood's interest in them has been entirely lost; nor for that matter have Old Testament characters ceased to be of interest to contemporary writers.[2] One needs only to be reminded of the portrayals of Moses in Gianfranco De Bosio's six-hour film *Moses: The Lawgiver* (1975) (the screenplay of which was written by no less a literary figure than Anthony Burgess), or of David in Bruce Beresford's film *King David* (1985) and Joseph Heller's novel *God Knows* (1984), to illustrate the point.[3] These films attracted the attention of major stars to play the leading roles (Burt

1.   The presentation of this sequence remains one of the most visually memorable of the film and has inspired a number of subsequent portrayals of the story. A good example is the comic book adaptation of *The Ten Commandments* issued as Classics Illustrated 135A in December of 1956, just in time to capitalize on the release of the film which took place the month before. The depiction of the crossing of the Red Sea within this comic book, which is adapted by Lorenz Graham and illustrated by Norman Nodel, is clearly influenced by De Mille's film. It is worth recording that the comic book has a full-page advertisement for the film on its inside back cover.

2.   A good discussion of the film genre is the recent study by B. Babington and P.W. Evans, *Biblical Epics: Sacred Narrative in the Hollywood Cinema* (Manchester: Manchester University Press, 1993).

3.   An interesting discussion of *God Knows* is found in D. Seed, *The Fiction of Joseph Heller: Against the Grain* (London: Macmillan, 1989), pp. 158-80.

Lancaster and Richard Gere, respectively), so they were hardly intended as 'grade B' movies.[1]

At times the impression of film is made by much less direct means; the impact does not require that a 'biblical' story be the main attraction in its own right. A good illustration of how Old Testament imagery can be subtly communicated to popular audiences via the cinema is the blockbuster film by Steven Spielberg entitled *Raiders of the Lost Ark* (1981). This is a film which blends fantasy with fast-paced action, mixing in a smattering of Old Testament history in the process. Ostensibly, it deals with one of the most perplexing of questions which arises out of the pages of the Bible: What happened to the Ark of the Covenant, the symbol of covenant faith for the Hebrew people? This has long been a subject of specialized interest among Old Testament scholars and an object of speculation among the population at large. In the words of G. Henton Davies, Principal Emeritus of Regent's Park College, Oxford:

> The fate of the ark is a bigger mystery than its origin.[2]

In his own way Spielberg answers precisely this question, tempting us with a possible (if highly imaginative!) answer. The mystery is a secret no longer, for Indiana Jones has come to the rescue and delivered the Ark into our hands, or at least those of the US government! What is remarkable about the film is the fact that so many people find it believable, at least in terms of the magical powers that the Ark is said to possess as an instrument of God's judgment. Perhaps this is not so difficult to understand. After all, are there not a number of places within the Old Testament where the destructive power of the Ark is made manifest?[3] And what about all of those visual touches within the film which build upon standard Old Testament ideas and present us with visual images of them? For example, we may recall that in the final climactic scene where the Ark of the Covenant is opened the German archaeologist wears garments deliberately designed to invoke thoughts of the Jewish High Priest with his breast-plate bearing the stones of the

---

1. D. Elley, *The Epic Film: Myth and History* (London: Routledge & Kegan Paul, 1984), pp. 25-41, discusses biblical epics depicting Old Testament stories.
2. Article on 'Ark of the Covenant', *IDB* I, p. 224.
3. As in 1 Sam. 5–6; 2 Sam. 6.6-7; Num. 4.15; Ps. 132; 1 Chron. 13.15-16; 1 Kgs 8; and Jer. 3.16-17.

Twelve Tribes of Israel. All of this suggests that film-making has had a long tradition of turning to the Old Testament as an important source of its subject material. It is remarkable how expressive modern films are of the myths and stories which have been part of our cultural heritage for centuries, stories which are sometimes operating at a subconscious level and are only brought to higher awareness by means of the film. At the same time there is much to be gained from re-reading the Old Testament stories in light of the cinematic interpretations which build upon it. We can discover how eternal some of the themes and ideas contained in modern cinema are, as well as finding out much about ourselves in the process.

2. *The Literary Works Selected*

There certainly exists what in the words of T.R. Wright is described as a 'creative tension' between theology and literature.[1] However, this tension need not necessarily be viewed as a negative thing; it can even become an instrument of our increased appreciation of both theology *and* literature as important aspects of authentic human existence, provided that we are able to avoid the tendency to posit truth absolutely in one domain or the other at the expense of its partner.[2] Within this volume I would want to say that there is much to suggest that the tension between theology and literature can indeed be creative, and I have attempted to demonstrate precisely that through the materials selected and discussed. There is much to be learned about the process of interpretation by means of such an exercise.

A brief word about how the various works of literature and films discussed within this book came to be chosen is in order. I suspect that a chapter on Cecil B. De Mille's *The Ten Commandments* will come as no surprise to anyone. Of all of the Hollywood blockbuster epics this is perhaps the most well known; it would be almost impossible to write about *The Old Testament and Film* without including some discussion

---

1.   *Theology and Literature* (Signposts in Theology; Oxford: Basil Blackwell, 1988), p. 1.

2.   Wright warns that in both disciplines we must avoid the danger of a literalism of approach which limits or defines meaning and forges too close a connection between meaning and language. As he says (*Theology and Literature*, p. 13), 'One of the main purposes of encouraging an interaction between theology and literature is to avoid the dangers of literalism'.

of this film since it set the standard for many that followed. However, rather than simply making a comparison between De Mille's vision of the life of Moses and that of the Pentateuch, interesting though that might be, I chose to compare it with the award-winning film series *Decalogue* by the Polish director Krzysztof Kieslowski. The difference between an attempt to *re-create* the Old Testament story and an attempt to *re-interpret* it using a modern setting will, I hope, be obvious to anyone who has seen both (sets of) films.[1]

The decision to include a chapter on John Steinbeck's *East of Eden* was an easy one to make. It clearly builds upon the story of Cain and Abel in Gen. 4.1-16 and recognizes how that particular story cries out for a modern re-telling. The fact that Elia Kazan's film version of the story has now become something of a cult classic, by the mere presence of James Dean within it, also makes *East of Eden* an obvious choice—people are familiar with the story and are interested in watching it. Lesser known, but well worth watching as an interpretation of Steinbeck's novel is the TV mini-series from 1981 directed by Harvey Hart.

Another chapter which takes as its starting point a story from the book of Genesis concerns the creation of man and woman, Adam and Eve (as recorded in Gen. 2–3). Here we trace the influence of the biblical myths of human creation upon Mary Shelley within her classic horror story *Frankenstein*. Shelley's nightmarish vision has been one of the most important resources for film-makers over the years, and popular knowledge of the story, or at least a rough idea of it as channelled through films, is virtually universal. Yet the biblical

1.   The essential point of difference is well made by David Jasper in connection with the life of Jesus as presented in the New Testament Gospels. In his book *The New Testament and the Literary Imagination* (London: Macmillan, 1987), p. 90, Jasper says, 'There are those, like Lloyd Douglas in *The Robe* and the Jewish author Max Brod in *The Master*, who have tried to update the gospels, implying that they are, fundamentally, biographical chronicles and producing works whose very historical brilliance is an obstruction to an encounter with Jesus Christ. Their historicism leads them into the realms of fantasy. Other novelists have been truer to the gospels, making no attempt to provide an historical image of Jesus. They begin rather with the experience of the contemporary world. Jesus stands behind the dramas of their novels, not directly, but reflected in character and patterning.' We could say that the difference between De Mille's presentation of the Ten Commandments and that of Kieslowski is an illustration from the Old Testament of precisely the same tension Jasper describes.

underpinnings of *Frankenstein* are easily overlooked or forgotten; among the scores of adaptations and variations of the story which are available for popular consumption, only occasionally is the creation motif of Genesis brought to the fore, central though it is to the original story itself. All of this means that Mary Shelley's *Frankenstein* provides an ideal opportunity to see how both literature and cinematic interpretations of it not only build upon biblical mythology, but invite a reconsideration of the biblical materials themselves.

The selection of Melville's *Moby-Dick* as a subject of discussion might, at first glance, seem peculiar. Many modern readers are put off by the sheer size of the book, prompting Woody Allen to include the line in his film *Zelig* that one of his life's ambitions was to finish reading it. Length is not the only problem, however. The fact that the novel seems to belong to a past age is also a consideration. Is it not really a tale of a previous time, difficult for a contemporary readership to follow because of its archaic language and in parts virtually incomprehensible in its use of nautical terminology? Yet, even though it was written over 140 years ago, the central theme of the novel is just as relevant as it ever was, if we take modern stories of the human struggle with the sea and its creatures as evidence. Ernest Hemingway's *The Old Man and the Sea* (1952) immediately comes to mind, relating the all-consuming desire of an old fisherman, Santiago, to bring home his catch despite the forces of nature raging against him. Indeed, some of the imagery within Hemingway's short story is remarkably reminiscent of portions of Melville's classic, suggesting that Hemingway wrote the work with a conscious eye toward *Moby-Dick*.[1] Even more of a parallel is Peter Benchley's best-seller *Jaws* (1974). The film version of this story, another gripping effort directed by Steven Spielberg in 1975, is testimony to the enduring power of the story of nautical monomania, setting box office records around the world. Is not the irascible Captain Quint a modern version of Captain Ahab, this time engaged in the 'quenchless pursuit' not of a Great White Whale but of a Great White Shark?[2] Both figures are scarred, physically as well as psychologically,

---

1.   A good example is the attack of the sharks on the Old Man's catch as he makes his way back to harbour. This is similar to the attack of the sharks on a killed whale in a chapter in *Moby-Dick* entitled 'Stubb's Supper'.

2.   Steven Spielberg is on record as describing Jaws as 'a great episode of *Sea Hunt* mixed with a little *Moby-Dick*' in T. Crawley, *The Steven Spielberg Story* (London: Zomba Books, 1983), p. 41.

by earlier encounters with malevolent creatures of the sea and both now live only to avenge themselves. In the end the fate of both Quint and Ahab is the same: both men are destroyed by their obsession. Other films dealing with the same basic subject, humankind's obsessive attempt to confront and conquer a force larger than itself, continue to catch the public imagination. Nor should we think that the theme is exhausted by excursions into a nautical setting; there is even a space-age version in the form of Gene Roddenberry's ever-popular creation *Star Trek*. In the second of the Star Trek feature films entitled *The Wrath of Khan* (released in 1982) we have a tale of obsession and revenge which is clearly based on Melville's *Moby-Dick*. The evil Khan is hellbent on destroying Captain Kirk to settle an old debt and takes Ahab, with his obsessive pursuit of the White Whale, as a hero figure to be emulated. Khan even spouts quotes from *Moby-Dick* as he seeks to blow up his own ship and destroy the Enterprise and its hated Captain.[1] Most people who see the film are aware that Khan is quoting from some famous work of literature, but it comes as a surprise to some that it is from something as (seemingly) inaccessible and dated as *Moby-Dick*. In a strange sort of way this itself stands as a testimony of the enduring power of Melville's story.

Finally, the choice of Ecclesiastes as the background for a discussion of Ernest Hemingway's *A Farewell to Arms* is a little more understandable, given the known affinity that Hemingway had for the biblical book. Ecclesiastes has enjoyed something of a revival of interest in recent years. This is due, in no small measure, to the fact that the uncertainties of modern life have driven us to search for meaning in every conceivable corner—no stone is left unturned, no possible source of help ruled out of bounds without consideration. Consequently, the Jewish wisdom literature has been rediscovered as offering valuable insight for life in these chaotic times. Ecclesiastes is generally regarded as belonging to that wisdom tradition, even though the author's answers to life's questions are far from orthodox, and there has been a renewed interest in what he has to say. As Robert Penn Warren once wrote:

---

1. Melville's *Moby-Dick* also serves as the inspiration for an episode within the original TV series of *Star Trek*, an episode from the second year of production (1967–68) which is entitled 'The Doomsday Machine'. See my 'The Cultural Veneer of Star Trek', *JPC* for a full discussion.

[The] story is the quest for meaning and certitude in a world which seems to offer nothing of the sort. It is, in a sense, a religious book; if it does not offer a religious solution it is nevertheless conditioned by the religious problem.[1]

Warren was writing about Hemingway's *A Farewell to Arms*, but the comment is equally applicable to Ecclesiastes. The fact that both books fit the bill so readily is sufficient in itself to warrant a comparison of them, despite the fact that their authors were separated by nearly twenty-two centuries.

As I mentioned in connection with the volume on *The New Testament in Fiction and Film*, I am aware that an approach to interpreting the biblical texts through the use of modern literature and cinema is in many ways a risky business. It is like conducting a military campaign on three separate fronts, constantly trying to protect against attacks from well-entrenched troops on each border. In attempting such a playful exercise one knowingly opens oneself to criticism from specialists in one or more of the three fields involved. For me, coming to this particular effort as a *New* Testament specialist, I am even more acutely aware than before of how far out on a limb I have placed myself by tackling the Old Testament. To add to the anxiety, there is always the worry that I have misunderstood, or misrepresented, the literary or cinematic material discussed within this volume. Nevertheless, I believe such an enterprise can prove stimulating, if for no other reason than that it drives the reader back to the biblical text again. I can only speak for myself in saying that I have found my understanding of, and my appreciation for, the biblical texts greatly increased through my study of the various works of literature, and their cinematic interpretations, which use biblical materials as an essential backdrop against which to tell their stories.

---

1. 'Ernest Hemingway', in H. Bloom (ed.), *Modern Critical Views: Ernest Hemingway* (New York: Chelsea House, 1985), p. 54.

Chapter 1

THE TEN COMMANDMENTS:
SOME MODERN FILM INTERPRETATIONS

The essential aim of this chapter is to note how two completely different approaches can be adopted in presenting a film version of one of the best known sections of the Old Testament, the Ten Commandments delivered to Moses on Mount Sinai. The first approach is that of director Cecil B. De Mille, whose name is probably forever linked with the ultimate Hollywood effort in this regard, the hugely successful film *The Ten Commandments* (1956). The second is that of the Polish director Krzysztof Kieslowski, who offers us an alternative vision of the Mosaic Law through his ten-part cycle *Decalogue* (1990). De Mille's approach is essentially one of biography—he tells the story of the Ten Commandments by giving us a dramatic re-creation of the life of Moses. In contrast, Kieslowski's approach is analogical in nature—he presents us with the Ten Commandments in the form of a series of modern parables about the commandments themselves. This second approach is characteristic of Kieslowski's cinematic work as a whole, perfectly illustrating the power of such cinematic parables to penetrate human defences and strike where we least expect it. He recently described his film-making technique with these words:

> Whatever stage I'm at with a film, whether I'm writing the script or editing, I always look at it from the point of view of the viewer—what he's expecting, the way he'd like me to entrap him and the way he'd like to be released from the trap, when he wants to be surprised, when he wants to laugh, when he wants to cry. You could describe my job as a game with the viewer—to give him what he wants but at the same time covertly to slip in something that he might not be expecting.[1]

1. Cited in an article entitled 'No End to the Enigma', by Jonathan Romney, *The Guardian* (Arts Section, 15 October 1993), p. 6.

Let us turn to consider Cecil B. De Mille's *The Ten Commandments* before moving on to summarize and discuss Kieslowski's lesser-known effort. In passing I shall also make reference to one other film interpretation of the life of Moses, that of Gianfranco De Bosio entitled *Moses: The Lawgiver* (1975) which continues the lead set out by De Mille in telling the Exodus story as if it were a biography of Moses.

1. *De Mille's* The Ten Commandments *(1923 and 1956)*

As a film-maker, legendary Hollywood director Cecil B. De Mille's name is synonymous with big-budget, biblical epics, as his two versions of *The Ten Commandments*, *The King of Kings* (1927), *The Sign of the Cross* (1932), *Cleopatra* (1934) and *Samson and Delilah* (1949) all testify. As De Mille himself explained:

> I like spectacles. I like to paint on a large canvas.[1]

De Mille had no less than two attempts at translating the *Ten Commandments* onto the silver screen. He made a silent version in 1923 and the more widely known version in 1956 which starred Charlton Heston in the role of Moses. Clearly the 1923 version of *The Ten Commandments* was envisaged by De Mille to be a film version of the biblical story which brought the essential message to a contemporary audience. Legend has it that De Mille sent a copy of the Bible to every employee of the Lasky Company working on the film with a memo which exhorted them:

> As I intend to film practically the entire book of Exodus…the Bible should never be away from you. Place it on your desk, and when you travel, stick it in your briefcase. Make reading it a daily habit.[2]

The attention to detail that De Mille brought to the project was amazing, and the filming was conducted with almost military precision. Filming took place on a variety of locations, including Hollywood, San Francisco and the Mohave desert, and lasted from May until July of 1923. There was great popular interest in ancient Egypt at the time, no doubt fuelled

---

1.   Cited in P.F. Boller, Jr, and R.L. Davis, *Hollywood Anecdotes* (London: Macmillan, 1987), p. 295.
2.   Cited in C. Higham, *Cecil B. De Mille* (New York: DaCapo Books, 1973), pp. 111-12.

by the discovery of the tomb of Tutankhamen by Howard Carter in November of the previous year. De Mille spared no expense in making the film as realistic and as historically accurate as he could, sending out researchers across the globe to bring back facts which he incorporated within the film; details of costuming, armoury, hair-styles and so forth, all filtered back into the visual presentation. The final bill for the project was some $1,200,000—a considerable amount above budgeted figures.

Yet, despite the conscious effort to base the film on the book of Exodus, *The Ten Commandments* takes a remarkably creative way of presenting the biblical story, combining a visualization of the ancient story of the Israelites' release from Egypt with a retelling of its essential truths which is set in modern times.[1] In effect it is a film within a film, a story set against a story, a modern parable based upon the biblical tale; insofar as it juxtaposes the biblical story with a modern one it anticipates the sort of approach that Kieslowski takes up and develops into the highly acclaimed *Decalogue* cycle. This juxtaposition of an ancient and a modern setting of the film is the idea of Jeanie Macpherson, a long-time friend and companion of De Mille's who worked with him on a number of projects over the years and who wrote most of the screenplay for the film in February and March of 1923. Macpherson explains that the problem is one involving 'translating the Ten Commandments into terms of modern, everyday life, with modern everyday people'.[2] The film premiered on 21 December 1923 in the George M. Cohan theatre in New York to critical acclaim. However, it is the second of De Mille's attempts to bring the story of the Exodus to screen which remains the one most associated with him in the public's mind.

The 1956 version of *The Ten Commandments* was De Mille's last film and was one in which he openly indulged himself, as exemplified in the fact that he opens the film with a two-minute long prologue in which he himself appears, emerging from behind a plush set of drapes at the front of a theatre and declaring,

---

1. There is much to suggest that De Mille is indebted to D.W. Griffith's classic film *Intolerance* (1916) in this regard.

2. This is discussed in Higham, *Cecil B. De Mille*, pp. 109-10. Babington and Evans, *Biblical Epics*, pp. 44-46, also discuss what they describe as the film's 'dual narrative' technique.

Ladies and gentlemen, young and old. This may seem an unusual proce-
dure, speaking to you before the picture begins. But we have an unusual
subject: the story of the birth of freedom, the story of Moses. As many of
you know, the Holy Bible omits some thirty years of Moses' life—from
the time he was a three-month old baby and was found in the bullrushes
by Bithiah the daughter of Pharaoh and adopted into the court of Egypt,
until he learned that he was Hebrew and killed the Egyptian. To fill in
those missing years we turn to ancient historians such as Philo and
Josephus. Philo wrote at the time that Jesus of Nazareth walked the earth,
and Josephus wrote some fifty years later and watched the destruction of
Jerusalem by the Romans. These historians had access to documents long
since destroyed, or perhaps lost, like the Dead Sea scrolls. The theme of
this picture is whether men ought to be ruled by God's law or whether
they are to be ruled by the whims of a dictator like Rameses. Are men the
property of the state, or are they free souls under God? This same battle
continues throughout the world today. Our intention was not to create a
story, but to be worthy of the divinely inspired story created three thousand years ago: the five books of Moses.

De Mille's narration continues throughout the film, from the reading of
the Old Testament stories in Genesis and Exodus to his explanations of
the various intrigues of plot within the house of Pharaoh.[1] As one recent
description of the film puts it:

> The story may be familiar, but De Mille rams it home as though he were
> telling it for the first time with his camera platform as a pulpit linked by
> direct line to the Deity.[2]

De Mille insisted that parts of *The Ten Commandments* be shot on
location in Egypt (including Mount Sinai). Filming in Egypt began in
November of 1954 and, after an unusually long final production period,
De Mille's second *The Ten Commandments* premiered in the Criterion
Theatre in New York on 8 November 1956. The film vastly overran its

---

1.   Some commercially available versions of the film also include an additional
trailer for the film in which De Mille appears and harangues the audience for some ten
minutes about the film, pontificating on everything from how it was that Michelangelo
came to sculpt his statue of Moses with 'horns' (based on a mistranslation of the
Hebrew text of Exod. 34), to Van Dyke's paintings depicting the life of Moses, to an
explanation of how the original path of Moses' journey through the Sinai desert
provided the basis for the filming schedule on location.

2.   Cited in an *Empire* magazine sales catalogue from September of 1993 offering classic films available from W.H. Smith.

budget, costing Paramount Pictures some $13,000,000, but it proved to be a wise investment because the film remains one of the all-time, top-grossing pictures ever released. It also served as the launching pad for the career of Charlton Heston, whose name is now synonymous with the big-budget biblical epic.[1] It won one Academy Award, for Best Special Effects, based largely on the sequence depicting the parting of the Red Sea.

De Mille set the film within the time of Pharaoh Rameses, casting a host of big-name actors and actresses in addition to Heston as Moses, including Yul Brynner as Rameses, Anne Baxter as Nefretiri, Edward G. Robinson as Dathan, Sir Cedrick Hardwicke as Seti, Yvonne De Carlo as Sephora, Vincent Price as Baka, and John Derek as Joshua. The scene depicting the crossing of the Red Sea remains one of the most dramatic ever filmed. It required 12,000 extras and 15,000 animals and prompted De Mille to list among the opening credits 'The Cavalry Corps of the Egyptian Armed Forces'. Dilys Powell, film critic for *The Sunday Times* for many years, describes the artistry that De Mille's film represents, the sheer grandeur that it embodies, with these words:

> one is compelled to respect the organization of the scenes of spectacle: the raising of the obelisk, the river of Israelites straggling off into the distance of the desert. And although the optical trick by which the fugitives appear to cross the seabed between the two harmless Niagras seems to me clumsy in execution, the passage is exciting to watch; Mr De Mille shows here that he has not lost the drive which, for nearly half a century, has kept him among the best-sellers.[2]

This is not to suggest, however, that the story line of the film is derived exclusively from the book of Exodus. Some additional complications of plot, as well as extra characters, are inserted into the retelling that De Mille presents to us, notably the rather far-fetched love triangle between

---

1. Details of the production, together with 18 photographs of the film, are provided in J. Rovin, *The Films of Charlton Heston* (Secaucus, NJ: Citadel Press, 1977), pp. 67-82. Much has been written about the physical similarity between Heston and the statue of Moses carved by Michelangelo which now stands in the church of St Peter in Chains in Rome, a similarity which may even have prompted De Mille to cast Heston in the part. Babington and Evans (*Biblical Epics*, p. 28) reproduce a publicity still which shows Heston sitting next to the famous statue of Moses, carved by Michelangelo in 1512–1516.

2. *The Dilys Powell Film Reader* (Oxford: Oxford University Press, 1992), p. 305.

Moses, Pharaoh Rameses and Queen Nefretiri. Faithful to the biblical account this certainly is not, but essential to Hollywood drama it without doubt was. In order to concoct such a story De Mille wove together features of several popular novels about Moses including *Prince of Egypt* by Dorothy Clarke Wilson, *Pillar of Fire* by J.H. Ingraham and *On Eagle's Wings* by A.E. Southon.

This is a film which is openly devotional; one could go so far as to say that it is, despite its portrayal of the *Old* Testament, essentially Christian in its piety. There is a clear Christian sub-theme running through the film, with barely veiled allusions to the story of the life of Jesus of Nazareth in abundance. The scene where Moses talks to Sephora and Joshua after he descends from Mount Sinai following his encounter with God has Moses speak of his experience in overtly Johannine terms. Moses speaks of how, through the experience with the burning bush, he had God's Word revealed to his mind, following this with such remarks as: 'and the Word was God', 'He is not flesh but Spirit, the Light of Eternal Mind', 'His light is in every man'. The film is also extremely conservative in its approach to interpreting the Old Testament. It attempts to put on the screen in a literalistic fashion all of the miraculous events recorded in the book of Exodus and allows nothing to chance; Moses encounters God in a *literal* burning bush which is not consumed by the fire, the Nile *literally* runs blood-red, the Red Sea is *literally* parted so as to allow the escape of the people of Israel, the pillar of fire representing the presence of God *literally* appears, and Moses *literally* hands over to Joshua the five books of the Torah in the final scene of the film before ascending the mountain to his death. In short, De Mille's *The Ten Commandments* (1956) becomes an arena for such spectacular pyrotechnic effects that it makes anything God himself might do look almost feeble in comparison!

A much more believable cinematic version of the life of Moses is that offered by director Gianfranco De Bosio entitled *Moses: The Lawgiver* (1975).[1] The scale of this production is much smaller than that of De Mille's extravaganza; it is much less opulent in terms of costuming and

---

1.   The film was originally broadcast as a six-hour TV movie. A shortened version lasting 136 minutes is available from Polygram Video Ltd. A novel based on the TV series is also available, written by Thomas Keneally, and entitled *Moses: The Lawgiver* (London: Collins, 1975). The book contains 79 photographs from the film (both black-and-white and colour).

set design, and all the more satisfying as a result. The number of Hebrew people being led in the exodus from Egypt is realistic, much less than a hundred, and the size of Pharaoh's army destroyed in the Red Sea is proportionally reduced. The film lends itself much more to a psychological interpretation of Moses' encounter with God in Sinai, something which is emphasized by the fact that the voice of Yahweh speaking out of the burning bush is clearly that of the actor portraying Moses (Burt Lancaster). Gone too are the post-production special effects which were used by De Mille to invoke a sense of the supernatural; instead here we are given a more naturalistic interpretation of the events of Moses' life and the events of the Exodus. For example, the burning bush episode is caused by a lightning bolt striking a tree, the miracle of the turning of Moses' staff into a snake is given as a dream-like sequence which takes place in Moses' imagination, the pillar of cloud which leads the Hebrew people by day across the desert wilderness is portrayed as a dust tornado, and the feeding of the people in the midst of the desert by means of quail and manna is explained by Moses himself as due not so much to a miracle as to his knowledge of the bird migration patterns and how and where the tamarind tree sheds its resin in the desert. Even the central theme of the giving of the Mosaic Law is made more credible, effectively demythologizing De Mille's version of it. De Bosio gives us Moses himself relating the substance of the Ten Commandments to the people before he ascends to Mount Sinai, and inviting their agreement to life under the covenant with the Lord God. All of this helps to make the film a much more credible portrayal of the life of Moses. In short, within *Moses: The Lawgiver* we have another example of a cinematic retelling of the story of the Ten Commandments which assumes a biographical approach, which manages successfully to avoid (with one or two exceptions such as the death of Dathan) simply becoming a showcase for Hollywood special effects.

In any event, these essentially biographical versions of the life of Moses are a far cry from the more subdued, yet infinitely more inviting approach to the Ten Commandments provided by Krzysztof Kieslowski. It is to this recent artistic effort that we now turn our attention.

2. *Kieslowski's* Decalogue *(1990)*

Kieslowski's approach to presenting the Ten Commandments is markedly different from that adopted by De Mille in his 1956 effort, although, as we have already noted, there are similarities to De Mille's earlier film of 1923. *Decalogue* is a series of ten one-hour long films directed by the Polish film-maker Kieslowski, a director who has long demonstrated an interest in translating social and political comment into cinematic art. *Decalogue* was filmed in Warsaw during 1988 and 1989 and was first broadcast in the United Kingdom on BBC2 in May of 1990 and then re-broadcast in 1991. Each of the films is designed to dramatize one of the Ten Commandments contained in Exod. 20.1-17 (and the parallel in Deut. 5.6-21), but to do so by presenting the commandment within a modern setting. Two of the series of films, namely *Decalogue Five* and *Decalogue Six*, were issued for general cinematic release in Britain in 1990 under the titles *A Short Film about Killing* and *A Short Film about Love*, both being slightly longer than the one-hour segments of the television versions.[1] The first of these general releases was critically acclaimed, winning awards at the Cannes Film Festival in 1988. The series as a whole also received the BAFTA award for Best Foreign Language Television Programme in 1990 and has been widely recognized to be one of the most significant cinematic contributions of the past few decades. The film series is available from Fox Video on four cassettes and is in Polish with English sub-titles.

The screenplay for the series was written by Kieslowski together with his friend and artistic colleague Krzysztof Piesiewicz over a period of twelve months during 1985–1986, a tense time for people living in Poland as the communist regime was in the process of disintegrating. The idea for the project was Piesiewicz's, who suggested that Kieslowski make a film about the Ten Commandments to serve as an illustration of the need to return to human values which had been destroyed by communism. The scripts for the ten films of *Decalogue*, together with an introduction to the work by Kieslowski, have recently been translated from Polish and published by Faber and Faber (1990),[2] who have also

1.   The longer versions of the twc films have recently been released on video in Britain and are available from Tartan Video as a limited-edition boxed set. *A Short Film about Killing* lasts 85 minutes; *A Short Film about Love* lasts 87 minutes. As expected the longer versions of the episodes add extra details which make them fuller expositions of the commandments under discussion and *A Short Film about Love* has a more optimistic ending. However, the essential message of the films remains consistent.

2.   The book contains a listing of the Ten Commandments (on p. xviii) which, unfortunately, divides them up badly and effectively misnumbers them as far as the *Decalogue* series is concerned. This has a disastrous effect upon the unwitting viewer who is attempting to fit the Commandment to the story of the particular episode. The

issued a book in their Film Director series entitled *Kieslowski on Kieslowski* (1993) containing a full discussion by the director about how the series came into being.[1]

Each of the ten segments of Kieslowski's *Decalogue* is linked in that all begin with an establishing shot of the same apartment block in the city of Warsaw; this is an ingenious touch which allows the housing estate to function as a microcosm of the world and all of its problems. The episodes all have a strong sense of right and wrong within them, all assuming that people have what Kieslowski describes as the moral 'inner compass'[2] which lies buried deep within the human heart. At the same time they all demonstrate what happens in human lives when one of the Commandments is broken; the films set out to portray the havoc that is wrought in personal relationships, the devastating consequences that result, when God's Commandments are not obeyed. Kieslowski explains the tentative connection between the films and the individual Commandments:

> The films should be influenced by the individual Commandments to the same degree that the Commandments influence our daily lives. We were aware that no philosophy or ideology had ever challenged the fundamental tenets of the Commandments during their several thousand years of existence, yet they are nevertheless transgressed on a routine basis.[3]

Thus, it is not so much with an attitude of moral crusade that Kieslowski presents his films to us, but by means of the complexities in the lives of the individual characters of a story he attempts to paint a realistic human portrait. If De Mille likened his films to painting on a large canvas, Kieslowski's approach might be said to be like painting miniature portraits, the emphasis always being on individual situations, the focus on the personal stories of the characters. Yet the ten individual stories do

---

viewer is better off following the listing of the Commandments which is given on the video-boxes for the ten segments of the *Decalogue*. Otherwise one ends up trying to interpret the films as expressions of the *wrong* Commandment.

1.   *Decalogue* is discussed on pp. 143-72 and eleven stills from five of the ten segments are given. Full production details of *Decalogue* are also given in the filmography section of the book on pp. 255-60.

2.   *Kieslowski on Kieslowski* (London: Faber & Faber, 1993), p. 150.

3.   K. Kieslowski with K. Piesiewicz, *Decalogue: The Ten Commandments* (London: Faber & Faber, 1991), p. xiv. The comment comes in the Introduction to the book and was written in Warsaw in 1990.

hold together and form part of a larger whole; at times we even see characters flitting in and out of the story which we recognize as having appeared in other episodes. In one instance there is a deliberate linking together of two of the stories: in *Decalogue Eight* the story line contained in *Decalogue Two* is related by one of the characters as a case study during an ethics class.

The ten instalments of *Decalogue* are such visual masterpieces that one is loath even to describe them and run the risk of ruining the viewer's enjoyment of them as individual efforts. I would certainly not want to spoil anyone's appreciation of the segments by imposing my own impressions about them, but a brief synopsis of each of the films, together with the citation of the relevant commandment from the Authorized Version of the book of Exodus, seems in order.

a. Decalogue One: *'I am the Lord thy God. Thou shalt have no other God but me.'*
This is essentially a story about how a father, named Krzysztof, comes to deal with the fact that his young son Pawel dies as a result of an over-reliance on his father's confidence in his ability to predict how life proceeds. The close relationship between father and son is wondrously presented, with the obvious aim of establishing the viewer's sympathy for the two. However, the father is overly confident about his ability to predict the strength of the ice on a frozen pond to support his son's weight—a fatal miscalculation which results in the boy's death when he goes skating one evening after school. In short, we have presented in a short, dramatic parable just what happens when people trust in their own abilities and assessments of life and all of its complications, a striking way of presenting the commandment against trusting one's abilities to solve the complexities of life without reference to God. Krzysztof's reliance upon science, as depicted by his trust in the mathematical and computational formulae he derives from his much-prized computer which is revered as infallible, proves to be his undoing; his own son takes him at his (reasoned) word and pays the ultimate price. Pawel, the trusting son, believes his father when he determines through the computer that the ice on the lake will hold someone three times the boy's body weight—not an unreasonable calculation given all of the data that he is able to gather from the meteorological office about the temperature, frost levels, and so on, over the past few days of a cold

spell. As a result Krzysztof tells his son that he can take his new ice skates onto the local pond but discovers, only too late, just what his foolhardy pursuit of life without God costs him. The ice on the pond breaks and the son is drowned. In contrast, Krzysztof's sister Irena, Pawel's aunt, lives her life with a conscious eye toward God. She prays, for example, and there is a scene in which she shows Pawel some pictures of her spiritual pilgrimage to the Vatican. She stands as someone who tries to offer an alternative perspective on life to the young and inquisitive Pawel who is just at the age when he is beginning to ask questions about life and death and the meaning of existence. In short, the film graphically portrays what it means for human beings to place the god of personal ambition and self-reliance at the centre of life. Life that relies absolutely upon science and rationality is ruined, as is powerfully conveyed by the striking image of ink from a cracked bottle spreading across Krzysztof's pages of scientific calculations. Tragedy and tears can be the only outcome of a life which shuts God out.

There are many features of this introductory episode of the *Decalogue* series which are later developed more fully in the series as a whole. There is, for example, the presence of a mysterious figure alongside the frozen lake, a man who sits at a fire. Within this episode the figure appears four separate times, always at moments in the story which might be said to invite the viewer to contemplate the presence of God (within the narration of the story). The same actor (identified in the screenplays as 'young man') appears in most of the ten episodes, always playing a part which is suitable to the particular story line of the segment. Kieslowski comments about the character,

> There's this guy who wanders around in all the films. I don't know who he is; just a guy who comes and watches. He watches us, our lives. He's not very pleased with us. He comes, watches, and walks on.[1]

The figure symbolizes (as far as I am able to determine) the presence of God, or perhaps even Christ, in the midst of the human situation. Since the appearance of this unnamed character is strategically placed in the stories so as to suggest divine presence, it is worth noting how and

---

1. *Kieslowski*, p. 158. The figure does not appear in *Decalogue Seven* (where he was edited out due to a bad take) or in *Decalogue Ten* (where Kieslowski admits that he probably should have been included in the screenplay).

where he comes in the story line. I shall keep track of him throughout my summaries, identifying him as the 'mystery man'.

b. Decalogue Two: *'Thou shalt not take the name of the Lord thy God in vain.'*

This story revolves around a middle-aged consultant physician who has as one of his patients a man named Andrzej who is terminally ill. The consultant, who lives in the Warsaw apartment block which serves as the focus for the series, is approached by the wife of the sick man who lives upstairs from the doctor. Dorota, as the woman is called, demands that she be told precisely what the prognosis is for her husband's case. It is clear that something is troubling Dorota deeply, and we eventually discover that she is three months pregnant, but that her husband has not fathered the child. The father is one of her colleagues from the Philharmonic Orchestra in which she plays and this tangle of relationships has brought her to the point of crisis; she has long been unable to have a child and she fears that she will never have another opportunity. However, she feels caught between the love for the two men in her life and she is desperately trying to get the consultant to let her know what the chances of survival are for her husband so that she can know what to do. If it appears that Andrzej will die then she wants to go on and have the child, but if it appears that he will live then she wishes to have an abortion, knowing that this decision will end any possibility of her being able to build a meaningful relationship with the father of the child in the future. Unfortunately the consultant is unable to make a definite prediction as to her husband's chances and this causes something of a rift to develop between him and Dorota. At one point the two have a short, but significant exchange:

Dorota:	Do you believe in God?
Consultant:	I have a God; there's only enough of him for me.
Dorota:	A private God?
Consultant:	*[nods slowly and drops his eyes.]*
Dorota:	Then ask him for absolution.

Eventually Dorota decides to go ahead and have an abortion and informs the consultant of her decision. He persuades her not to do so, because the latest laboratory tests indicate that her husband's illness is progressing rapidly and it does not seem that he will live very much longer. In a crucial exchange between the two of them, an exchange which provides us with the link to the Second Commandment, she demands that the consultant swear before God that he is telling the truth about her husband's impending death. He does so, and the situation seems resolved.

However, against all odds the husband begins to recover from his illness. As a moving and creative image of his recovery we are presented with a close-up shot showing a honeybee attempting to extricate itself from the syrup of a jar of fruit into which it has fallen; the bee struggles valiantly to pull itself up a spoon which is resting in the jar and ultimately cleans its wings so that it can fly away. As the bee escapes, so too does Andrzej recover. Andrzej has a final conversation with the consultant about his miraculous recovery, thanking him and leaving him with the suggestion that knowledge of the fact that he and Dorota will soon have a child has given him the will to live. A final question by Andrzej to the consultant helps put the whole story in focus. He asks, 'Do you understand what it means to have a child?' 'I do', replies the doctor, his face expressive of internal sadness, providing the viewer with a powerful image of the struggle that the case has represented to him as well. Several scenes which have taken place earlier in the film now are filled with new meaning, notably the conversations that the consultant has with his housekeeper about how he lost his family, including two children, in a bombing raid in the war. In the end, we are aware that this has been a story of how one's narrow vision of God can make one blind as to the possibilities that exist in life, and to swear by, to take the name of, just such a narrow conception of God is to run the risk of missing out on much that life offers. The God by whom the consultant swears his oath, this self-proclaimed *private* God who was only big enough to answer the needs of his own faith, is insufficient in its conceptualization, standing as but a pale reflection of the true God who is full of infinite possibilities. In short, to swear by such a narrow vision of God is to break the Second Commandment, for, above all else, it privatizes God and fails to take him seriously for who he is, the Lord of *All*.

One or two other nice touches are found within the film which make it a visual masterpiece, including the way in which Dorota destroys the living things around her, such as her house plants, as an evocative image of her intention to have the abortion; this is made to stand in stark contrast to the attitude of the consultant who surrounds himself with all manner of plants and animals. In this episode the mysterious figure, whom I suggested above might be seen as a symbol of the presence of God, makes his appearance as a doctor observing the interactions of the various characters of the story.

c. Decalogue Three: *'Honour the Sabbath day.'*
This story takes place on Christmas Eve, a fitting symbol of a Sabbath or holy day within a Catholic country like Poland. This episode revolves around the relationship between a taxi driver named Janusz and a former lover of his named Ewa. Janusz, now happily married, is talked into leaving his own family late in the evening so that he can help Ewa find her husband Edward who has left her. In order to do this Janusz makes up a story about his car being stolen and persuades his wife and mother-in-law that he needs to leave their flat within the apartment block to go in search of the car. However, it quickly becomes clear that Ewa is not altogether stable mentally, and that she has something of a destructive streak within her. As we watch the pair visit various places where Edward might be found (hospitals, jails, train stations, etc.) we become less and less convinced of Edward's continuing presence in Ewa's life. At the same time we learn that Janusz and Ewa had once been caught by Edward sleeping together in a hotel room. This had happened three years earlier, and had caused the two of them (Ewa and Janusz) to break up and not see each other again. The experience is one from which Ewa has obviously never fully recovered, and she appears to need Janusz to help her discover how she is going to make sense of her life now. Janusz suspects her deceit, but does not know the full extent of it; he obviously goes along with it out of some residual sense of love for her. In the end, Ewa admits the truth to Janusz, the fact that she lives alone and that Edward has been happily married for several years to another woman now living in Krakow. She admits that she has been conducting an elaborate charade just to keep Janusz with her so that she will not have to spend Christmas Eve on her own. As she explains, 'It's difficult to be alone on a night like this'. The sad truth within this story is that Janusz can attempt to help Ewa in the midst of her anguish only by weaving a web of deceit over his own family and spoiling the celebrations of Christmas Eve which rightly should be spent with them. In this instance Janusz's failure to 'remember to keep the Sabbath holy' sets up a heart-breaking scene with which the episode concludes. He returns home on Christmas morning to find the children asleep in their

beds and his wife sleeping fitfully on the sofa. She asks, with a simplicity which betrays deep insight and understanding of the situation, 'Ewa?' He answers in the affirmative, which prompts her to reply with another question, 'You'll be going out again in the evenings?' 'No. No, I won't', he answers.

Once again there are some ingenious features of this episode that are worth mentioning. The 'mystery man' makes his customary appearance, this time as a driver piloting a tram which Janusz nearly collides with as he follows the mad suggestion of Ewa that he drive the car so fast that it might be involved in an accident so that the agony the two of them feel about their respective situations might be ended. Secondly, there is a scene in the opening sequences in which Janusz is dressed up as Santa Claus so that, suitably disguised, he can deliver presents to his two children in the family flat set within our familiar apartment block. As he enters the particular stairwell he runs into Krzysztof, the rationalist scientist whose son Pawel died in *Decalogue: One*. An uneasy exchange between them takes place, the impression being given that for Krzysztof family celebrations of Christmas are now emptied of meaning.

d. Decalogue Four: *'Honour thy father and thy mother'*.
This story revolves around the relationship that Anka, a twenty-year-old college student, has with her father, Michal. Anka's mother died five days after her birth, leaving Michal to raise the baby girl; he has never remarried and the two, father and daughter, live together in the Warsaw apartment block. The happy relationship that the two share is radically disturbed when Michal goes away on a business trip and Anka finds within his papers an envelope with the words 'Not to be opened before my death' written on it in his hand. Her curiosity is aroused, although she is unsure whether it is right for her to open the envelope. Eventually, after some days of agonized soul-searching, she does open the envelope only to discover that it contains another envelope addressed to her by her mother (we discover later that it was written to Anka while her mother lay on her deathbed). When her father returns from his trip he is greeted frostily by the daughter who reveals to him that she has found and read her mother's letter and that it informs her that he is not her true father. This new knowledge causes a severe strain on their relationship, with neither knowing how to treat the other any longer. Anka admits to Michal that she has always found relationships with other men difficult, confessing that sleeping with someone had

made her feel guilty, as if she was betraying her father. He too admits to her that he had always suspected that he might not be her father, but never knew for sure how to let her know about his doubts, let alone the feelings that he had for her which were outside the bounds of the normal father–daughter relationship. Anka tries to seduce Michal, but he does not respond to her advances, fearing that he is still in some way her father, and the two go to their separate rooms in the flat. In the morning Anka awakens to find that Michal has left the house and, looking out of the window, sees him walking away from the housing estate. She is frightened that he is leaving her, unable to continue to live with her in view of the change in circumstances. She calls out of the window to him, catches his attention, and then frantically runs down the stairs and out of the building to catch up with him. Here she admits that she never opened the letter from her mother and that she had made up the whole story. The final scenes of the episode show the two of them, father and daughter, burning the envelope containing the letter from Anka's mother. Only one charred fragment remains, which reads, 'My darling daughter. I would like to tell you something very important. Michal isn't...'; the rest of the line is burnt.

Anka's search for identity lies at the heart of this episode, a search no doubt brought on by a number of factors, including the facts that she has not had the advantage of having a mother in her life, and that she finds relationships with her boyfriends unfulfilling. There are several scenes which are designed to suggest her fascination for older men, making for a strong reversed-oedipal theme throughout. This episode is a complex one, offering an interesting exploration not only of how deceit operates (in that father and daughter both lie to each other in various ways), but how fragile the definition of precisely what it means to be a parent can be. In the end we are left unsure as to whether Michal is indeed Anka's father, but perhaps that is as it should be given the fact that they have lived as father and daughter for twenty years. We are also left in two minds about what one should do in a situation such as this to honour one's parents; is the burning of the letter the proper way to honour Anka's mother or not? Would the reading of it, by either Anka or Michal, be an honourable act, or a dishonourable one?

The 'mystery man' makes two appearances in this film; first in a scene where Anka is sitting alongside a lake trying to decide whether she should open the letter, and also in the scene where Anka admits to

Michal that she has never really opened the letter and that she lied in telling him what she did about its contents.

e. Decalogue Five: *'Thou shalt not kill.'*

This segment of *Decalogue* was singled out by the Cannes Film Festival of 1989 as deserving of special note, winning the prestigious Jury Prize for the year. It has been described as a powerful statement against murder on the part of the individual as well as against the use of capital punishment by the State, and perhaps that is its greatest message. The film chronicles the murder of a taxi driver, named Waldemar Rykowski, by a twenty-year-old youth named Jacek Lazar. The brutality of the murder, and Jacek's guilt in performing it, are never in dispute in the film; what is at stake is the right of a retributive (or deterrent) form of capital punishment by the State. Thus the film intersperses the narrative of how Jacek comes to perform the murder with the musings of Piotr Balicki, the young lawyer assigned to defend him, about the appropriateness of capital punishment as a deterrent within modern society. To illustrate the nature of the debate, the film opens with a voice-over narration as Balicki faces the judgment of the Council of Defence lawyers who are considering his application to join their ranks. He wrestles internally with the reason why anyone would wish to become a lawyer. Piotr gives voice to the central issue, which dominates the focus of the film as a whole, when he says,

> The law should not imitate nature, the law should improve nature. People invented the law to govern their relationships. The law determines who we are and how we live. We either observe it, or break it. People are free. Their freedom is limited only by the freedom of others. Punishment means revenge. In particular when it aims to harm, but it does not prevent crime. To whom does the law avenge? In the name of the innocent? Do the innocent make the rules?

The film opens with the taxi driver, who lives on the Warsaw housing estate, going to wash his taxi at the beginning of the new working day. One of the remarkable things that the film does is illustrate how involved *all* of the characters are in human wickedness and sinfulness. No one is without guilt in some form within the film, including the taxi driver who is murdered, since he is depicted as exhibiting his own carelessness, even wickedness, in how he treats some of his potential clients. Time and time again we are presented with images of human failing, human wickedness, human self-centredness as the film progresses. It is as if to say that we are all involved in the human condition and that each of us, in his or her own way, is implicated in the descent into murder that ensnares Jacek. At the same time the arbitrariness of the murder of Waldemar by Jacek is highlighted repeatedly; if only Waldemar had taken the fare of two passengers who had waited patiently for him to finish washing his taxi, he would have never picked up the murderous Jacek. Irony is also given voice, by the fact that the defence lawyer Piotr happens to be present in the cafeteria wherein Jacek plans his murder of Waldemar by winding the rope he uses to strangle the taxi driver around his hand (this scene is brought out more explicitly in the cinematic version of the film, a scene which helps explain Piotr's curious reference to his presence in the cafe in the TV version of the film which remains something of an enigma without full knowledge of the longer cinematic version).

The 'mystery man' makes two appearances within this film. The first is when he is shown to be a traffic construction worker holding a sign with which he stops the taxi containing the ill-fated Waldemar and his passenger Jacek. The mystery man looks at Jacek within the taxi as if to challenge him about his proposed action. The second appearance takes place when Jacek is in prison awaiting execution for his crime. Here the mystery man enters the prison carrying a ladder just as the young lawyer Piotr meets the judge of the trial on his way to speak to Jacek immediately before the execution. The anti-capital punishment theme comes through most clearly in the final emotive scenes between Jacek and his lawyer Piotr. Piotr not only declares defiantly to the prison guards that he will never be ready for the execution to be carried out, but declares (in the final spoken words of the film) that he abhors the idea of killing—a classic declaration against state executions if ever there was one.

f. Decalogue Six: *'Thou shalt not commit adultery.'*
This episode details the story of a young, nineteen-year-old postal clerk named Tomek who has an obsession for an older woman who lives in the building opposite him within the Warsaw housing estate. The woman's name is Magda and it is clear from the start that she is very much a woman of the age, freely engaging in a sexual relationship with a man who visits her regularly. This stands in stark contrast to Tomek who lives with his landlady from whom he rents a room within which he has a telescope trained on Magda's apartment opposite. In effect Tomek is a voyeur, a peeping-tom who derives much delight in disrupting the

romantic relationship Magda has with her lover by means of telephone calls and fictitious reports of gas leaks in her flat to the relevant authorities who arrive at a delicate moment of intimacy. It is clear that he does not find it easy to accept her involvement with another man and he does everything possible to courage it.

However, Tomek's interest in Magda is not merely one of detached sexual lust; it is not simply that he wishes that he himself was sexually involved with her. He truly loves Magda and is desperate to find an appropriate way of expressing this to her. Eventually he finds enough courage to speak to her face to face about his feelings for her and this establishes a different relationship between them. She mocks his interest in her, inviting her lover over to her flat and revealing to him as they prepare to make love that they are being watched from across the way. The result is that Tomek is humiliated and beaten up when he is confronted by the angry lover who storms out of Magda's flat and demands that Tomek present himself on the grounds between the two blocks of flats. Eventually Magda invites Tomek to her flat and attempts to seduce him, discovering in the process that he has never been with a woman before and ridiculing him when he cannot perform sexually as one might expect. He flees from her apartment and tries to commit suicide by slashing his wrists with a razor blade. Fortunately Tomek's landlady finds him and calls an ambulance which takes him to the hospital. Magda begins to realize the depths of Tomek's love for her and slowly, painfully, is made to face the fact that her treatment of him is shameful. The final scenes of the film have Magda confront Tomek after he has been released from the hospital. He tells her that he is no longer watching her apartment, the implication being that the love which he had for her is no longer alive. The shock on Magda's face tells all—she has realized what she has lost in spurning the love and affections of the inexperienced Tomek in the way that she has. The episode leaves us wondering about the nature of sexual encounters between human beings, and what it means to fall in love with someone. In a sense we could say that Magda's flippant treatment of Tomek is a form of adultery inasmuch as he loves her and is chaste towards her, even though he is not formally married to her or sexually involved with her. Magda is forced to realize that her casual dismissal of love in favour of promiscuous sex is inherently dissatisfying.

The 'mystery man' makes an appearance within this episode confronting Tomek just after he has taken on a milkman's round in an effort to be closer to Magda. The scene is one of exhilaration for young Tomek, since he has now discovered a way to speak to the woman he has come to love. Soon, however, the exhilaration will give way to despair as his love is spurned by Magda.

g. Decalogue Seven: *'Thou shalt not steal.'*
The essence of this episode is the struggle between Majka and her mother, Ewa, over a six-year-old girl named Ania. The relationships between the three are not as they first appear, for we soon come to realise that Ania is in fact the daughter of Majka, even though she has grown up believing that Ewa was her mother and that Majka was merely her older sister. Clearly Ewa, a formidable headmistress at a local school, is the engineer of this complex web of deceit and the one who brought superficial stability to a potentially disastrous situation. She is the dominant figure in the household where the three females live with Majka's father, Stefan, in the Warsaw apartment block. We learn as the story unfolds that Ania was born as a result of an illicit relationship between Majka and one of the teachers at the school, a man named Wojtek; Majka was only sixteen years old at the time. Majka is tired of living the lie and obviously is on a painful journey of self-discovery, wishing to emigrate to Canada and reconstruct her life there with her daughter. Majka manages to 'kidnap' the impressionable Ania during a school play and takes her to a remote village where she knows Wojtek lives as a maker of toy teddy bears, having rebuilt his life following Majka's pregnancy. However, he does not want to have anything to do with Majka's rather flawed and desperate plan and he tries to encourage Majka to contact her mother and at least explain what is happening and that the child is safe. Our sympathy for Ania is promoted by the fact that she cannot go to sleep at night without crying, obviously because she is in some deep emotional trauma brought about by her anomalous predicament, perhaps instinctively feeling that something is not right within the family set-up.

There is a great deal of resentment within Majka concerning the situation, resentment which is focused on Ewa whom she feels has 'stolen' her daughter from her to meet her own emotional needs. The crucial line of dialogue that brings the episode to its climax is a rhetorical question which is uttered by Majka to Wojtek as she contemplates what she is doing in taking Ania away from her home: 'Can you steal something that's yours?' In a way *both* Majka and Ewa have broken the seventh commandment against stealing, not least because they have treated little Ania as a mere possession, something to be owned. In one sense we could say that this facet of the episode is rather forced for we generally would not describe human beings in such terms. Yet, at the same time, and in a rather clever fashion, it opens up for our consideration what the true nature of theft involves: the all-consuming desire for possession. And most striking of all within this film is the way in which Majka is continuing in her relationship with Ania the cycle of domination and self-centredness that she experienced at the hands of her own mother Ewa. In effect, both women are stealing that which does not, in the strictest sense of the term, 'belong' to them.

As mentioned above, the 'mystery man' sequence of this particular episode had to be cut from the film because of the poor quality of the filming. However, we know from the published screenplay where he was supposed to have appeared in the story. In fact, he was to have made two brief appearances, both in scenes where Majka struggles to define her relationship with Ania. The first was to have occurred early on in the film, as Majka picks up Ania from the playground at school, where the 'mystery man' slowly makes his way past them supporting himself by crutches. The second was to have occurred as one of the last scenes of the film just as Majka boards a train to take her away from the daughter she cannot seem to have and the mother who prevents her from finding fulfilment as a parent. Here the 'mystery man' gets off of the train, again supported by crutches, and looks over towards Majka and her mother. The fact that he is in both instances disabled may underline the psychological state of both Majka and Ewa, not to mention that of the emotionally traumatized Ania who cannot get to sleep at night without crying.

h. Decalogue Eight: *'Thou shalt not bear false witness.'*
This episode is unique within the *Decalogue* in that it grounds its ethical parable in a concrete historical setting. In this case we are dealing with some of the ethical dilemmas presented by the Second World War, particularly those arising out of the persecution of the Jews by the Gestapo during the German occupation of Poland. The episode concerns the relationship between an elderly professor, named Zofia, who lives in the apartment block and teaches ethics at the University of Warsaw, and a younger researcher from New York named Elzbieta Loranz who comes to visit the professor and sit in on some of the professor's

lectures as part of a cultural exchange programme. We discover as the two are introduced to one another by the Dean of the University that they have in fact already met in the United States when Elzbieta served as Zofia's translator and guide during a recent lecture tour she made there. As we watch, however, we begin to suspect that the relationship between the two women is much more involved than we first suspected; the furtive glances between them, and the strained conversations they share, lead us to this conclusion. We are led to believe that Zofia is a kind-hearted woman who is well-disposed towards the people that she lives with in the apartment block. We are treated to a couple of scenes, for example, in which she demonstrates a polite interest in the stamp collection of one of her fellow residents.

The story comes to a climax when Elzbieta sits in on one of Zofia's classes and relates an ethical problem for the class to consider; in fact she tells her own story. She sets the scene as February of 1943, when a little six-year-old Jewish girl is being taken to a house in a suburb of Warsaw by a guardian who has been sheltering her in the family cellar in an outlying village. However, the Gestapo are due to move into the village soon and new arrangements for the safety of the little girl have to be made. The girl is being taken to Warsaw in order to meet a couple who have agreed to assist her in escaping from the Gestapo by becoming her adoptive godparents and then arranging her safe conduct to another family. They have agreed to do this on one condition: that the girl have formal documentation of her Christian baptism. The necessary paper-work has been prepared and a sympathetic Catholic priest found to perform the ceremony. When the girl arrives at the flat in Warsaw with her guardian she is told by the (prospective) adoptive godparents that they are unable to go through with the ceremony and give as their excuse the fact that they did not want to bear false witness and break the Eighth Commandment. As Elzbieta explains, 'The false witness they were about to commit was incompatible with their principles'. The adoptive godparents were, of course, Zofia and her husband and their refusal to go forward with the religious fiction meant that they were sending the little girl into almost certain death. Only now, after some forty years have passed, does Zofia realize that the little girl has survived the war and now stands before her, named Elzbieta. This revelation leads to a renewed friendship between the two, and Zofia, having invited Elzbieta to stay with her in her flat, eventually explains why she and her husband acted as they did that fateful night in 1943. She relates how news had come to them that the underground network with which they worked was due to be compromised through the acceptance of the little Jewish girl and that they sacrificed her for the sake of the continuance of the resistance organization. This brings a new perspective to the situation for Elzbieta and she realizes the anguish that Zofia has had to live with all these years, feeling a deep sense of guilt that her action led (at least as far as she could determine) directly to the death of an innocent child. Elzbieta wishes to meet the people who offered to take her in and hide her following the Christian baptism and Zofia arranges this. However, the man, who now works as a tailor on the other side of the city, does not remember Elzbieta, or at least refuses point-blank to talk to her about anything that happened in the war. It is obvious that the memories are too painful for him.

In two ironic but powerfully presented twists in the story line the implications of bearing false witness are brought home. First, Elzbieta is presented as a devout and believing Christian, praying at her bedside before going to sleep in Zofia's flat; we are given several scenes in which she unconsciously fingers a necklace bearing a cross around her neck, a symbol of Christian belief. The irony of this is that the reason originally given for rejecting her was that a Christian baptism would have implicated Zofia and her husband in false witness. Secondly, we learn that the couple who were to hide Elzbieta following her baptism were themselves the victims of false accusations being made against them with the result that the man, the tailor who refused to discuss the war with Elzbieta, spent many years in prison as an alleged Gestapo agent. In short, we see the devastating effects of bearing false witness against others worked out in the lives of its victims.

The 'mystery man' makes an appearance as one of the students in Zofia's class, watching intently the conversation that takes place between her and Elzbieta.

i. Decalogue Nine: *'Thou shalt not covet thy neighbour's wife.'*
This episode chronicles the tragic marriage of Roman and Hanka as they have to deal with problems surrounding sexual relationships and the love and trust which is contained within them. Roman is a talented surgeon who discovers that he has a medical condition which means that he is impotent, physically incapable of making love with his wife. This causes all sorts of questions to arise in his mind about the stability and permanence of their relationship and he tells Hanka that it will be

necessary for her to take a lover. This idea she rejects, saying that what they have is much more important than what they do not have. In fact, however, the problem has been going on for some time and she already has a young lover, named Mariusz. Hanka manages to keep her illicit relationship with Mariusz secret from Roman although he begins to suspect something. Roman is desperately trying to deal with the perceived loss of his manhood and starts to catch Hanka in her affair, listening to her telephone conversations, reading her mail, and rummaging through her handbag. Eventually he does follow Hanka to her mother's apartment where she is meeting Mariusz. Roman sits outside on the staircase while the two are inside in bed, uncertain about what he should do.

However, it is clear that Hanka is not satisfied with the situation and that her affair with Mariusz has hardly been an easy decision for her. The next week Hanka arranges to meet Mariusz again at the same place in order to break off the relationship; what she does not realize is that Roman is hidden in the wardrobe and is watching the proceedings. After she dismisses Mariusz, turning him away despite his offer to marry, she discovers Roman in his hiding place and confronts him about his presence there. This leads to a reconciliation between them in which she promises never to hide anything from him again and not to force him to secrete himself in a wardrobe as he has. The two agree that they will try and rebuild their lives together and adopt a child. They also decide that they need some time away from each other. Hanka books a skiing holiday in the mountains near Zakopane and Roman returns to work at the hospital. Soon after she goes on her trip, however, Roman happens to see Mariusz loading some skiing equipment into his car. This causes doubts to rise in Roman's mind about Hanka's trust and he writes a note to her, presumably to end their relationship, which he leaves by the telephone in their flat. Hanka is surprised to discover that Mariusz has come independently to the ski resort and quickly deduces what his presence there means as far as her relationship with Roman is concerned; if Roman were to find out, he would falsely presume she was continuing the affair with Mariusz. She tries to telephone him at the hospital but cannot reach him, and decides to travel back to Warsaw on the next available bus. Meanwhile Roman has made a half-hearted bid at suicide while cycling and is lying on a bed in the emergency ward of the hospital, fearing the worst as far as his wife's fidelity is concerned. He is told by one of the nurses that Hanka had telephoned earlier and that she was returning to Warsaw. He telephones home and speaks with her, the trust re-established and their love for each other confirmed.

The 'mystery man' makes two appearances in the film, both while riding a bicycle. The first occurs while Roman is returning from a hospital in Krakow and he nearly skids off of the road while driving his car; the 'mystery man' cycles by. The second occurs while Roman is himself riding his bicycle to work out his frustration and attempt suicide by riding off a bridge after discovering that Hanka and Mariusz are both in Zakopane.

j. Decalogue Ten: *'Thou shalt not covet thy neighbour's goods.'*
The final episode picks up one of the incidental characters we met in an earlier segment, the stamp collector of *Decalogue Eight*, and builds its story around his stamp collection; in effect the collection becomes the 'neighbour's goods' of which the Commandment speaks. Within the story the old stamp collector, known as 'Root', has died and his collection has gone to his two surviving sons, named Jerzy and Artur. The sons have never had much of an interest in their father's hobby and certainly did not suspect that it was one of the most extensive private collections in the country with which their father had won several international competitions. The two sons, one of whom is a white-collar businessman and the other the lead singer in a popular rock band, decide to sell the collection and approach a stamp dealer with this in mind. They are astonished to discover that the collection is priceless and are somewhat embarrassed when another collector, who was a friend of 'Root', chastises them about breaking the collection up and for failing to appreciate that this was their father's life obsession—to sell it for simple profit is to dishonour his memory. He tells Jerzy and Artur that one set in particular is very valuable but that it is incomplete; one stamp out of the three-value set needs to be obtained in order to increase the value of the collection as a whole. The two brothers enter into the closed world of high-class philately, a world in which stamps are not so much bought or sold for cash but exchanged by serious collectors who wish to fill out their own collections and follow up their own interests. Through one of the dealers they befriend they are told of a way that they could obtain the missing stamp from their set, a rare pink Austrian Mercury from 1851. It could be obtained through a complicated series of trades among collectors which ultimately means that Jerzy must donate one of his kidneys so that the daughter of one of the collectors might live

independently of daily dialysis treatments. The pursuit of this rare stamp begins to take over the lives of the two brothers, with Jerzy finding relationships with his wife and son strained and Artur having to give up a tour with the band to help take care of the stamp obsession. Eventually Jerzy agrees to undergo the kidney operation although not without some reservations; Artur helps him to justify it to himself as a humanitarian gesture. While Jerzy is in the hospital, with Artur faithfully visiting him and waiting for his recovery from the surgery, the rest of the stamp collection is stolen by thieves who break into their father's apartment. Artur is devastated, but does not tell his brother until Jerzy is discharged from the hospital. In the end, the brothers get the rare pink Austrian mercury, but it is of limited value now that the rest of the collection is gone. Soon they are at each other's throats, each accusing the other before the police investigator of arranging the theft. Not only has the pursuit of the rare Austrian Mercury cost Jerzy his kidney and possibly his family, and Artur his career as the lead singer with his band, but the two brothers find their friendship tested to its very limits.

In the end they are reconciled to each other, and to the fact of human obsession about owning possessions, when they both happen to buy the latest, cheap Polish stamp issue. In a touching scene, with which the film closes, the two are seen looking at the latest, cheap, three-value stamp set that they have bought at the local post office. We are left feeling that they have found each other and lost everything else.

Summary

Within this chapter I have briefly examined several widely differing cinematic interpretations of the Ten Commandments, notably those of the American director Cecil B. De Mille and the Polish director Krzysztof Kieslowski. Both Kieslowski's *Decalogue* and De Mille's 1956 version of *The Ten Commandments* received critical awards following their general cinematic release and are well worth viewing. The Oscar-winning film by De Mille I have characterized as a highly fictionalized biography of Moses while the *Decalogue* cycle by Kieslowski I have described as essentially parabolic in nature, grounding its message, as it does, in contemporary settings and dealing with modern situations.

There is much to be gained from a critical, comparative viewing of the work of the two directors as they attempt to bring the Old Testament Mosaic Law to life. The main advantage of such a juxtaposition of the two film interpretations of the Ten Commandments is the insight into their ability to confront the viewer with the challenges contained within Exod. 20.1-17. We are left with an interesting question to ponder. Which of the two styles better confronts us with the meaning and message of the Ten Commandments? The answer we give is probably itself an indication of our own cultural assumptions and expectations, a hint about what we expect film to be and what we want it to do. No doubt the 1950s had a vastly different understanding of biblical history than would be found today, and the assumption that such history had been written *as it really was* and therefore could be presented as such would have been accepted in a way that few would find credible nowadays. It surely is no accident that the rise of the so-called Biblical Theology movement coincided with the heyday of the Biblical Epic in cinema; neither is it coincidental that both movements fell out of favour at about the same time. And yet, I wonder if perhaps in a few years time we will look back on Kieslowski's work and see with the benefit of critical hindsight how much his interpretation was shaped by the historical framework out of which it arose, the dying years of a communist society where moral ambiguities abounded and everything seemed dark and gloomy, the future uncertain.

Nevertheless, in many ways Kieslowski's effort is, in my opinion, much to be preferred as a means of engaging the meaning of the Mosaic Law since it involves the audience in the all too human dramas depicted, replete as they are with all of the complexities and dilemmas presented by life in our late twentieth-century world. On the other hand, the sheer grandeur of De Mille's spectacle can hardly be topped, and his attempt to translate literally the story of Moses, complete with burning bush and the very finger of God writing the Commandments into stone like a fire-bolt from heaven, remains in the memory for a long time. The same quality which today makes so many of Steven Spielberg's films such box-office successes is in operation here. It may indeed be pure escapism, a retreat into the shrouded (but safe and secure!) mists of ancient history, but it is all entertaining, not to say visually compelling, nonetheless.

Perhaps more than anything else we are presented, by means of a careful viewing of the work of both De Mille and Kieslowski, with an object lesson of how captivating the Old Testament can be when real imagination is put to work in bringing the story to cinematic expression. At the same time we also see, especially through De Mille's extravaganza, how easy it is to have the hermeneutical flow reversed and approach the

stories contained in the Bible through our own cultural expressions of
them. I wonder how many of us inadvertently find ourselves reading the
words of the story of Moses and the Exodus with the images of
Charlton Heston and De Mille running through our mind's eye? One
can but hope that Kieslowski's *Decalogue* film cycle will have such a
widespread distribution that it too will become part of our mental
heritage and help frame our understanding of the Ten Commandments
and their challenge to our lives.

Chapter 2

MOBY-DICK: ENCOUNTERING THE LEVIATHAN OF GOD

We generally associate whales with the story of Jonah in the Bible. Without doubt the miraculous deliverance of Jonah from what the author of the book describes in 2.2 as 'the belly of Sheol' makes the biblical story the most famous one about mammoth sea creatures ever written; this despite the fact that 'whale' is a rather inaccurate and, scientifically, an entirely misleading translation of the Hebrew words דָּג גָּדוֹל in Jon. 2.1 (they are translated rather more accurately as 'a great fish' in the AV).

If Jonah stands as the most famous of 'whale stories', then it would probably be fair to say that Herman Melville's *Moby-Dick; or, The Whale* (1851) ranks as number two in this regard. There is certainly much that can be learned about *Moby-Dick* by a careful consideration of how the story of Jonah is used within it. At the same time, I would also like within this chapter to explore briefly another biblical work which provides an opportunity to appreciate Melville's novel from a slightly different angle, one involving the difficult question of theodicy, the presence of suffering and evil in the world and how humans are reckoned to survive in the face of it. I refer, of course, to the book of Job, in many ways the most contemporary of all the Old Testament wisdom writings. By using the book of Job in the way that he has, Melville can join a select band of literary figures who might justly bear the title of 'The Modern Job'.[1] There is much to be gained from an examination of how Melville grapples with the central themes of the book of Job, interpreting them for his own day and, it must be admitted, arriving at some rather unorthodox and pessimistic conclusions. Most importantly of all, I would like to suggest that a key lesson about the significance of the epilogue of the book of Job can be gleaned by a

1. M. Friedman ('The Modern Job: Melville, Dostoievsky, and Kafka', *Judaism* 12 [1963], pp. 436-55) discusses this.

careful consideration of the way Melville's *Moby-Dick* uses this portion of the book of Job in *Moby-Dick*.

At first glance, the selection of these three pieces of literature as the focus of a comparative study may seem somewhat foolish. What do they have in common, after all, to warrant the comparison? The answer is quite simple: each, in its own way, uses the image of a man's encounter with Leviathan, the whale, as a means of framing its story. We could go so far as to suggest that in each case the encounter with the Leviathan is a window through which the book's whole message is to be glimpsed and its purpose recognized.

In keeping with the theme of this present study we shall also be looking at how Melville's *Moby-Dick* is itself interpreted by some of the more popular plays and films which are based upon it. The way that these adaptations handle the material invites us to consider afresh the meaning of the central image of Leviathan which unites Jonah, the book of Job and Melville's classic novel.

I shall pursue the task at hand in four parts: (1) The Writing of *Moby-Dick*; (2) The Biblical Sources of *Moby-Dick*; (3) Theatrical and Cinematic Interpretations of *Moby-Dick*; (4) Theological Symbolism in *Moby-Dick*.

1. *The Writing of* Moby-Dick

In a letter to Richard H. Dana Jr, author of another famous sea-faring tale, *Two Years before the Mast* (1840), we have Melville's first recorded mention of *Moby-Dick*. The letter was written on 1 May 1850 while he was midway through writing the novel; Melville describes his tale of the White Whale as 'a strange sort of a book'.[1] Elsewhere he describes it as a 'romance of adventure',[2] a description which perhaps reveals more about the novelist than it does about the novel itself. Certainly it is true that Melville's lifetime falls within the Romantic period; but it is difficult to describe *Moby-Dick* as a 'romance of adventure' and leave it at that. As a piece of literature Melville's *Moby-Dick* has been variously described. It has been labelled an epic romance, a tragedy, a moral fable, a symbolic poem in prose, a theological allegory,

1. *The Letters of Herman Melville* (ed. M.R. Davis and W.H. Gilman; New Haven: Yale University Press, 1960), p. 108.
2. In a letter to his English publisher Richard Bentley, dated 27 June 1850, in which Melville offers *Moby-Dick* for publication.

an American national epic, a 'disorderly elegy to democracy',[1] a spiritual autobiography, and, most interestingly, an 'apocalypse of the White Whale'.[2] Certainly it contains elements of all of these literary types, and more; yet it conforms to no one, single genre. This is one of the strengths of the work and one which has made it endlessly fascinating for subsequent literary interest, particularly within the last fifty years or so. The range of literary figures who praise *Moby-Dick* is quite astonishing. D.H. Lawrence greatly admired Melville, describing him as 'the greatest seer and poet of the sea'[3] and *Moby-Dick* as 'the greatest book of the seas ever written'.[4] W.H. Auden reckoned that the book was perhaps the best available to study 'the romantic conception of the relation between objective and subjective experience'.[5] E.M. Forster went so far as to suggest that a new category of literature was needed to describe it (which he labelled 'Prophecy'), and enrolled Melville alongside Fyodor Dostoyevsky, Emily Brontë and D.H. Lawrence as writers of such works. William Faulkner once remarked that *Moby-Dick* was the one book that he wished he had written, particularly as it details the turmoil within the central figure Ahab and traces what Faulkner poetically describes as his 'Golgotha of the heart'.[6] Jean-Paul Sartre described *Moby-Dick* as an 'imposing monument', ranking it alongside James Joyce's *Ulysses* as a literary work of enduring importance for today.[7]

Melville worked on *Moby-Dick,* his most famous novel, for nearly two years, from early 1850 until late summer of 1851.[8] For the most

---

1.   A. Delbanco, 'Introduction', to Herman Melville's *Moby-Dick or, The Whale* (London: Penguin Books, 1992), p. xxi.

2.   L. Buell, *'Moby-Dick* as Sacred Text', in R.H. Brodhead (ed.), *New Essays on Moby-Dick* (Cambridge: Cambridge University Press, 1986), p. 64.

3.   'Herman Melville's Typee and Omoo', in R. Chase (ed.), *Melville: A Collection of Critical Essays* (Englewood Cliffs, NJ: Prentice-Hall, 1962), p. 11.

4.   'Moby Dick, or the White Whale', in M.R. Stern (ed.), *Discussions of Moby-Dick* (Boston: D.C. Heath & Co., 1960), p. 43.

5.   'The Romantic Use of Symbols', in M.T. Gilmore (ed.), *Twentieth-Century Interpretations of Moby-Dick: A Collection of Critical Essays* (Englewood Cliffs, NJ: Prentice-Hall, 1977), p. 9.

6.   'View Points', in Gilmore (ed.), *Moby-Dick,* p. 109.

7.   'Herman Melville's *Moby-Dick'*, in Gilmore (ed.), *Moby-Dick,* p. 94.

8.   A recent discussion of the composition of *Moby-Dick* is J. Barbour, '"All My Books Are Botches": Melville's Struggle with *The Whale'*, in J. Barbour and

part the book was written at his farmhouse in Arrowhead near Pittsfield, Massachusetts where Melville lived with his wife and family of four children. He based much of it on his own experience of sailing on the whaling ships *Acushnet*, *Lucy Ann* and *Charles and Henry* during 1841–1843, although he filled this out with considerable research and investigation into every aspect of whaling, exhausting available libraries to make his account more realistic and factual. The book was first published in three volumes in London by Richard Bentley on 18 October 1851, with an American edition appearing in New York published by Harper's and Brothers a month later on 14 November. Even by Melville's considerable standards it was an enormous book (635 pages in the American edition and containing 135 chapters plus an Epilogue!). The novel was his sixth pursuing a nautical theme, following the pattern set by his earlier works *Typee* (1846), *Omoo* (1847), *Redburn* (1849), *Mardi* (1849) and *White-Jacket* (1850), but it was not a commercial success, going out of print in America in 1887 having sold a total of only 3180 copies. For the most part the public ignored it, much to the author's great dismay. It was generally adjudged to be an uneven work, caught in the twilight-zone between fact (the materials on whales and whaling) and fiction (the story of the pursuit of Moby-Dick).[1]

One of the great ironies is that Melville spent the last 20 years of his life working as a customs official in New York with his talent unrecognized. He died on 8 September 1891 in relative poverty, virtually forgotten by the literary world. It was not until after the turn of the century that he was to be rediscovered as a writer of immense importance, largely on the basis of *Moby-Dick*. The simple fact of the matter is that it was a book ahead of its time and it took a later generation to recognize its worth. Now *Moby-Dick* is consistently ranked as one of

---

T. Quirk (eds.), *Writing the American Classics* (London: University of North Carolina Press, 1990), pp. 25-52.

1.   So marked are some of the narrative tensions (and inconsistencies!) within the novel that some scholars have suggested that Melville changed the direction of the work in the course of writing it. Of crucial importance in the issue is Melville's relationship with Nathaniel Hawthorne and the influence of Hawthorne upon Melville's developing story-line. On the question see: G.R. Stewart, 'The Two *Moby-Dicks*', *AL* 5 (1954), pp. 417-18; J.M. Loving, 'Melville's Pardonable Sin', *NEQ* 47 (1974), pp. 262-78; R. Chase, 'Melville and *Moby-Dick*', in R. Chase (ed.), *Melville: A Collection of Critical Essays* (Englewood Cliffs, NJ: Prentice-Hall, 1962), pp. 49-61; J. Barbour, 'The Composition of *Moby-Dick*', *AL* 47 (1974), pp. 343-60.

the three or four most important American novels of the nineteenth century and has earned Melville a rightful place in literary history.

The book is filled with a host of references and allusions to people, places and works of literature. Melvillian scholars have had a field-day attempting to track down and identify the sources for the novel. Chief among them has been, of course, the Bible, without doubt the major background source for all of Melville's stories. However, many other important sources can also be identified, including various plays of Shakespeare (notably the tragedies *King Lear*, *Macbeth* and *The Tempest*), Milton's *Paradise Lost*, Coleridge's *Rime of the Ancient Mariner*, Thomas Carlyle's *Sartor Resartus*, Edgar Allen Poe's *The Narrative of Arthur Gordon Pym*, and several of the novels by Melville's friend and neighbour Nathaniel Hawthorne, to whom he dedicated the work.[1] Chief among these are Hawthorne's *Twice-Told Tales*, *Mosses from an Old Manse* and *The Scarlet Letter*. However, we must confine our attention to the biblical materials so foundational to the novel. Let us now turn to consider more fully some of the quotations and allusions within *Moby-Dick* to the biblical books of Jonah and Job.

2. Moby-Dick *and the Bible: The Twin Sources of Melville's Leviathan*

The Penguin Classics edition of *Moby-Dick* (first published in 1986) acknowledges the importance of both Jonah and the book of Job as sources for Melville's work.[2] Harold Beaver, who edited the text and provides an extensive commentary to accompany it, discusses about a dozen places in the novel where Jonah and the book of Job are either alluded to or quoted.[3] I shall use his commentary as a basic guide to the

---

1. The relationship between Melville and Hawthorne is fully discussed in Barbour, 'Composition', pp. 32-39.

2. Quotations from *Moby-Dick* within this study are taken from this edition. Throughout the discussion I shall identify the major quotations by their chapter number and title; thus the first chapter appears as '1. Loomings'. In 1992 Penguin Classics also issued what is described as 'The Definitive Text' of the work, *Moby-Dick or, The Whale*, with an Introduction by A. Delbanco and Notes and Explanatory Commentary by T. Quirk.

3. H.B. Franklin (*The Wake of the Gods: Melville's Mythology* [Stanford: Stanford University Press, 1963]) puts forward an interesting case for the ultimate reliance of Melville upon the Egyptian myth of Osiris for his theme in *Moby-Dick*,

discussion here, although I will occasionally mention additional passages from *Moby-Dick* which also allude to or quote Jonah and Job. To be fair, there are other biblical passages which are likewise used by Melville to significant purposes within the novel, notably 1 Kings 16–22 which provides the name of his central character Ahab, and Isa. 27.1 which probably provides the title for the fated ship of the narrative, the *Pequod*.[1] But it is Jonah and the book of Job which are most important for our consideration, and on these we will concentrate.

What unites Jonah and the book of Job within *Moby-Dick* is the fact that they both include discussion of a mythological beast known as 'Leviathan'. In short, Melville is ultimately reliant upon the biblical texts for his use of the term 'Leviathan' as a description of the White Whale (which he uses some 104 times within the book). This is true despite the fact that, technically, 'Leviathan' appears nowhere in the book of Jonah, although it does occur in Job 3.8 and 41.1[2] and in Isa. 27.1.[3] The

---

arguing (p. 97) that 'Melville saw Egyptian mythology as the direct source of the Hebrew mythology'.

1. W.G. Braude, 'Melville's *Moby-Dick*', *Exp* 21 (1962–63), n. 23, suggests that Melville derived the name of the ship from the Hebrew verb translated 'shall punish' (*yi-pequod*) in Isa. 27.1.

2. The term 'Leviathan' also appears in Pss. 74.14 and 104.26, while whales are also referred to in 1.21. It is worth noting that on the opening page of *Moby-Dick*, in the so-called 'Extracts', Melville also cites, in addition to these five scriptural references, several other important works of literature which make reference to this mythological beast. Included are lines from Milton's *Paradise Lost*, Hobbes's *Leviathan*, and Dryden's *Annus Mirabilis*. Melville nowhere cites Job 3.8, probably because he was reliant upon the AV which mistranslates the reference to Leviathan. The connection between Leviathan and whales should be retained (at least as far as Melville's use of Job 41.14 is concerned) despite the fact that some recent commentators feel the animal being described in Job 40–41 is a hippopotamus (D. Atkinson, *The Message of Job* [Leicester: Inter-Varsity Press, 1991], pp. 148-51) or a Nile crocodile (C.S. Rodd, *The Book of Job* [EC; London: Epworth Press, 1990], p. 79). Other commentators have taken the beasts Behemoth and Leviathan to be any number of natural creatures. J. Day (*God's Conflict with the Dragon and the Sea* [Cambridge: Cambridge University Press, 1985], pp. 62-87) disagrees, arguing that both Behemoth and Leviathan are purely mythological creatures and that the descriptions in Job 40.15–41.26 do not fit any known natural creature, be it whale, crocodile, hippopotamus or dolphin. J.C.L. Gibson ('A New Look at Job 41.1-4 [English 41.9-12]', in R.P. Carroll [ed.], *Text as Pretext: Essays in Honour of Robert Davidson* [JSOTSup, 138; Sheffield: JSOT Press, 1992], pp. 129-39) concurs. Gibson remarks (p. 130) that Leviathan's role is 'to be the embodiment of evil' and

mythological beast 'Leviathan' was also a subject of considerable speculation among later Jewish writers, usually as the main course at the banquet meal celebrating God's victory over his foes (see *1 En.* 60; *4 Ezra* 6.38-52 and *2 Bar.* 29.3-4). Melville cites none of these subsequent developments of the idea of 'Leviathan' within his work and appears to have been unaware of them. For him it is Jonah and Job which formed the basis for his creative adaptation of the 'Leviathan' myth.

not to denote some living creature. Also see his 'On Evil in the Book of Job', in L. Eslinger and G. Taylor (eds.), *Ascribe to the Lord: Biblical and Other Essays in Memory of Peter C. Craigie* (JSOTSup, 67; Sheffield: JSOT Press, 1992), pp. 399-419; J.V.K. Wilson, 'A Return to the Problems of Behemoth and Leviathan', *VT* 25 (1975), pp. 1-14; N.C. Habel, *The Book of Job* (OTL; London: SCM Press, 1985), pp. 568-74; H. Rowold, 'Leviathan and Job in Job 41:2-3', *JBL* 105 (1986), pp. 104-109, for more on the subject.

3. Scholarly debate has ranged far and wide about the precise meaning of this cryptic verse in Isa. 27.1 and its place within the eschatological section of Isa. 24–27, a section generally regarded as foundational for much of the later eschatological work produced by Jewish writers. The threefold description of the monster is particularly intriguing. Do the three monsters described represent three separate nations oppressing Israel, and if so, which ones? Do the two 'Leviathans' represent the two rivers of Assyria and Babylon, the Tigris and the Euphrates? Or perhaps we should follow the lead of Ps. 74.13-14 where the nation Egypt is portrayed as both the dragon of the sea and the beast of the deep, Leviathan. This seems to be precisely the direction that the author of the Targum of Isaiah takes when he alters the two 'Leviathans' into two human figures, the Pharaoh of Egypt and King Sennacherib of Assyria and Babylonia. It has also been suggested that Leviathan is a symbol for Tyre, and that God's judgment on the city is portrayed by means of his victory over the beast. Others have suggested that we would do better to take the threefold description as referring not to nations or rivers, but to an unspecified, representative foe of God's people. These and other questions have perplexed scholars for many years, and no doubt will continue to do so. What does seem clear is that the author of the passage is equating the restoration of the nation Israel with the mythological story about God's conquest of the primaeval monster(s) of chaos. As the author of the most recent, detailed study of the passages (D.G. Johnson, *From Chaos to Restoration: An Alternative Reading of Isaiah 24–27* [JSOTSup, 61; Sheffield: JSOT Press, 1988]) has affirmed (p. 84): 'In light of the fact that the author understood exile as a collapse into chaos, it is appropriate that he argues that 24:21–27:1 was written during the exile when the prophet looked forward to the future destruction of Babylon by Yahweh'.

a. *Jonah and* Moby-Dick

Robert Carroll points us in the right direction when he says,

> As no text can be read without taking into account the many levels of
> interpretation which it has been granted through time...a reading of the
> book of Jonah will inevitably entail reading Herman Melville's novel,
> *Moby-Dick*, which enhances the Jonah legend of the great fish.[1]

It is clear that Melville had the story of the prophet Jonah in mind while
composing his novel, for he alludes to it at several places, most notably
the sermon by Father Mapple at the beginning of the book, in '9. The
Sermon'.[2] Indeed, one of the most creative things Melville does within
the whole of the novel is to rewrite Psalm 18 into a hymn of Jonah's
deliverance from the whale and place it at the beginning of this sermon.[3]
Father Mapple takes as his main text Jon. 1.17: 'And God had prepared
a great fish to swallow up Jonah'. This helps set the tone for all that is to
follow as the story of Captain Ahab's vengeful battle with the whale is
unfolded. One critic goes so far as to suggest that

> Melville establishes an antithesis between the doctrine of Father Mapple's
> sermon and the conduct of Captain Ahab. Jonah and Ahab react in oppo-
> site ways to a similar incident: the attack of a whale.[4]

Yet one of the most interesting things about Melville's use of Jonah
within Father Mapple's sermon is the fact that it is only chs. 1–3 which
are discussed within the preaching. The repentance of Nineveh and the

---

1.   'The Discombobulations of Time and the Diversities of Text: Notes on the
Rezeptionsgeschichte of the Bible', in Carroll (ed.), *Text as Pretext*, p. 64.

2.   N. Wright, *Melville's Use of the Bible* (Durham, NC: Duke University Press,
1949), pp. 82-91, offers a good introduction on the importance of the character of
Jonah in the novel.

3.   D.H. Battenfield, 'The Source of the Hymn in *Moby-Dick*', *AL* 27 (1955), pp.
393-96, discusses this at some length.

4.   T.W. Herbert, Jr, 'Calvinism and Cosmic Evil in *Moby-Dick*', *PMLA* 84
(1969), p. 1613. Similarly, R. Stewart ('The Vision of Evil in Hawthorne and
Melville', in N.A. Scott, Jr [ed.], *The Tragic Vision and the Christian Faith* [New
York: Association Press, 1957], p. 256) remarks, 'Father Mapple's sermon about
Jonah gives us a yardstick by which to measure the sin of Ahab'. D. Hoffman
('*Moby-Dick*: Jonah's Whale or Job's?', in Gilmore [ed.], *Moby-Dick*, p. 63) says,
'Melville consistently presents Ahab, his Anti-Christ in the guise of an unrepentant
Jonah'.

mercy of God are not included within the sermon,[1] perhaps simply because they distract attention from Jonah himself, or more likely because Melville here wants to have a go at the harshness of the Calvinism which Mapple represents.[2] A powerful image of the remoteness of Calvinism is made within the narrative as Father Mapple ascends to the prow-like pulpit, drawing the rope ladder up behind him. As Melville comments, alluding to the closed theological system of Calvinism, 'this pulpit…is a self-contained strong-hold'. Embedded within passages like this which purport to defend and support traditional Christian views is a powerful critique of religious orthodoxy, lying so still and well hidden that the critique is often overlooked. Father Mapple's sermon on Jonah certainly contains much more than is at first glance visible; indeed, it may well be that Lawrance Thompson is right in describing it as a 'trap' set by Melville early on in *Moby-Dick* to test the religious discrimination of his readers.[3]

The next reference to Jonah within the book is a passing comment in '32. Cetology', a long chapter given over to a discussion of scientific questions dealing with whales. Here the witness of the biblical prophet is brought in to dispute the opinion of the scientist Linnaeus that whales are separate from fish. Melville, through his narrator Ishmael, counters, 'I take the good old-fashioned ground that the whale is a fish, and call upon holy Jonah to back me'. The question of the literalness of the account of Jonah being swallowed by a whale is the focus of several other references to the prophet within *Moby-Dick*, notably the three times his name appears in '82. The Honor and Glory of Whaling' and the dozen mentions of Jonah in '83. Jonah Historically Regarded'. Throughout these two chapters Melville appears to be concerned with defending the traditional interpretation of Jonah having been swallowed by a real whale against mythical or symbolic interpretations of it. He shows in the course of his discussion awareness of some of the

---

1. Josephus, *Ant.* 9.208-14, also omits the theme of repentance within his retelling of the story of Jonah.

2. J. McIntosh ('The Mariner's Multiple Quest', in Brodhead [ed.], *New Essays*, p. 42) says, 'By involving Mapple in this misreading of Jonah, Melville undercuts Mapple's claim to authority and invites the reader to view Mapple's Christianity ironically'.

3. *Melville's Quarrel with God* (Princeton, NJ: Princeton University Press, 1952), p. 10.

arguments of contemporary biblical scholars of his day on the matter. However, most scholars agree that Melville is actually making a tongue-in-cheek criticism of such orthodox defenders of the literalness of the story of Jonah's encounter with the whale by purporting to be defending it.

Two passing references to Jonah are also contained in '55. Of the Monstrous Pictures of Whales', although they do not really contribute anything to how Jonah is used by Melville in connection with his symbol Moby-Dick. These two references merely demonstrate again the basic tradition of Jonah being swallowed by a whale. A similar occurrence comes in '75. The Right Whale's Head—Contrasted View' where Melville, through the narrator Ishmael, gives us an anatomical tour of a whale which had been killed and butchered by the crew of the *Pequod*. As he comes to describe the large, gaping jaw of the whale he asks, 'Good Lord! is this the road that Jonah went?' Similarly, in '102. A Bower in the Arsacides' Jonah is mentioned twice as the narrator Ishmael confesses himself a rather second-rate witness as to what the insides of a whale look like when compared to Jonah. Here, once again, the focus is on the anatomy of whales, and the historicity of the story of Jonah being swallowed by the whale is assumed as the basis for the discussion. In '104. The Fossil Whale' Melville mentions an old legend associating the prophet Jonah with the Temple of Dendara in Egypt. According to the legend, it is at the base of this temple that the whale vomited Jonah onto the shore. Throughout *Moby-Dick* Melville plays with this idea of Jonah being literally inside the 'belly of the whale', inserting his equivalents of it (such as Tashtego falling inside the sperm whale's severed head in '78. Cisterns and Buckets').

Another interesting allusion to Jonah appears in '19. The Prophet' where the character Elijah explains how it was that Ahab first encountered Moby-Dick off the coast of Cape Horn. It was here, the wild-eyed prophet Elijah explains, that Ahab lost his leg to the White Whale and 'lay like dead for three days and nights'. The allusion is straight from Jon. 1.17, where the fleeing figure of Jonah is said to lie 'in the belly of the fish for three days and nights'. Once again the text upon which Father Mapple's sermon was based comes to the fore in the story.[1]

---

1.   Rarely do commentaries on Jonah mention Melville's *Moby-Dick* as having any basis in the biblical story. A quotation from Father Mapple's sermon on Jonah

b. *Job and* Moby-Dick

The past two decades have witnessed a flood of new commentaries, monographs and articles being published on the book of Job; one recent commentary lists over 1000 such works as available for study of the book.[1] Questions about the precise place that Job has within the wisdom literature of Judaism have long been raised as a matter of considerable scholarly debate.[2] The book itself presents notoriously difficult textual problems, with considerable differences between the MT and the LXX versions. Questions of authorship, provenance, structure, source composition (the relationship between the prose and poetic sections of the book; the place of the Elihu speeches), integrity[3] and, above all, the meaning of the book of Job are all hot topics of discussion. Yet the book of Job remains a literary gem and has served as the inspiration for some recent fiction works, including Albert Camus' *The Plague* (1947), Archibald MacLeish's Pulitzer Prize-winning *J.B., a Play in Verse* (1958), Neil Simon's *God's Favourite* (1975) and Muriel Spark's *The Only Problem* (1984),[4] as well as a creative poem by Robert Frost entitled 'A Masque

appears at the beginning of the commentary section of J. Sasson, *Jonah* (AB, 24B; Garden City, NY: Doubleday, 1990), p. 65, although it is not discussed within the commentary itself.

1. D.J.A. Clines, *Job: 1–20* (WBC, 17; Waco, TX: Word Books, 1989). C.S. Rodd ('Which is the Best Commentary?: Job', *ExpTim* 97 [1985–86], pp. 356-60) offers an assessment on some of the available commentaries.

2. R. Gordis, 'Wisdom and Job', in S. Sandmel (ed.), *Old Testament Issues* (London: SCM Press, 1969), pp. 213-41, offers a good introduction to this topic.

3. See: J.A. Baker, 'The Book of Job: Unity and Meaning', in E.A. Livingstone (ed.), *Studia Biblica I (1978)* (JSOTSup, 11; Sheffield: JSOT Press, 1979), pp. 17-26; J.F.A. Sawyer, 'The Authorship and Structure of the Book of Job', in Livingstone (ed.), *Studia Biblica I*, pp. 253-57; Y. Hoffman, 'The Relation between the Prologue and the Speech-Cycles in Job: A Reconsideration', *VT* 31 (1981), pp. 160-70; R.D. Moore, 'The Integrity of Job', *CBQ* 45 (1983), pp. 17-31.

4. MacLeish's play is briefly discussed in J.L. Crenshaw, 'The Wisdom Literature', in D.A. Knight and G.M. Tucker (eds.), *The Hebrew Bible and its Modern Interpreters* (Philadelphia: Fortress Press, 1985), p. 387. Spark's work is discussed in H. Pyper, 'The Reader in Pain: Job as Text and Pretext', in Carroll (ed.), *Text as Pretext*, pp. 234-55; and D. Jasper, *The Study of Literature and Religion: An Introduction* (London: Macmillan, 2nd edn, 1992), pp. 132-35. We could perhaps also add science-fiction writer R.A. Heinlein to our discussion. His book *Job: A Comedy of Justice* (New York: Ballantine Books, 1984) provides us with a space-age version of the title character.

of Reason' (1945).[1] No doubt all of this says something about the newly discovered relevance and importance of the book of Job to the modern situation. Yet within this flood of new material given over to the book it is difficult to find theologians taking much notice of Melville's indebtedness to it. This is so despite the declaration by Professor James Barr that 'Job is an outstanding example of a biblical book which has to be evaluated as literature',[2] and Melville's *Moby-Dick* provides an ideal starting point for accomplishing just that.

One sometimes wonders if the biblical specialists are even aware of Melville's *Moby-Dick* at all, so rarely is it discussed as being dependent upon the book of Job. One would think that it ought to warrant a footnote or two at least, particularly within the commentaries which are, after all, supposed to help make Job accessible to the average 'person in the pew'.[3] Indeed, there is much to be said for associating Melville's adventurous, sea-faring tale with the book of Job, at least as the source for the novel's central symbol. As Melville rhetorically asks in '24. The Advocate', 'Who wrote the first account of our Leviathan? Who but the mighty Job!' The basic plot of the novel is even summarized by an evocative allusion to the book of Job at one crucial point in the story, in '41. Moby-Dick', where Ahab is described as 'this grey-headed, ungodly old man, chasing with curses a Job's whale round the world'. Another immediately obvious connection is the naming of the character of Captain Bildad, one of the Quaker owners of the fated whaling-ship *Pequod*; this unusual name is from the book of Job (Bildad the Shuhite is one of Job's three friends who first comes to comfort him in 2.11). Little wonder that many specialists in English literature (as opposed to theologians!) have turned to the book of Job as a means of entering into Melville's absorbing story.[4]

1.   Contained in *Selected Poems* (ed. I. Hamilton; London: Penguin Books, 1973), pp. 229-47. The poem is briefly discussed by R.E. Murphy, *The Tree of Life: An Exploration of Biblical Wisdom Literature* (AB Reference Library; Garden City, NY: Doubleday, 1990), p. 45, and by R.A.F. MacKenzie and R.E. Murphy, 'Job', in R.E. Brown, J.A. Fitzmyer and R.E. Murphy (eds.), *The New Jerome Biblical Commentary* (London: Geoffrey Chapman, 1991), p. 486.
2.   *The Bible in the Modern World* (London: SCM Press, 1973), p. 56.
3.   The one recent commentary which shows a recognition of Melville's work is the two-volume effort by D.J.A. Clines, *Job* (WBC, 17-18; Waco, TX: Word Books, 1989–forthcoming).
4.   The literature on this is quite extensive: Wright, *Melville's Use of the Bible*, pp. 105-108; F.X. Carfield, '*Moby Dick* and the Book of Job', *CW* 174 (1952), pp.

There are clear indications of the work helping to frame the background for much of what Melville is trying to accomplish within his novel, which, like the book of Job, explores the moral ambiguities of the tragedy which is life. C. Hugh Holman goes so far as to state that Job is 'pervasive and controlling' to Melville's composition.[1] Indeed, there are several notable clues to the importance of the book of Job as a source, not only for characterization, but also for much of the powerful imagery and penetrating theological exploration which dominates Melville's *Moby-Dick*.

The influence of passages from the book of Job can be detected at several points in the story. For instance, the curious reference in Job 1.7 to Satan 'going to and fro in the earth' in his bid to tempt humankind is alluded to twice within *Moby-Dick*. Both instances occur in veiled fashion, but to great effect. The first of these is found in '36. The Quarter Deck', where it is used to describe Ahab's stumping around the deck of the *Pequod* on his ivory leg:

> Soon his steady, ivory stride was heard, as to and fro he paced his old rounds, upon planks so familiar to his tread, that they were all over dented, like geological stones, with the peculiar mark of his walk.

The second allusion occurs in '73. Stubb and Flask Kill A Right Whale and Then Have a Talk Over Him' where Melville combines the image of Satan asking God for permission to tempt Job with Marlowe's and Goethe's adaptations of it wherein the Devil asks permission to tempt their title character Faust. Note this section from the chapter in which Stubb is speaking to his mate Flask:

> I don't know, Flask, but the devil is a curious chap, and a wicked one, I tell ye. Why, they say as how he went a sauntering into the old flag-ship once, switching his tail about devilish easy and gentleman-like, and inquiring if

254-60; C.H. Holman, 'The Reconciliation of Ishmael: *Moby-Dick* and the Book of Job', *SAQ* 57 (1958), pp. 477-90; T.Y. Booth, '*Moby Dick*: Standing up to God', *NCF* 17 (1962–63), pp. 33-43; N. Wright, '*Moby-Dick*: Jonah's or Job's Whale?', *AL* 37 (1965), pp. 190-195; J. Stout, 'Melville's Use of the Book of Job', *NCF* 25 (1970–71), pp. 69-83; E. Behnken, 'The Joban Theme in *Moby-Dick*', *IR* 33 (1976), pp. 37-48; Hoffman, '*Moby-Dick*', pp. 59-75; A. Holstein, 'Melville's Inversion of Job in *Moby-Dick*', *IR* 35 (1978), pp. 13-19; W.A. Young, 'Leviathan in the Book of Job and *Moby-Dick*', *Soundings* 25 (1982), pp. 388-401.
    1.   Holman, 'The Reconciliation of Ishmael', pp. 477.

the old governor was at home. Well, he was at home, and asked the devil what he wanted. The devil, switching his hoofs, up and says, 'I want John.' 'What for?' says the old governor. 'What business is that of yours,' says the devil, getting mad,—'I want to use him.' 'Take him,' says the governor—and by the Lord, Flask, if the devil didn't give John the Asiatic cholera before he got through with him, I'll eat this whale in one mouthful.

'John' is, of course, a thinly disguised Job and the passage has Job 1.6-12 as its backdrop; it has accurately been described as 'a travesty of the story of Job'.[1] Melville sets this within a discussion between Stubb and Flask about the presence of the mysterious Fedallah, a stowaway smuggled on board the *Pequod* by Ahab for his private service, whom the whalers take to be the Devil in disguise. In effect, Fedallah is given the role of the great tempter Satan with Ahab playing the part of Job/Faust/John who is subjected to the temptation with its disastrous consequences.

Another interesting passage which seems to be dependent on Job 40 occurs in '132. The Symphony'. We read in Job 40.7-9 of God's coming to Job in a whirlwind and asking him a series of humbling questions:

7 Gird up thy loins now like a man: I will demand of thee, and declare thou unto me. 8 Wilt thou also disannul my judgment? Wilt thou condemn me, that thou mayest be righteous? 9 Has thou an arm like God? Or canst thou thunder with a voice like him?

The key phrase is contained in v. 9: 'Hast thou an arm like God?' The idea is picked up a few verses later, in v. 14, where God concludes his rhetorical questioning of Job with a promise that if Job can answer all of these things, 'Then will I also confess unto thee that thine own right hand can save thee'. It is immediately following this declaration that Behemoth and Leviathan are introduced into the discussion (40.15–41.34). Melville picks up on this idea of the 'arm of God' as an image of divine power and uses it as a means whereby Ahab seemingly acquiesces to God's questioning. Thus in '132. The Symphony', on the eve of his fateful encounter with Moby-Dick, Ahab raises his voice to heaven in similar rhetorical fashion:

1.   Herman Melville, *Moby-Dick* (A Norton Critical Edition; ed. H. Hayford and H. Parker; New York: Norton, 1967), p. 276.

> Is Ahab, Ahab? Is it I, God, or who that lifts this arm? But if the great sun
> move not of himself; but is an errand-boy in heaven; nor one single star
> can revolve, but by some invisible power; how then can this one small heart
> beat; this one small brain think thoughts; unless God does that beating,
> does that thinking, does that living, and not I.

Here we see Ahab apparently submitting to divine power and surren-
dering free will.[1] In pursuing Moby-Dick he declares himself to be under
the control of Divine Fate. Thus, in '37. Sunset' Ahab defiantly
challenges those who would deflect him from his purposes:

> Swerve me? ye cannot swerve me, else ye swerve yourselves! man has ye
> there. Swerve me? The path to my fixed purpose is laid with iron rails,
> whereon my soul is grooved to run.

In '132. The Symphony' Ahab reflects on his forty years of whaling
and says to Starbuck,

> By heaven, man, we are turned round and round in this world, like yonder
> windlass, and Fate is the handspike.

Similarly, in '134. The Chase—Second Day' he again declares to
Starbuck, who tries to persuade him to give up the hunt,

> This whole act's immutably decreed. 'Twas rehearsed by thee and me a
> billion years before this ocean rolled. Fool! I am the Fates' lieutenant; I act
> under orders.

Chapter 41 of the book of Job, containing God's discourse with Job on
the beast Leviathan is, understandably, of special significance.[2] The
unusual words contained in Job 41.12, 14 seem to underlie the whole of
'74. The Sperm Whale's Head—Contrasted View' where Ishmael gives
us the guided tour of the severed head. The verses certainly seem an
appropriate introduction to the contents of the chapter:

> I will not conceal his parts, nor his power, nor his comely proportion. Who
> can open the doors of his face. His teeth are terrible round about.

---

1.   R.L. Cook, 'Big Medicine in *Moby-Dick*', in Stern (ed.), *Moby-Dick*, pp. 20-
21, argues that this is not to be taken as a sign of Ahab's acceptance of God's
omnipotence in these matters, but is used by him to gain the obedience of the crew in
pursuing the White Whale by means of quasi-religious ritual and magical
incantations.

2.   Wright, *Melville's Use of the Bible*, p. 11, notes that this passage is heavily
marked in Melville's own copy of the AV Bible. Holman, 'The Reconciliation of
Ishmael', pp. 479-80, provides details as to which verses are annotated.

Similarly, in '32. Cetology' Melville creatively uses Job 41.1-4, 9 to illustrate the inscrutability of nature, the fathomless depths of God, and the limits of human reason. The relevant passage from Job reads as follows:

> 1 Can you draw out Leviathan with a fishhook,
>   or press down his tongue with a cord?
> 2 Can you put a rope in his nose,
>   or pierce his jaw with a hook?
> 3 Will he make many supplications to you?
>   Will he speak to you soft words?
> 4 Will he make a covenant with you to take him for your servant
>   for ever?
> 9 Behold the hope of man is disappointed;
>   he is laid low even at the sight of him.

The passage is again part of the Second Discourse of the Lord to Job (40.6–41.34) in which the human being is challenged to explain divine actions. The passage does present some textual problems, mainly revolving around the difficulty of identifying the 'monsters' under discussion and maintaining a continuity of description. The Hebrew is at points very obscure, making readings difficult, and various solutions have been attempted to make the passage more understandable. For instance, the NEB moves 41.1-6 to follow 39.30, effectively making 41.7-8 refer not to Leviathan, but to the crocodile (Behemoth) of 40.15.[1] Most commentators do not follow this transposition, but feel that the connection between 41.1-6 and 41.7-34 makes perfect sense and that the normal order should be retained. In any event, Melville turns the description of Leviathan to his own purposes, having his narrator/character Ishmael attempt to describe the majestic world that is the whale:

> To grope down into the bottom of the sea after them; to have one's hands among the unspeakable foundations, ribs, and the very pelvis of the world; this is a fearful thing. What am I that I should essay to hook the nose of this leviathan! The awful tauntings in Job might well appal me. 'Will he' (the leviathan) 'make a covenant with thee? Behold the hope of him is vain!'

---

1.   Day (*God's Conflict*, pp. 66-67) notes that the alteration was made under the influence of the NEB editor G.R. Driver, who wanted to support his contention that Leviathan was a crocodile and therefore moved this section (which seemed inappropriate) to another place.

In effect, one could go so far as to say that for Job to be able to 'hook the nose of Leviathan' is for him to be able to discover the rationale of evil in the world and plumb the depths of the nature of God in so discovering it. James Barbour remarks at this point,

> In writing about the whale, Melville had gone from cetology to theology and had arrived at the hieroglyph that God used as a self-symbol of his otherness in speaking to Job out of the whirlwind.[1]

This 'hieroglyph' is a means whereby the incomprehensibility of God is portrayed and the limitations of human beings are established—the only response to God's questioning about the Leviathan is a humble acceptance of God's sovereignty and our small place within it.[2]

In '81. The *Pequod* Meets the Virgin' we find another interesting use of the book of Job. The relevant passage reads,

> Is this the creature of whom it was once so triumphantly said—'Canst thou fill his skin with barbed irons? or his head with fish-spears? The sword of him that layeth at him cannot hold, the spear, the dart, nor the habergoen: he esteemeth iron as straw; the arrow cannot make him flee; darts are counted as stubble; he laugheth at the shaking of a spear!' This is the creature? this he? Oh! that unfulfilments should follow the prophets. For with the strength of a thousand thighs in his tail, Leviathan had run his head under the mountains of the sea, to hide him from the *Pequod*'s fish-spears!

The quotations from the book of Job embedded within this passage are a montage of phrases from 41.7, 26-29, and arise as a comment by the narrator as the boat crews of the *Pequod* hunt an old sperm whale. They are said in a spirit of mockery as it is clear that this particular whale is going to meet his doom. Moby-Dick will, however, be an altogether different story, which perhaps explains why the quotation from Job does not go on through to v. 34!

Thornton Y. Booth has offered a fascinating study of the contrast between Job and Melville's *Moby-Dick* on the crucial question of divine omnipotence and the presence of evil, suggesting that we today may

---

1. 'All my Books are Botches', p. 32.
2. Commenting on the Calvinists of Melville's day, T.W. Herbert, Jr (*Moby-Dick and Calvinism: A World Dismantled* [New Brunswick, NJ: Rutgers University Press, 1977], p. 133) remarks, 'To the orthodox, the leviathan in Job was an image not only of God's power but of his transcendent mystery, an image proposed to humble man's pride of knowledge'.

find Ahab's solution to the question of theodicy more satisfying than Job's.[1] Booth argues that a deliberate contrast between Ahab and Job is being inserted by Melville in how the two figures handle the great beast Leviathan:

> God asks Job if Leviathan can be drawn out with a hook; Ahab has suc-
> cessfully hunted whales all his life, has had his companions make a ban-
> quet of them, has stirred them up, has filled their skins with barbed hooks
> and their heads with fish spears.[2]

Not all agree with so simple a contrast between the two characters, Ahab and Job; few would deny, however, that the main themes being dealt with in the two pieces of literature, *Moby-Dick* and the book of Job, are closely related. Whether we feel justified in arguing for a literary symmetry between the characters of Ahab and Job is, however, another matter. It may well be that the truest Job-like figure in *Moby-Dick* is found in '100. Leg and Arm' where we encounter the English Captain Boomer of the *Samuel Enderby*. He, like Ahab, has lost a limb to the White Whale, but has reconciled himself to the fact and faces life with much more equanimity and a greater serenity of spirit. In any event, most would agree with the opinion of Thomas Woodson on what Melville has managed to accomplish within the novel:

> Perhaps the greatest of Melville's achievements in writing *Moby-Dick* is to
> make us see in Ahab the naked dramatic identity of creative and destructive
> impulses within the human soul.[3]

Melville's vision of humanity is a heroic one; the individual is capable of great goodness, but also capable of great destruction. This applies even to Ahab, who though he is consumed with hatred for Moby-Dick and is motivated by an obsessive desire to kill the whale, can still demonstrate compassion for the cabin boy Pip, and can feel such affection for his

---

1. '*Moby-Dick*', pp. 33-43. Stout ('Melville's Use of the Book of Job', pp. 76-77) disagrees, arguing that to pursue this line of thought is to distort the meaning of Job. The character Ishmael, she suggests, is a more Job-like figure in *Moby-Dick*.
    2. '*Moby-Dick*', p. 40.
    3. 'Ahab's Greatness: Prometheus as Narcissus', *ELH* 33 (1966), p. 356. Woodson goes on to suggest the classical figure of Prometheus as a perfect type of Ahab, citing the words at the end of 'The Chart', and commenting, 'Ahab is Prometheus, not stealing fire from the gods, but suffering the agony of an internal vulture' (p. 361).

family back in Nantucket that he can shed a tear into the sea for them ('132. The Symphony').

There is perhaps an important allusion to Job 41.7 contained within the final chapter ('135. The Chase—Third Day'). The verse speaks of Leviathan and has God challenge Job with the words: 'Canst thou fill his skin with barbed irons? or his head with fish spears?' If we take the whaling equivalent of 'barbed irons' to be harpoons,[1] then the final words of Ahab in the novel take on a Job-like meaning. As Ahab is astride Moby-Dick, thrusting at him with his harpoon, he says,

> Towards thee I roll, thou all-destroying but unconquering whale; to the last I grapple with thee; from hell's heart I stab at thee; for hate's sake I spit my last breath at thee. Sink all coffins and all hearses to one common pool! and since neither can be mine, let me then tow to pieces, while still chasing thee, though tied to thee, thou damned whale! *Thus*, I give up the spear!

The connection with Job seems certain when we also note 41.29b, which has God describe Leviathan's mocking reaction to such barbs/harpoons/ spears: 'He laugheth at the shaking of a spear'.

An even more significant use of Job within *Moby-Dick* is the appearance of the phrase 'And I only am escaped alone to tell you'. These words are repeated four times to Job by four of his servants as they report the disasters which have befallen them and the family of Job (1.15, 16, 17, 19), and help to set the tone for Job's own struggle to survive the testing of God. In *Moby-Dick* the words appear in the 'Epilogue' and are applied to the sailor/narrator Ishmael. It is Ishmael alone who is rescued by the crew of the *Rachel*, the very ship that Ahab refused to help following their encounter with Moby-Dick.

In terms of the 'credibility' of the story the Epilogue is extremely important, for it provides us with the answer as to how the fate of Captain Ahab, the *Pequod* and her crew have come to be known—there is one survivor. It is difficult to imagine the story having quite the same impact without this Epilogue. Yet, strange as it may sound, the English edition of 1851 was published without it. It appears that the editor of the English edition, Richard Bentley (or one of his staff), excised it for some reason, inflicting a great injustice on Melville's

---

1.   Habel, *The Book of Job*, p. 554, renders שֻׂכּוֹת as 'harpoons' and צִלְצַל דָּגִים as 'fishing spears', noting that both terms occur only here in the MT.

purposes. Fortunately the Epilogue was re-inserted in a subsequent edition.[1] I shall have more to say about the interpretation of the Epilogue below. Let us now turn to consider some artistic interpretations of Melville's tale.

3. *Theatrical and Cinematic Interpretations of* Moby-Dick

The story line of Moby-Dick lent itself to dramatic interpretation, and adaptations for dramatic readings, plays and films quickly appeared. Given the setting of much of the drama (on board a ship at sea), it is not an easy story to adapt to theatre. How does one portray a whale on the stage, after all? Nevertheless, some very interesting adaptations were attempted to overcome this problem, including the clever, two-act drama by Orson Welles entitled *Moby Dick* (1955). Welles set the whole drama up so that the play is a rehearsal for a production of Melville's story—effectively a play within a play. Thus the actors are able to practise their lines and move about the stage as they would in the 'real' performance, but do so without having to bother with all of the props and sets which would be so difficult to produce; only some ropes suspended from the ceiling suggest the deck of the *Pequod*. The rest Welles leaves for the most part to the imagination of the audience, adding just enough sound effects to help the audience along. The play opened on 6 June 1955 at the Duke of York Theatre in London with Welles himself cast in the role of Captain Ahab. Theatre critics were for the most part enthusiastic about the production, readily acknowledging its creativity and ingenuity. An interesting thing that comes through in Welles's adaptation is the close connection between Melville's story and Shakespeare's play *King Lear*. As one actor is made to remark about the White Whale within Act One:

> The whole thing is like the storm in 'Lear'—it's real, but it's more than real;—it's an idea of the mind.[2]

In the end, Welles makes explicit in the dialogue that which is only hinted at within Melville's novel—Moby-Dick dies as a result of its

---

1.   H.D. Hetherington ('Early Reviews of *Moby-Dick*', in Stern [ed.], *Moby-Dick*, pp. 5-6) discusses some of the hostile reviews by British critics based on the (erroneous) notion that Melville had 'drowned his narrator'.

2.   O. Welles, *Moby Dick Rehearsed: A Drama in Two Acts* (London: Samuel French, 1965), p. 9.

encounter with Ahab and the crew of the *Pequod*. Yet, true to Melville's book, only Ishmael survives the avenging White Whale.[1]

A play adaptation of the story was written by Henry Reed in 1947 and was first broadcast on BBC Radio 3 on 26 January 1947. The major departure within the play from Melville's story line concerns the fate of Ishmael. In short, Reed allows Ishmael to perish along with the rest of the crew of the *Pequod*, inadvertently committing the same grievous mistake that the English editors of the novel did nearly 100 years before by (effectively) amputating the Epilogue. Reed acknowledges freely that this is a deliberate falsification of Melville's story, but justifies it because, as he puts it, 'I cannot make up my mind whether there is much more point to his survival than that he must be left to tell the tale'.[2] However, this is to miss the deliberate contrast between the fates of the obsessive Ahab and the more reasoned Ishmael that Melville builds into the very structure of the novel.

Among the first of the cinematic versions was a silent classic entitled *The Sea Beast*, produced by Warner Brothers in 1925 and riding the wave of new-found interest in Melville characteristic of that decade. The film was directed by Millard Webb and starred John Barrymore as Captain Ahab. The integrity was spoiled somewhat by the gratuitous insertion of a love interest for Ahab, the effect of which was to detract from the obsession with the White Whale. The same misreading of Melville's story occurred in the 1930 version entitled *Moby-Dick*, directed by Lloyd Bacon and again starring John Barrymore. In both instances a happy ending was imposed upon Melville's story with Ahab killing the whale, marrying the leading lady and living happily ever after. This stands in sharp contrast to the slaughter-filled finale of the novel itself. It appears that Hollywood just could not stand to have its heroes die in the final reel! In contrast, a version of *Moby-Dick* was released by Stylus Video in 1987 as part of their Classic Children's Stories. This version lasts just under an hour, but is much more faithful to Melville's story, including the death-filled finale.

1. Melville's story continues to attract theatrical interest as Cameron Macintosh's recent West End musical *Moby-Dick* testifies. This production, which first opened in Oxford in 1990, will hardly win any critical praise for its penetration to the heart of what has made Melville's story a classic, but it does seem to have struck a popular chord and is doing well in spite of the hostile reviews by theatre critics.
2. *Moby Dick: A Play for Radio from Herman Melville's Novel* (London: Jonathan Cape, 1947), p. 10.

Far and away the most influential of all dramatic adaptations was John Huston's film *Moby-Dick*, made in 1956, again for Warner Brothers, and starring Gregory Peck in the role of Captain Ahab.[1] Huston had first read Melville's story as a teenager and had long harboured the desire to translate it onto the silver screen. The screenplay for this version was written mainly by a man most famous for his science-fiction writing, Ray Bradbury, although he shared screen-writing credits with Huston.[2] The film was shot during 1954–55 mainly in Ireland, Wales and London with the sea footage being done in the tempestuous Irish Sea, often in storm conditions (which helps add to the realism of those scenes in the film). The final climactic confrontation between Moby-Dick and Ahab was filmed, in part, off the coast of the Canary Islands, where the sea was warmer and the weather kinder. Because of a number of production disasters, including nearly losing the film's star Gregory Peck in the fog when a cable towing the latex model of Moby-Dick (on which the actor was precariously perched) snapped, Huston described the film as the most difficult he had ever made in his long and distinguished career.[3]

There is an interesting connection with one of the theatrical adaptations of *Moby-Dick* (mentioned above), for Huston cast Orson Welles to play the role of Father Mapple. The sermon on Jonah preached by Mapple is fairly faithful to Melville's original story and provides one of the best sequences in the film, even though it only lasts five minutes. Remarkably, the scene was shot in two takes and is adjudged by many to be one of the best performances of Welles's career.[4]

Huston is fairly faithful to Melville's story line, although he does add some sections which help pace the story dramatically. For instance, there is a scene added in which the three mates of the *Pequod*, Starbuck,

1.   J. Griggs, *The Films of Gregory Peck* (London: Columbus Books, 1984), pp. 139-43, contains a discussion and six photographs from the film.

2.   The artistic tension between the two men over the screenplay is discussed in L. Grobel, *The Hustons* (London: Bloomsbury, 1990), pp. 416-23. Two others, Roald Dahl and John Godley, also worked on the screenplay but they found the temper tantrums of Huston impossible to bear and quit the project after a short time.

3.   J. Huston, *An Open Book* (London: Columbus Books, 1988), pp. 251-58, discusses the making of the film. Also see Boller and Davis, *Hollywood Anecdotes*, pp. 188-89, describing the incident involving Gregory Peck.

4.   C. Higham, *Orson Welles: The Rise and Fall of an American Genius* (London: New English Library, 1985), p. 286, discusses the performance.

Stubb and Flask, discuss whether it is wise to continue to follow Ahab's mad pursuit. The scene takes place in the mates' cabin shortly after Ahab has ordered the crews to leave a fine hunting ground and set sail after Moby-Dick. The dialogue demonstrates the theological issues which Huston feels are central to the story:[1]

Starbuck: I do not fear Moby-Dick. I fear the wrath of God.
Stubb: The wrath of God?
Starbuck: It is our task to kill whales and furnish up their oil for the lamps of the world. If we perform that task well and faithfully, we do a service to mankind that pleases Almighty God.
Stubb: Aye!
Starbuck: Ahab would deny all that. He has taken us from the rich harvest we were reaping to satisfy his lust for vengeance. He is twisting that which is holy into something dark and purposeless. He is a champion of darkness. Ahab's red flag challenges the heavens.

The climactic ending of Huston's *Moby-Dick*, with Ahab being killed by the White Whale, was the brain child of Bradbury. As he explains,

My inspiration was to have Moby-Dick take Ahab down and wind him in the coiled ropes and bring him up among the harpoons on this great white bier, this great cortege, this funeral at sea. Then we see, 'My God, these two should be together forever through eternity, shouldn't they—Ahab and the white whale?' It's not in the book, but I do believe that Melville would have approved.[2]

The survival of Ishmael is something which is stressed very much within the film. Two scenes help prepare the audience for it; the first taken from Melville's book and the second created by the film-makers. The first is based on '19. The Prophet' where Ishmael and Queequeg are confronted by the prophetic figure of Elijah just prior to shipping on-board the *Pequod*. As in the novel Elijah warns them of the dangers of sailing with Ahab. However, an additional dialogue is given to Elijah which does not appear in the book. Elijah prophesies,

At sea one day you'll smell land where there be no land, and on that day Ahab will go to his grave. But he'll rise again within the hour. He will rise and beckon. Then all...all...all, save one, follow!

1. Grobel, *The Hustons*, p. 422, discusses this scene (which was written by Huston himself). The director describes it as 'the heart of the story'.
2. Cited in Grobel, *The Hustons*, p. 418.

The second scene is a wholly created one, a conversation between
Ishmael and Ahab just prior to the final confrontation with the White
Whale (within the novel no conversation between Ahab and Ishmael
ever takes place). Ahab has announced to the crew that he can smell
Moby-Dick, a smell reminiscent of an island. This prompts Ishmael to
remember Elijah's prophecy.

> Ahab: An island to himself is the White Whale.
> Ishmael: Elijah!
> Ahab: What say ye lad?
> Ishmael: The day we sailed...a man...Elijah his name was...
> Ahab: Well?
> Ishmael: He said...he said 'a day will come at sea when you smell land
>   where there be no land. And on that day Ahab will go to his
>   grave. But he will rise and beckon. Then all...all...all, save one,
>   follow.'

This prophetic heightening of the disaster which is to befall them, along
with the pronouncement of a single survivor, is carried through to the
end of the film. Not only are we presented with the image of Ahab's
body tied to the back of Moby-Dick by harpoon lines, his one loose arm
flapping about in a gesture of beckoning, but we have the survival of
Ishmael, floating on the top of Queequeg's coffin. Huston handles the
Epilogue of the book very cleverly, altering the contents of it to good
effect. The result is that instead of having the quotation from Job 1.17
introducing the Epilogue, we have the words of Job 1.17 now becoming
the very last things heard in the film. Ishmael's voice-over comes as we
watch him climb onto the coffin:

> The coffin! Drowned Queequeg's coffin was my life-buoy. For one whole
> day and night it sustained me on that soft and dirge-like main. Then a sail
> appeared. It was the *Rachel*—the *Rachel* who in her long, melancholy
> search for her missing children found another orphan. The drama is done.
> All are departed away. The great shroud of the sea rolls over the *Pequod*,
> her crew, and Moby-Dick. *I only am escaped alone to tell thee.*

Huston's film version of *Moby-Dick* premiered on 27 June 1957,
appropriately enough, in the Massachusetts town of New Bedford, the
home port for the fictional whaling ship *Pequod*. For many people
today it remains the main vehicle of exposure to Melville's classic novel
and is generally regarded as the definitive artistic adaptation of the work.

4. *Theological Symbolism in* Moby-Dick

Melville aptly notes in '104. The Fossil Whale',

> To produce a mighty book, you must choose a mighty theme. No great
> and enduring volume can ever be written on the flea, though many there
> would be who have tried it.

One of the features of Melville's novel which has established it as an
acknowledged classic is its use of evocative symbols and representative
characters as the author grapples with the 'mighty theme' contained
within it. But what is this theme? What ties the complex symbolism
together? Is it the whale of the titles? D.H. Lawrence remarked about
the meaning of the whale Moby-Dick, 'Of course he is a symbol. Of
what? I doubt if even Melville knew exactly. That's the best of it.'[1]
Critics have been unanimous in acknowledging the creative use of
metaphor and symbol to express moral and theological ideas within the
work. In particular, '42. The Whiteness of the Whale' is often discussed
in this regard since 'whiteness' represents in *Moby-Dick* what has been
described as 'the infinity of possibilities', both good and evil, not so
much the fulness of colour, but the complete *absence* of colour.[2]
Similarly, in '24. The Advocate' whales are said to embody the
'interlinked terrors and wonders of God!' As one critic rhetorically
queries, 'Might it not have been Melville's own intention to invest his
great symbolic leviathan with a plurality of meanings?'[3] The answer to
this must surely be 'Yes!'; in Melville's *Moby-Dick* we have image piled
upon image, symbol after interlocking symbol, so that the final product
is a labyrinth of interpretative possibilities rarely equalled in modern
literature. Kafka's *The Trial* and *The Castle*, T.S. Eliot's *The Wasteland*,
Joyce's *Ulysses* and some of the novels of Jorge Luis Borges are
possible comparisons, but even they cannot match Melville in the sheer
magnitude of what is accomplished in *Moby-Dick*. Melville demonstrates
again and again his ability to attach multiple interpretations to key
images throughout the work ('99. The Doubloon' is a prime example

1.   'Moby Dick', p. 35.
2.   J.J. Mayoux, *Melville* (New York: Grove Press, 1960), pp. 76-78, suggests
that Melville was dependent upon Edgar Allen Poe's *A Narrative of Arthur Gordon
Pym* (1838) for the metaphor of whiteness.
3.   R.E. Watters, 'The Meanings of the White Whale', in Stern (ed.), *Moby-Dick*,
p. 77.

with each crew member offering an interpretation of the gold coin according to his own insights and desires). The result is that for the reader the book has a certain fluidity about it, an open-endedness of meaning which is both exhilarating and frightening at the same time as he or she tries to take it all in.

Melville has been able not only to bring together a fascinating entourage of human figures, a memorable cast of characters (Ishmael, Queequeg, Starbuck and above all Captain Ahab), but to place them within a nautical setting where the sea, the ship, the elements and, most importantly, the whale Moby-Dick all have profoundly symbolic meanings. In short, Melville is acknowledged as a master in his use of symbol throughout the novel, but nowhere is this more in evidence than in Ahab's struggle with the whale.[1] A wide variety of interpretative approaches have been applied to *Moby-Dick* as students of Melville's work have sought to unlock its treasures.

Some critics have focused on the internal struggle within Ahab and suggest a psychological interpretation of the novel, where the Captain of the *Pequod* is attempting to overcome the emotional sickness which is Obsession. In the words of Richard Chase, '*Moby-Dick* (is) a book about the alienation from life that results from an excessive or neurotic self-dependence'.[2] Closely connected to discussions about the meaning of the pursuit of Moby-Dick by Ahab is the question of what light that may shed about the author himself. Are we to see the personality of Melville lurking behind his characterization of Ahab? Or is the author to be found more in the character of Ishmael? How far should the psychological approach be taken? Freudian and Jungian interpretations of Melville's work have had a field day, seeing, for example, the amputation of Ahab's leg as a symbol of psychic castration, or his destructive attitude to Moby-Dick as an extreme instance of the psychological process known as projection. This is hardly surprising given that Melville's novels are so symbol-laden and lend themselves readily to such an analysis.

Others have felt that the sociological angle to interpreting *Moby-Dick*

1.   Sister Mary Ellen, 'Duplicate Imagery in *Moby-Dick*', *MFS* 8 (1962), pp. 252-64, offers a very illuminating discussion about Melville's use of key symbols and images in his description of both Ahab and Moby-Dick. This is, she suggests, a way of integrating the two within the narrative; they become effectively mirror-images of each other. McIntosh, 'The Mariner's Multiple Quest', pp. 23-52, also contains an excellent discussion of this.

2.   'Melville and *Moby-Dick*', p. 56.

yields more fruit and have approached the work in that way. Is Melville striking a blow at Emersonian individualism?[1] By means of his portrayal of Ahab's fateful egotism is he demonstrating what happens when this notion of self-reliance is taken to its extreme? It is, after all, an egotism which not only causes his death but also slaughters virtually his entire crew. And, building upon these sociological considerations, how far can we legitimately reconstruct Melville's political philosophy based upon *Moby-Dick*?[2]

Still others have come at *Moby-Dick* from a theological standpoint. Could it be that Melville is making a declaration about his own Calvinistic heritage by means of the obsessive chase after, and death-struggle with, Moby-Dick? Is Henry A. Murray right when he says that 'Melville, in the person of Ahab, assailed Calvinism in the Whale'?[3] There is much to be gained from a careful consideration of Melville's religious heritage and the impact that would undoubtedly make upon his written compositions. Indeed, one prominent Melvillian scholar, Lawrance Thompson, in his seminal book entitled *Melville's Quarrel with God* (1952), has argued that Melville's religious experience, particularly growing up in the Dutch Reformed Church, is absolutely determinative for his literary work, not least his composition of *Moby-Dick*. While many will disagree with Thompson's controversial interpretation of Melville,[4] he is correct in asserting that the Calvinistic background of

1.   W. Braswell, 'Melville as a Critic of Emerson', *AL* 9 (1937), pp. 317-34; H.C. Horsford, 'The Design of the Argument in *Moby-Dick*', *MFS* 8 (1962–63), pp. 233-51; Stewart, 'The Vision of Evil', pp. 238-63; and R.E. Watters, 'Melville's "Isolatoes"', in Stern (ed.), *Moby-Dick*, pp. 107-14, all offer some discussion on this. H.N. Smith, 'The Image of Society in *Moby-Dick*', in Gilmore (ed.), *Moby-Dick*, pp. 27-41, offers a different view, arguing that, generally speaking, in *Moby-Dick* society is evil, thus making Melville's position not dissimilar to Emerson's.

2.   A. Heimart, '*Moby Dick* and American Political Symbolism', *AQ* 15 (1963), pp. 498-534, discusses this. Also see: M. Bewley, 'Melville and the Democratic Experience', in Chase (ed.), *Melville*, pp. 91-115; R. Slotkin, '*Moby-Dick*: The American National Epic', in Gilmore (ed.), *Moby-Dick*, pp. 13-26; R.H. Brodhead, 'Trying all Things: An Introduction to *Moby-Dick*', in Brodhead (ed.), *New Essays*, pp. 2-3.

3.   'In Nomine Diaboli', in Stern (ed.), *Moby-Dick*, p. 32. Murray makes this comment while pursuing a Freudian interpretation of Melville's work.

4.   See, for example, the assessment by M. Davis, *RES* (July 1954), p. 327. R.B. Sewall, '*Moby-Dick*', in Gilmore (ed.), *Moby-Dick*, pp. 51-53, also offers some discussion.

Melville is an important source for much that lies at the heart of *Moby-Dick*.[1] One of the most revealing confirmations of this is found in Melville's review of his friend Nathaniel Hawthorne's *Mosses from an Old Manse* (1846). Melville's review was first published anonymously in the journal *Literary World* in August of 1850. Within the review Melville describes one of the prominent images within Hawthorne's work, that of 'blackness', with these words:

> this great power of blackness in him derives its force from its appeals to that Calvinistic sense of Innate Depravity and Original Sin, from whose visitations, in some shape or other, no deeply thinking mind is always and wholly free...it is that blackness in Hawthorne...that so fixes and fascinates me.[2]

For my purposes it is this underlying theological dimension of the narrative in *Moby-Dick* which is the most important. This can be seen most clearly in the two main streams of interpretation offered for the central struggle between Captain Ahab and Moby-Dick, thought by most to be the hermeneutical key to the novel as a whole. We can label these two basic approaches according to their differing interpretations of the figure of the White Whale, as being either a demonic or a divine agent.[3] This then also leads us to consider how the two main human characters, Ahab and Ishmael, might be interpreted theologically. Let us take up these four interpretative stances in turn.

a. *Moby-Dick as Agent of a Demonic God*
Some interpreters have taken Moby-Dick to be representative of evil, a personification of Satan, with Ahab representing the struggle that humankind has with that evil. Clearly Ahab blames God for the existence of evil, which has been visited upon him in the form of Moby-Dick's 'dismasting' of his leg; hence he vows that he will 'dismember his dismemberer'. Ahab's inability to accept either that evil can be

---

1.   The fullest discussion of this is Herbert, *Moby-Dick and Calvinism*. Herbert remarks (p. 2), 'In writing *Moby-Dick*, Melville confronted a spiritual conflict that had been generated during his childhood and youth'. Also see his articles, 'Calvinism and Cosmic Evil in *Moby Dick*' *PMLA* 84 (1969), pp. 1613-19; 'Calvinist Earthquake: *Moby-Dick* and Religious Tradition', in Brodhead (ed.), *New Essays*, pp. 109-40.
2.   'Hawthorne and His Mosses', in Melville, *Moby-Dick*, pp. 540-41.
3.   Thompson, *Melville's Quarrel with God*, p. 171 remarks, '(Melville) took delight in recognizing Leviathan as an ambiguous Satan-God symbol'.

localized in himself or necessarily accepted as part of the created world order, means that he must revolt against God—whom he views as the ultimate source of evil. Nowhere is this more clearly demonstrated than in a celebrated passage from '36. The Quarter-Deck', where, in a heated tirade directed at chief-mate Starbuck, Ahab describes the immortal Moby-Dick as both a mask of the Divine as well as a wall separating him from God:

All visible objects, man, are but pasteboard masks. But in each event—in the living act, the undoubted deed—there, some unknown but still reasoning thing puts forth the mouldings of its features from behind the unreasoning mask. If man will strike, strike through the mask! How can the prisoner reach outside except by thrusting through the wall? To me, the White Whale is that wall, shoved near to me. Sometimes I think there's naught beyond. But 'tis enough. He tasks me; he heaps me; I see in him outrageous strength, with an inscrutable malice sinewing it. That inscrutable thing is chiefly what I hate; and be the White Whale agent, or be the White Whale principal, I will wreak that hate upon him.[1]

It is the unashamed defiance—the Promethean-like striking out at God, the removing of a mask after the fashion of Shakespeare's *King Lear*—which is so stunning here. The passage shows Melville at his creative best, revealing the agony of Ahab's soul. William Braswell comments perceptively on this passage,

When Ahab strikes at Moby-Dick, the symbol of all spiritual as well as all physical evil, he does so in a mad desire for revenge on God, whom he holds responsible for its existence.[2]

At heart this is the stuff of pure tragedy, at least in Sophoclean terms of tragedy as 'the encounter of man with more-than-man'.[3] Perhaps this is

---

1. J.D. Young ('The Nine Gams of the *Pequod*', in Stern [ed.], *Moby-Dick*, p. 100) remarks, 'Whether the White Whale be agent or principal, divine justice is fulfilled; the very naming of God at the Whale's appearance, almost an incantation of the Christian deity, reflects Ishmael's comprehension of the secret portion of the story: "Jesu, what a whale! It was Moby-Dick."'

2. *Melville's Religious Thought: An Essay in Interpretation* (Durham, NC: Duke University Press, 1943), p. 58. By contrast, Ishmael, in '86. The Tail' is able to accept the fact that he cannot see the face of God, a passage which Melville deliberately builds upon the story of Moses' encounter with God (Exod. 33.20).

3. As E.H. Rosenberry, *Melville* (London: Routledge & Kegan Paul, 1979), p. 78, notes.

one point at which the difference between Job and Ahab can be seen most clearly. Both characters are caught in the tragic web of life, and both perceive the hand of God to be somehow intimately involved in, not to say responsible for, their circumstances; yet they respond quite differently. As Richard B. Sewall puts it, 'It was the Person in the impersonal that Job loved and could not repudiate—and which mono-maniac Ahab hated and spat upon'.[1] At the same time, such profound hatred of God is not presented by Melville as something unique to Ahab, but has its roots in the mists of time, going back to Adam. In short, Ahab's hatred is theologically explained as being connected to Original Sin (Hawthorne's 'blackness' again!), with the mad Captain having a virulent case of the disease affecting us all. As Melville writes, in another celebrated passage from '41. Moby-Dick' which brings together Ahab and Adam in a creative fashion,

> All that most maddens and torments; all that stirs up the lees of things; all truth with malice in it; all that cracks the sinews and cakes the brain; all the subtle demonisms of life and thought; all evil, to crazy Ahab, were visibly personified, and made practically assailable in Moby Dick. He piled upon the whale's white hump the sum of all the general rage and hate felt by his whole race from Adam down; and then, as if his chest had been a mortar, he burst his hot heart's shell upon it.

Taken to its extreme, such an interpretative approach makes Ahab himself 'the embodiment of evil' as he is driven by his lust for revenge . There is more than a little substance to this interpretation within the novel itself, for at times it is clear that Ahab's actions are openly Satanic: he blasphemously sets sail in the *Pequod* on Christmas Day; he spits in the communion chalice to show his contempt; he conducts a black mass on the deck of the *Pequod* for the crew; he baptizes the harpoon with which he intends to kill Moby-Dick with the blood of the pagan harpooners, invoking as he does so not the name of God, but the name of the Devil; he offers 'the worship of defiance' to God, never bowing his knee to anyone or anything; in the midst of the storm when the flames of St Elmo's fire flash around the ship he mocks the Trinity; he asserts that he, and he alone, is lord and master over the *Pequod* and her crew; he even takes it upon himself to forgive his own callous refusal

---

1.   'The Book of Job', in P.S. Sanders (ed.), *Twentieth-Century Interpretations of the Book of Job* (Englewood Cliffs, NJ: Prentice-Hall, 1968), p. 30.

to help search for the lost son of the captain of the *Rachel*.[1] Judged simply from the standpoint of the character of Ahab alone, *Moby-Dick* is precisely what Melville describes it as to his friend Hawthorne: 'a wicked book'.[2]

b. *Moby-Dick as Agent of Divine Judgment*
Others have taken the whale to be representative of God, with Ahab's battle with Moby-Dick representative of man's rebellion against Heaven, the point being that Ahab supremely represents human defiance of God.[3] Indeed, one character in the novel, the mad prophet Gabriel in '71. The Jeroboam's Story', goes so far as to say that Moby-Dick is 'the Shaker God incarnated' and that Ahab is a blasphemer in attempting to pursue him, the crew of the *Pequod* 'sacrilegiously assailants of his divinity'. William A. Young suggests that Melville is influenced on this point by Calvin's interpretation of the Leviathan in the book of Job as the personification of God's wrath.[4]

It is clear that at times in *Moby-Dick* the White Whale does indeed seem to function as the instrument of God's judgment. Perhaps the best example of this is contained in '54. The *Town-Ho's* Story', where the tale of the conflict between the characters Radney and Steelkit is unfolded. The *Town-Ho* is a whaling ship and is one of the nine ships encountered by the *Pequod* during her search for the White Whale; the story of Radney and Steelkit is told as a flashback by Ishmael when the two ships meet. Radney is chief-mate aboard the *Town-Ho* and has an altercation with the sailor Steelkit which eventually escalates into a full-scale mutiny aboard the ship. The mutiny is put down and Radney flogs Steelkit, who breathes revenge against Radney and plots to kill him. At

1. H.A. Murray, 'In Nomine Diaboli', in Stern (ed.), *Moby-Dick*, pp. 28-29, discusses these matters.
2. *Letters*, p. 142.
3. Thompson, *Melville's Quarrel with God*, is a good example of this. J. Stanonik, *Moby Dick: The Myth and the Symbol* (Ljubljana: Ljubljana University Press, 1962), pp. 143-51, also offers a discussion.
4. 'Leviathan', p. 389. Young goes on to suggest that Melville challenges orthodox interpretations of the Book of Job just as he does the traditional interpretations of Jonah being literally swallowed by the whale. Melville, he suggests, is equally as dismissive of orthodox interpretations of Scripture as he is of more liberal ones which were being promulgated during his time. According to Young, these two main interpretations of Christian faith (Calvinistic orthodoxy and liberalism) are represented by the characters Ahab and Ishmael respectively.

this critical juncture the *Town-Ho* comes across the White Whale and in the ensuing chase, Radney falls overboard and is drowned. Thus, justice is accomplished not by man (Steelkit), but by God (through his agent Moby-Dick).[1] As Melville explains within the chapter, 'Heaven itself stepped in to take out of his hands into its own the damning thing he would have done'.

c. *Ahab: Victim and Victor*

Yet, is Ahab (to borrow a phrase from '130. The Hat') 'sinning or sinned against' as he pursues with 'fatal pride' the White Whale? How closely should we draw the parallel between Job and Ahab at this point? Is Ahab meant to be seen as an innocent sufferer, victim of a conspiracy between God and Satan? The dialectic between good and evil is not as easy to pin down in *Moby-Dick* as it might first appear. In '49. The Hyena' Ishmael remarks at one point about Ahab's pursuit of Moby-Dick; he describes himself as being implicated in 'a devil's chase'. This is an interesting description in that it does not tell us precisely who the 'devil' is in this instance. Is the 'devil' the subject or the object of the chase? Is it Ahab or Moby-Dick? The most obvious interpretation would be to see Ahab as the devil and to add definition to the pursuit of Moby-Dick as an evil action being promulgated by a satanically inspired man. An interesting variation of this would reverse the roles played by Ahab and Moby-Dick, making the 'all-destroying but unconquering' whale the embodiment of divine evil and Ahab the instrument attempting to cleanse the world of it. This is precisely the interpretation which John Huston adopts within his film *Moby-Dick*. The director himself explains that his work was in one sense a blasphemy: 'The message of *Moby-Dick* was hate. The whale is the mask of a malignant deity. Melville doesn't choose to call the power Satan, but God.'[2]

---

1.   S. Paul, 'Melville's "The *Town-Ho's* Story"', in Stern (ed.), *Moby-Dick*, pp. 87-92, and D. Geiger, 'Melville's Black God: Contrary Evidence in "The *Town-Ho's* Story"', in Stern (ed.), *Moby-Dick*, pp. 93-97, both discuss this chapter along these lines. Crucial for the setting of the story is the mysterious leak below water line in the *Town-Ho* which the crew cannot find and plug; it serves as a symbol of the depths of God which humans cannot reach.

2.   Cited in Grobel, *The Hustons*, p. 423. In his *An Open Book*, p. 251, Huston himself offers his summary interpretation of Melville's novel: 'Ahab saw the White Whale as a mask worn by the Deity, and he saw the Deity as a malignant force. It was

It is with this in mind that we should perhaps turn to another reveal-ing passage from '132. The Symphony' wherein God himself is brought into the dock for his role in allowing evil to afflict humankind. Ahab asks Starbuck, 'Where do murderers go, man! Who's to doom, when the judge himself is dragged to the bar?' Here, Ahab becomes the accuser of the Accuser in a manner which is, for me, later powerfully echoed by Nobel Prize-winning author Elie Wiesel. In his *Night* (1958) Wiesel explains that his experience in a Nazi concentration camp led him to the conclusion that 'I was the accuser, God the accused'.[1] From this perspective Melville's character Ahab, like Job before him and Wiesel after him, is easily viewed as 'sinned against', and hence the victim of Heaven's wrath. But is there any way that he might also be thought of as enjoying victory in the midst of his agonies?

One final question is worth considering in this regard: Could we extend the idea of Ahab as an instrument of God to suggest that Melville intends a deliberate association between Ahab and Jesus Christ? Might we thereby draw together Ahab's unjust suffering at the hands of a (malignant?) deity with the ultimate victory these sufferings will achieve? Could not Ahab parallel Jesus Christ at this point, and rule as victor strapped to the back of the White Whale just as Christ ruled as the supreme victor even while nailed to the cross? There are one or two provocative passages which do appear to point in this direction.

First, we should not forget that the reference to Jonah spending 'three days and nights in the belly of the whale' (Jon. 1.17) has significant New Testament applications. In a cryptic passage from Q (Mt. 12.39-40/Lk. 11.29-30) this so-called 'sign of Jonah' is used as a symbol of Christ's death and resurrection from the dead three days later.[2] And as I have already noted above in the discussion on Jonah, the 'three days and three nights' motif is used in '19. The Prophet' with reference to Ahab and his battle with Moby-Dick.

God's pleasure to torment and torture man. Ahab didn't deny God, he simply looked on him as a murderer—a thought that is utterly blasphemous.'
1.   *Night*, p. 79. Wiesel goes on to describe how his horrific experience caused him to lose his trust in God's care and provision for humankind.
2.   See J.A. Fitzmyer, *The Gospel according to Luke (X–XXIV)* (AB, 28A; Garden City, NY: Doubleday, 1985), pp. 929-38, and W.D. Davies and D.C. Allison, *The Gospel according to Saint Matthew* (ICC; Edinburgh: T. & T. Clark, 1991), II, pp. 353-59, for discussions of the 'Q' passage.

Secondly, the use of imagery drawn from Jesus Christ's passion by Melville in his description of Ahab is quite striking in *Moby-Dick*. In '28. Ahab' Ishmael says that he 'stood before them with a crucifixion in his face' and that he 'looked like a man cut away from the stake', perhaps another veiled allusion to the cross. In '44. The Chart' his fitful and tormented sleep is described: 'He sleeps with clenched hands; and wakes with his own bloody nails in his palms', echoing descriptions of Christ's nail wounds to his hands. In '37. Sunset' Ahab sits in his cabin watching the sun set through his windows and says to himself,

> The diver sun—slow dived from noon,—goes down; my soul mounts up!
> she wearies with her endless hill. Is, then, the crown too heavy that I wear?
> this Iron Crown of Lombardy.

The connection with Christ's crucifixion is cleverly hidden here and can easily be missed. Not only is there in the 'endless hill' an allusion to Golgotha, but the Iron Crown of Lombardy clearly points to the passion in that this crown of Constantine the Great was traditionally thought to have been made from the nails with which Jesus was affixed to the cross. It is only a short step to move from here to seeing Ahab's battle with the White Whale as his equivalent of Christ's battle with the cross. And just as the cross can become transformed in Christian theology into a symbol of victory, so too can Ahab's death by the agency of Moby-Dick become the platform for proclaiming him as victor.

In summary, it seems clear that there is ample material for interpreting Ahab as the instrument of God, perhaps even a malevolent God; in this sense he is a victim. At the same time the association of Ahab with the passion of Christ might also open the door for our describing him as a victor, one who suffers in a righteous cause which brings about his 'crucifixion', but also gives him the assurance of having surrendered himself to God's purposes. The fact that Ahab can bear so many different meanings is again testimony to Melville's creative genius.

d. *Ishmael: Survivor and Orphan*

It is unanimously agreed that the deletion of the Epilogue from the first English edition of *Moby-Dick* was a mistake. Not to have it as the final page is to amputate the story and run the risk of losing the key to interpreting the whole of the novel. As C. Hugh Holman states, 'This unique salvation of Ishmael is essential to the theme of the novel'.[1] Precisely what that theme is, and why the survival of Ishmael contributes to it, are extremely difficult questions to answer; understandably, the one-page Epilogue of the novel has been the subject of an extraordinary amount of debate among Melvillian scholars.

For Holman the survival of Ishmael is crucial to his interpretation of *Moby-Dick* because it proves that the character learns humility and comes to accept all of the ambiguities of life, just as Job had to learn to do. In other words, the survival of Ishmael is seen as an extension, one might even say the logical conclusion, of the all-pervading influence of the book of Job on *Moby-Dick*. So Holman concludes,

> Like Job, Ishmael has rebelled against the order of the universe; like Job, too, a vast inscrutable symbol of incomprehensible reality has loomed before him in the form of a great whale.[2]

However, it is important to note that Ishmael is not simply described as a survivor in the Epilogue but also as an orphan ('orphan' is in fact the last word in the novel). The whole point of the symbolic name given to the rescuing ship, the *Rachel*, is to emphasize this fact, echoing as it does both Jer. 31.15 and its quotation in Mt. 2.17-18. Both of these biblical passages have to do with the symbolic Rachel's mourning over children that have been lost; the first through the exile and the second at the murderous hands of Herod the Great who slaughtered the innocents. If Ishmael is recognized not simply as a survivor but as an orphan, the whole tone of the passage (and hence the meaning of the novel) is subtly, but significantly, altered. As T. Walter Herbert, Jr puts it,

> Ishmael is not 'saved' because he has discovered the ground of a triumphant Goodness which overcomes Ahab's triumphant evil. He is rescued by chance, escaping alone to tell us of a catastrophe in which divine Truth is struck down as a moral standard.[3]

---

1. Holman, 'The Reconciliation of Ishmael', p. 490. B. Yu ('Ishmael's Equal Eye: The Source of Balance in *Moby-Dick*', *ELH* 32 [1965], p. 120) argues that Ishmael's survival provides a balance to Ahab's death within the structure of the novel as a whole.

2. Holman, 'The Reconciliation of Ishmael', p. 490.

3. *Moby-Dick and Calvinism*, p. 169.

Indeed, for the attentive reader, Ishmael's ultimate status as an abandoned orphan does not come as a complete surprise, for some clues to his condition as such have been provided very early on. We read, for example, in '1. Loomings' of Ishmael's feeling of 'a damp, drizzly November in my soul' which prompts his decision to 'get to the sea as soon as I can...my substitute for pistol and ball'. The ideas within this passage of loneliness and isolation, which lead to thoughts of suicide, are obvious, as the immediately following reference to the Roman Cato throwing himself on his sword makes clear. Thus, William Rosenfeld remarks about Ishmael, the rescued orphan of the Epilogue, 'He is still the sad outcast—the orphan in the wilderness—whom we found in the opening passages of the novel'.[1] In other words, the isolated orphan motif provides a framework for the beginning and end of the book, bringing to a climax that fated state of despair which had been hinted at in the very first few pages of the novel.

Pearl Chester Solomon extends the significance of the orphan theme of the ending to *Moby-Dick*, which she describes as Melville's 'allegory of man'. She contrasts the destiny of humankind represented by Ahab, a humankind which seeks after the Father (God) in a Fatherless cosmos only to find that it is annihilated, with the destiny of humankind represented by Ishmael, a humankind which finds itself cast out and rejected. Thus, Solomon concludes, on a decidedly pessimistic note,

> The old order is past, but perhaps a new one will come; perhaps a new relationship can take the place of the old familial one, one which will begin, perhaps, with the recognition that all men are now orphans.[2]

However gloomy a picture of ultimate meaning the salvation of Ishmael leaves us with at this point, it should not come as a complete shock. Melville has hinted at such a despairing view of life at several points earlier within the novel. Perhaps the most important of these is the rescue of the cabin-boy Pip in '93. The Castaway'. During a whaling run Pip falls overboard and is left for some time in the open sea, where he discovers the 'awful lonesomeness', the 'heartless immensity' of the sea, which is metaphorically linked to God. This is all too much for the

---

1. 'Uncertain Faith: Queequeg's Coffin and Melville's Use of the Bible', *TSLL* 7 (1965), p. 323.
2. *Dickens and Melville in their Time* (New York: Columbia University Press, 1975), p. 4.

young boy. He goes mad as a result of his experience, and even though he is eventually rescued (by chance!) he is never the same again. Pip discovers through this the void that lies at the heart of the universe, the ocean of meaninglessness which mocks life. That the story of Pip is intended to be taken as prelude to Ishmael's own experience is confirmed by the words with which the chapter closes: 'in the sequel of the narrative, it will then be seen what like abandonment befell myself'. Similarly, in '49. The Hyena' Ishmael is made to speak of how he must accept the meaningless absurdity of life and recognize that all of the trials one faces are but 'jolly punches in the side bestowed by an unseen and unaccountable old joker'. In short, the meaning of Ishmael's survival as an orphan, and the extraordinary means whereby it is achieved (through Queequeg's coffin, which Ahab in '127. The Deck' has scornfully rejected), is an entirely fitting way for Melville to conclude this heavily symbolic work. Ahab himself admits that the coffin may mean more than he realizes: 'A life-buoy of a coffin! Does it go further? Can it be that in some spiritual sense the coffin is, after all, but an immortality-preserver!' The significance of this 'life-buoy/coffin' as a means for defining the relationship between Ahab and Ishmael is often overlooked. Yet some have seen in this final evocative symbol an important point of contrast between the Job-like Ishmael and the unbelieving Ahab. Louis Letter, for example, states,

> Ishmael, who sees and describes death as an intimate part of life, is saved by the coffin Ahab has scorned. The book, a complex metaphor, presents a vision of existence as a procession of death.[1]

Many other commentators are much more sceptical about the (supposedly) pessimistic position to which Melville ultimately comes at the conclusion of the novel and deny the suggestion that Ishmael exhibits Job-like qualities throughout. Can there be a more fatalistic conclusion than this Epilogue, which at first glance seems to fly in the face of the way that Job accedes before God? Dare we assume that

---

1. 'Queequeg's Coffin', *NCF* 13 (1958–59), p. 250. B.H. McClary, 'Melville's *Moby-Dick*', *Exp* 21 (1962–63), n. 9, calls attention to the motif of the coffin as the instrument of Ishmael's salvation by citing a passage early on in the novel. In '3. The Spouter Inn' Ishmael, at his first sight of Queequeg, exclaims, 'Landlord, for God's sake, Peter Coffin!...Landlord! *Coffin!* Angels! *save me!*' (Italics are McClary's). This suggestion lends support to the contention that the means of Ishmael's deliverance was part of Melville's literary plan all along.

Ishmael is ultimately Job-like in his acceptance of God's control of and care for the world and all of its pain and suffering? Could it not be that Melville is infinitely more honest when he says, in effect, that there is no simple solution and that humankind is left alone and isolated by an indifferent God? As Michael T. Gilmore has put it,

> By ending *Moby-Dick* with the word 'orphan', Melville reemphasizes the impossibility of finding a conclusive solution to the riddle of the universe. Ishmael himself says that all men are figurative orphans who seek in vain for the secret of their paternity.[1]

It is surely no accident that Melville chose the name 'Ishmael' for his narrator/character, recalling the outcast son of Abraham by his bond-servant Hagar (Gen. 16–25). For Melville humankind, as represented by Ishmael, is an outcast, a castaway adrift at sea, both literally and figuratively. In this respect, *Moby-Dick* comes to an answer about the central problem of evil in the world which is essentially at odds with that discovered by Job following his confrontation with Yahweh who speaks to him out of the whirlwind. Ishmael comes to the conclusion that nothing has meaning or certainty; Job comes to the conviction that only God does.[2] This leads us to consider in more detail the significance of the Epilogue to Melville's story; perhaps it also gives us a clue as to the comparable prose section with which the book of Job concludes (42.7-17).

Scholars have long debated whether this passage is by the same hand as the opening prose section (chs. 1–2) and what its relationship is to the poetic parts of the book.[3] The Epilogue seem to run in the face of the

---

1.　'Introduction', in Gilmore (ed.), *Moby-Dick*, pp. 7-8.

2.　It is worth noting that G.B. Shaw's celebrated comment about God's assertion 'I can make a hippopotamus!' being no answer to the problems of evil in the world actually falls short of understanding the meaning of the Leviathan image in the book of Job. As A.C. Thiselton (*New Horizons in Hermeneutics* [London: HarperCollins, 1992], p. 14) perceptively remarks, alluding to Shaw's comment: 'To suggest that Job can leave in God's hands the threat of the untamable chaos-monster, the Kraken, the primeval force which threatens to dissolve the order of the cosmos into confusion and meaninglessness, is to say more than that Job cannot create a hippopotamus'.

3.　H.H. Rowley, 'The Book of Job and its Meaning', *BJRL* 41 (1958–59), pp. 167-207, and J. Barr, 'The Book of Job and its Modern Interpreters', *BJRL* 54 (1970–71), pp. 28-46, give details of how the issue has been handled by OT scholars over the years.

basic argument of the book as a whole, reinstituting, as it were, a theological framework in which faith is rewarded and unbelief punished. Little wonder that in terms of the theological teaching of the bulk of Job, the Epilogue of 42.7-17 presents real difficulties. There are certainly some theological tensions between what is said in this Epilogue and teaching elsewhere within the Dialogue (3.1–41.6). To cite but one instance: can the high praise of Job by God in 42.7-8 *really* be reconciled with Job's impious tirades against the justice of the Most High in the poetic chapters? Many think not; or at least, that it cannot easily be reconciled. Therefore, many have argued that the Epilogue of Job be excised, just as Melville's English editor excised the Epilogue to *Moby-Dick*. Such excision may be a drastic solution, but there is some merit in it, at least as far as it allows a consistent theological message to be found within the book. However, this solution is not acceptable, or necessary, in the opinion of other scholars who argue that within the book of Job, as it now stands, the Epilogue is integral to the structure of the work. Indeed, one of the most recent full-scale commentaries on the book of Job, that of Norman C. Habel, stresses the plot development of the work as a whole and the place of the prose Epilogue within it. As Habel says, 'With Job's restoration, long life, and happy death the author achieves a traditional closure with a final artistic touch'.[1] Many commentators feel that the interpretation of the book of Job as a literary document must proceed on this basis, whatever insights source-compositional studies might reveal about it. Be that as it may, it was no doubt felt somewhere along the tortuous path of the book's textual history that it was not enough simply to have the final note of the book be one of repentance on Job's part in the face of God's overwhelming arguments—there must also be restitution to fill out that repentance.

---

1. *The Book of Job*, p. 580. Habel is here applying the insights of R. Alter (*The Art of Biblical Narrative* [London: Allen & Unwin, 1981]) to his study of Job. Also worth consulting on this point are: Habel's 'The Narrative Art of Job', *JSOT* 27 (1983), pp. 101-11; A. Brenner, 'Job the Pious? The Characterization of Job in the Narrative Framework of the Book', *JSOT* 43 (1989), pp. 37-52; and A. Cooper, 'Reading and Misreading the Prologue to Job', *JSOT* 46 (1990), pp. 67-79. Interestingly, H.H. Rowley ('The Book of Job', p. 186) remarked, 'The Epilogue was not demanded by the message of the book; but it was demanded by its form'. Many would dispute the too-casual separation between form and content that this comment implies.

And what a restitution is provided! In fact, vv. 12-13 tell us that Job was given exactly double the number of possessions and sons he had before the debacle of 1.13-19. However much we may feel that this sort of ending 'spoils' the story, or casts doubts upon the integrity of the God it is purporting to reveal; however much we may want to remove the Epilogue altogether and not get caught in the rewards-for-repentance trap which it seems to imply, we cannot deny that the Epilogue is there and that it radically affects the interpretation of the book of Job as a whole. Little wonder then that David Clines, in an extremely stimulating and thought-provoking essay,[1] concentrates attention on the Epilogue and argues that these last eleven verses of the book actually allow the meaning of the book as a whole to be deconstructed, overturned and undermined.[2] In other words, the dismissal of the doctrine of retribution, which has been argued out so persuasively throughout the Dialogues, is accomplished by 42.7-17 as the deeper meanings (the narrative structures) of the text are discovered and 'deconstructed'. It is all strikingly reminiscent to me of Melville's oft-repeated exhortation to his readers that they 'dive deeper' and 'dive to a lower level' to discover the meaning of *Moby-Dick*. A hint of this is made in the very first chapter of the novel ('1. Loomings') where Melville has a provocative use of the classical story of Narcissus and his deadly fascination for his own image as reflected in water. Melville explains,

> And still deeper the meaning of that story of Narcissus, who because he could not grasp the tormenting, mild image he saw in the fountain, plunged into it and was drowned. But that same image, we ourselves see in all rivers and oceans. It is the image of the ungraspable phantom of life; and this is the key to it all.

It may well be that the key to understanding *Moby-Dick* lies in confronting this 'ungraspable phantom of life' by plunging headlong into

---

1. D.J.A. Clines, 'Deconstructing the Book of Job', in M. Warner (ed.), *The Bible as Rhetoric: Studies in Biblical Persuasion and Credibility* (London: Routledge, 1990), pp. 65-80. This article offers one of the best explanations I have read about how a deconstructionalist approach can be usefully applied to the biblical materials. Also worth noting is the discussion of the article in Thiselton, *New Horizons*, pp. 120-21.

2. This all builds upon the insights brought to biblical interpretation by the rise of structuralism which called attention to the formal rules governing the way in which stories are told and narratives are related.

the hidden, deeper structures of meaning contained within the text. Or, as Melville puts it in '32. Cetology' when he shifts to an architectural image and describes the novel as an unfinished construction, 'small erections may be finished by their first architects; grand ones, true ones, ever leave the copestone to posterity'. If ever there was a text which invites a deconstructionalist approach along the lines of what has been suggested concerning the book of Job, this grappling with the deeper meanings of a text, it is Melville's *Moby-Dick*! Perhaps it is our task as a subsequent generation to work on the copestone of the literary 'building' which Melville has created. There is much within the book that becomes clear only when it is recognized that passages do, indeed, undermine the essential ideas which the book elsewhere asserts; in this respect the deconstructionalist approach has much to offer in helping us to interpret it, as indeed it does for helping us to interpret the mysteries of the book of Job.

Thus, in a curious way the book of Job parallels Melville's *Moby-Dick* in that they each have a controversial conclusion to their respective stories; an ending which invites, even demands, further consideration. It is within the Epilogues of the two works that we find the most tantalizing point of comparison between them as works of literature which are interpreted by modern readers. The two narratives meet at the crossroads labelled 'Epilogue', but take off in very different directions afterwards. The book of Job's Epilogue is wholly conditioned by faith in the God of Israel who, in the final analysis, far from abandoning Job, actually blesses him beyond belief; Job discovers in the midst of his suffering a greater realization of the presence of God in his life. *Moby-Dick's* Epilogue is left floundering on a sea of scepticism which allows its character Ishmael to know no such personal experience of the abiding presence of God or of his grace. At least, there is a fundamental difference between the Epilogues of the book of Job and *Moby-Dick* insofar as we concentrate on Melville's *intended* ending; those published editions of *Moby-Dick* which for one reason or another omit or change the Epilogue, either through the folly of the publishing editor's knife or the pen of a Hollywood screenwriter motivated by the need for a happy ending, effectively do to Melville's work what the final editor of the book of Job does to his work by adding the disputed Epilogue. We could even say that Job's twofold recovery of property and family has its equivalent in the early Hollywood film versions of Melville's book where Ahab kills the whale, marries the girl, and lives happily ever after. It may be a nicely sanitized, Hollywood-style ending to Ahab's encounter with the whale, but it badly misinterprets *Moby-Dick*. It also fails to record just how marked a contrast there is between the book of Job and *Moby-Dick* on this vexing matter of how human beings should respond to the presence of evil and suffering in the world.

Paradoxically, it could be argued that the role that the Epilogue plays in the message of *Moby-Dick* is exactly the opposite of that which it plays in the book of Job. In *Moby-Dick* it needs to be retained if the body of the work is to make sense and the narrative framework of the novel is to have any credibility; the prevailing atmosphere that remains is one of tragedy and despair. In Job, by contrast, we nearly reach the point that the Epilogue needs to be removed if the message contained in the body of the book is to have any theological credibility, for what we are left with here is, quite simply, a fairy-tale ending. The only alternative is to follow, as David Clines has attempted, the hermeneutical pathway of a deconstructionist approach and try to make sense of Job in that way. To summarize, the importance of the Epilogue within the interpretation of both *Moby-Dick* and the book of Job can hardly be overstated.

It is important to note one final thing about the Epilogue of *Moby-Dick* and the quotation of the line from Job 1.15-17, 19 which opens it. Ishmael is clearly meant to invoke memory of the four messengers who survived the various calamities which befell Job from every corner of the compass. But let us not forget that their ominous words 'And I only am escaped alone to tell you' were directed to the character of Job himself. The critical question remains: To whom does Ishmael direct his statement of survival? The answer must surely be (and this is the wonder of what Melville has accomplished within the Epilogue) to you and I as the readers of the novel—we are Job, still faced with all of the ambiguities and challenges of life.

Both figures, Job and Ishmael, are united in that it is their encounter with the Leviathan of God which helps drive them to the crisis point of realization within their respective stories. On that score one cannot overestimate the importance of the book of Job for Melville's great contribution to literature, his self-described 'wicked book', *Moby-Dick*.[1]

---

1. In a letter to Nathaniel Hawthorne dated 29 June 1851, Melville speaks suggestively of his novel of *Moby-Dick*: 'This is the book's motto (the secret one),—*Ego non baptismo te in nomine*—but make out the rest yourself'. He is, of course,

5. *Summary*

I began this study of Herman Melville's *Moby-Dick* by describing something of how the novel came to be written. I discussed briefly how it was that Melville was able to draw upon his experience on board whaling ships and on his wide reading to help him with the novel's composition. Yet he managed to create something entirely new and different within this work, undoubtedly his most famous novel. I noted especially Melville's reliance upon two biblical documents, Jonah and the book of Job, for its central motif—the White Whale Moby-Dick, the Leviathan. Several key places where these two biblical books are either quoted or alluded to within *Moby-Dick* were cited, with particular attention being paid to how Melville blends together reference to these passages within his own narrative purposes. I then examined some of the theatrical and cinematic attempts to translate *Moby-Dick* for popular audiences, including Orson Welles's critically acclaimed *Moby-Dick Rehearsed* (1965), as well as some of the early silent film versions of the story.[1] Most importantly, I discussed at some length John Huston's film *Moby-Dick* (1956), perhaps the single most important vehicle for public familiarity with Melville's classic today. In each instance I tried to point out where the adaptation of the work diverges from Melville's novel and offered an interpretation of its own. Particularly important was the ending that was put to the story in these adaptations—who survived the encounter with Moby-Dick and how was this portrayed? Finally, I explored *Moby-Dick* as a work which is filled with a complex symbolism, with many of the key symbols manifestly containing more than one meaning. I listed some of the many approaches which have been applied in interpreting the meaning of *Moby-Dick* and suggested that the central theme of Ahab's vengeful quest for the White Whale is especially interesting as a symbol with theological overtones. The same holds true for the characters Ahab and Ishmael, both of whom have been interpreted as Job-like figures. The Epilogue of the novel, with its description of Ishmael's chance rescue after the sinking of the *Pequod* by Moby-Dick, led us to reconsider the place of the Epilogue of the

---

alluding to the baptism passage in '113. The Forge' where Ahab baptizes his crew in the name of Satan as they follow their unholy task of killing Moby-Dick.

1.   Notably the silent classics *The Sea Beast* (1925) and *Moby-Dick* (1930).

book of Job within the structure of that work. Points of similarity and points of contrast exist when one considers the role played by the Epilogue within the book of Job and *Moby-Dick*.

In closing, I would like to point out the way in which one recent commentator on the book of Job concludes his discussion about the Epilogue of the book and contrast that with how Melville ends the body of his *Moby-Dick*. J.H. Eaton summarizes his discussion of the Epilogue, and how it grapples with the thorny question of unjust suffering on Job's part, with these words:

> The story has told of a great suffering for which there was a reason in God's purpose, but not a reason known on earth. So the last word is not given to anarchy in human fates, however anarchical things seem. But for man there remains the inexplicable. *He has to suffer in the dark and keep faith when all the waves of chaos roll over him.*[1]

The passage is remarkably suggestive of Melville's concluding words in '135. The Chase—Third Day', where the same image of rolling ocean waves is applied to humankind's fate. Ahab and the *Pequod*, together with all of the crew, have been sucked into the vortex caused by Moby-Dick (we do not yet know of Ishmael's escape). Then we have these words:

> Now small fowls flew screaming over the yet yawning gulf; a sullen white surf beat against its steep sides; then all collapsed, and the great shroud of the sea rolled on as it rolled five thousand years ago.

The reference to 'five thousand years ago' is, of course, indicative of the belief, commonly held by people in Melville's day, that the flood of Noah took place five thousand years ago. It is as if to say that the struggle with evil, as symbolized by the waters of chaos and destruction which come upon people as a death-shroud, has been going on since primaeval times, and will continue to do so.

Thus, in like manner both the book of Job and *Moby-Dick* grapple with some of the key questions of life itself. One could go so far as to say that the encounter with the Leviathan of God which is portrayed within these two works of literature stands as a window through which the two books can be viewed by the reader. Both explore how humanity deals with, and responds to, God's Leviathan and both go a long way in

---

1.   *Job* (OTG; Sheffield: JSOT Press, 1985), p. 49. The italics are mine.

summarizing the essential ideas about value and purpose in life when human beings are faced with the presence of evil and suffering in the world.

Chapter 3

EAST OF EDEN: LIFE IN THE LAND OF NOD

Then Cain went away from the presence of the Lord, and dwelt in the land
of Nod, east of Eden. (Gen. 4.16)

The power of the mythic story of Cain and Abel to evoke the human
imagination has long been recognized, particularly by specialists in world
literature. A good study of its importance is the recent book entitled *The
Changes of Cain* by Ricardo J. Quinones, a Professor of English and
Comparative Literatures who attempts to trace the story's influence
through the literature and art of Western civilization. Not surprisingly,
John Steinbeck's novel *East of Eden* has a prominent place within
Quinones' discussion, particularly as it expresses what he describes as
the American experience in which 'the character of Cain becomes
something of a national type'.[1] In this regard it is fitting to note that
Steinbeck (1902–1968) was an American and almost all of his fictional
work is set in the United States.

While critics of Steinbeck's work are quick to point out the importance of the biblical story underlying it, it is much more difficult to find
Old Testament commentators who point to *East of Eden* as a modern
retelling of the story of Cain and Abel. Indeed, the only place which I
have been able to find which discusses Steinbeck's work in any depth is
the recent commentary on Genesis by Walter Brueggemann, who
rightly suggests that 'interpretation would do well to consider
Steinbeck's handling of the theme as a way of entering the text'.[2]
Brueggemann's suggestion is one that I would like to take up here.

Within this short study I would like to call attention to some of the
ways in which Steinbeck's novel creatively adapts the biblical material.

1. R.J. Quinones, *The Changes of Cain* (Princeton, NJ: Princeton University
Press, 1991), p. 135.
2. *Genesis* (IC; Atlanta: John Knox Press, 1982), pp. 58-59.

In particular, I aim to demonstrate how Steinbeck's handling of one special feature of the Genesis story of Cain and Abel may even help us move toward resolving one of the most perplexing problems arising from the passage, the meaning of the troublesome phrase at the end of 4.7: 'sin is couching at the door; its desire is for you, *but you must master it*' (RSV). Steinbeck's fictional exploration of this verse alerts us to the concepts of human freedom and responsibility which lie deeply embedded within the story as a whole. At the same time, the cinematic interpretations of Steinbeck's novel also offer insight into the ways in which the central theme of human responsibility contained within the novel has been communicated to the popular audience. As I shall demonstrate, the two available film adaptations of Steinbeck's *magnum opus* offer differing interpretations of the novel which, in some ways, fail to communicate the central theme (or do so badly) and thereby do injustice to the novel, and indeed to the underlying message of Genesis itself. Recognition of this shortcoming drives us in turn to consider how some of our interpretations, and translations, of Genesis 4 might similarly fail to grasp the key teaching about human relationships expressed in the story of Cain and Abel following the expulsion of Adam and Eve from the Garden of Eden by God. Thus the hope is that, by turning to Steinbeck's novel and its cinematic interpretations, we may discover something new and fresh about the meaning of the story of Cain and Abel and come to a greater understanding of the biblical teaching on human freedom and responsibility in relationships as a result.

I shall pursue this study under four headings: (1) The Symbolic Title of the Novel; (2) The Biblical Sub-Plot in *East of Eden*; (3) The Film Adaptations of *East of Eden*; (4) The Philosophical Core of *East of Eden*: 'Thou mayest' (Gen. 4.7c).

1. *The Symbolic Title of the Novel*

Steinbeck wrote the novel between 29 January and 1 November 1959, mostly in the house on 72nd Street in New York City where he lived with his third wife Elaine. The book was first published in September of 1952 and was an immediate success, quickly establishing itself as a national best-seller. It was to be his longest work, over 265,000 words, the manuscript converting into nearly 1000 typed pages in the original draft and the published work running to over 650 pages in its first edition. It contains four major parts, and is divided into 55 chapters, many of which are divided into several subsections.[1]

Steinbeck was convinced that *East of Eden* would be his best effort, and knew that the project would absorb him completely. He describes it thus: 'I think perhaps it is the only book I have ever written. I think that there is only one book to a man'.[2] It is clear that Steinbeck felt that for him *East of Eden* was his 'one book', or as he sometimes described it, '*The* Book'. That he felt this novel was his artistic peak, his crowning achievement is evident. As he remarked:

> If *East of Eden* isn't good, then I've been wasting my time. It has everything in it I've been able to learn about my art or craft or profession in all these years.[3]

Essentially *East of Eden* is a full-bodied saga of two American families, the Hamiltons and the Trasks, over the course of three generations. The story line spans the whole of the country, the Trasks in the East in Connecticut and the Hamiltons in the West in California, and covers some 50 years or so, beginning with the American Civil War of the 1860s and concluding with events surrounding the First World War. The novel narrates the triumphs and tragedies of the two families, relating how they each dealt with the tremendous changes of the time in their own way and how they eventually came to find the family histories intertwined within the Salinas Valley of central California.

Initially Steinbeck planned to highlight the interconnection between the Hamiltons and the Trasks by alternating material about them within the chapters of the novel, imposing an intercalation upon the story as a whole. This was eventually abandoned under the sheer weight of the narrative, although the reader can easily detect vestiges of it remaining. *East of Eden* is in many ways an overly ambitious effort; some critics have described it as seriously flawed, sprawling in content and discursive in style. Steinbeck struggles throughout to keep control of the work, as it goes off in all directions and involves nearly a dozen major characters. Nevertheless it is a noble attempt to portray the American movement to

---

1. Quotations from the novel are hereafter identified by chapter and subsection; thus 3:1 means subsection 1 of chapter 3. The edition used is *East of Eden* (London: Mandarin Books, 1990).

2. *Journey of a Novel* (London: Mandarin Books, 1991), p. 5.

3. Quoted in B. Kale, 'The Author', *Saturday Review* 35 (20 September 1952), p. 11.

the West, although clearly underlying the surface story line is Steinbeck's wrestling with the deeper issues of life and their meaning. Here we see the struggle between good and evil set forth, the strengths and weaknesses of human character being portrayed, the hopes and frustrations of life exposed in a quite powerful fashion.

Steinbeck originally intended to entitle the novel *The Salinas Valley*. However, in the course of writing it he came to feel that the themes dealt with within the book were not best served by a limiting reference to the local Californian valley in which he grew up, despite the fact that the valley is the geographical focus for much of the novel. There is clearly a large autobiographical dimension within the story (the key character Samuel Hamilton was in fact his maternal grandfather and Steinbeck himself makes an occasional childhood appearance in the story line, as well as functioning as the narrator throughout).[1] Nevertheless, Steinbeck felt that the ideas contained in the work were much more universal and he wisely decided to look for an alternative title for the book.

From the beginning he had conceived of the novel as a modern retelling of the story of Cain and Abel from Genesis 4, and thus it is not surprising that Steinbeck turned to Genesis for inspiration for a title. His own thoughts on the matter are perhaps best put on the lips of the character Lee, the Trasks' Chinese philosopher-cook, within the novel. Commenting on the Genesis story, Lee, who often functions in the novel as the mouthpiece for Steinbeck's own thoughts and ideas, is made to remark (22:4),

> I think this is the best-known story in the world because it is everybody's story. I think it is the symbol story of the human soul...I think this old and terrible story is important because it is a chart of the soul—the secret, rejected, guilty soul.[2]

Fortunately we have an invaluable means of examining more closely Steinbeck's own soul during the production of the novel. He kept a fascinating diary of his thoughts while writing the book, effectively a writer's log with an entry for virtually every working day spent on the

---

1. See, M.H. Cox, 'Steinbeck's Family Portraits: The Hamiltons', *SQ* 14 (1981), pp. 23-32, for a discussion of this.

2. For a discussion of the narrative role that Lee plays within the novel, see R.C. Bedford, 'Steinbeck's Uses of the Oriental', *SQ* 13 (1980), pp. 5-19.

book. The diary was for Steinbeck a 'literary warm-up' for the daily demands of writing the novel, his way of starting the creative juices flowing and an important means of concentrating his mind to the task at hand. The diary was directed to his friend and publishing editor Pascal Covici. Published posthumously in 1969 under the title *Journey of a Novel: The East of Eden Letters*, these entries offer great insight into what he was trying to accomplish within the novel. For instance, he tells us of his struggle to find a title and framework for the book:

> I thought about the book a great deal yesterday…its framework roots from that powerful and perplexing story in Genesis of Cain and Abel…With this in mind I went back to Genesis. I do not want a direct quotation but if I can find a symbol there which is understood on sight and which strikes deep, I will have my title. The punishment of Cain is a strange and perplexing one. Out of Eve's sin came love and death. Cain invented murder and he is punished by life and protection. The mark put on him is not placed there to punish him but to protect him. Have you ever thought of that? And this is the best known mark in the world. So I suggest as a title for my book *Cain Sign*. It is not a direct quote, it is short, harsh, memorable and nearly everyone in the world knows what it means.[1]

Eventually he moved beyond *Cain Sign* and settled on the title *East of Eden*, still drawing upon the imagery of Genesis 4 and using a suggestive phrase from it as the symbolic basis for his long-sought title. The phrase selected crystallized the sense of wandering and expectation contained within the novel, a wanderlust which finds the characters attempting to create in the Californian valley a new Eden. As Steinbeck says later in his working journal,

> And now I had set down in my own hand the 16 verses of Cain and Abel and the story changes with flashing lights when you write it down. And I think I have a title at last, a beautiful title, *East of Eden*. And read the 16th verse to find it.[2]

He wrote in a similar vein to film director Elia Kazan (a close friend and artistic colleague with whom Steinbeck had worked on the Oscar-winning film *Viva Zapata!* and who was later in 1955 to direct the first film version of *East of Eden*) about his struggle to come up with a suitable title for the book:

1.   *Journey of a Novel*, p. 107. The entry is dated 22 May 1951.
2.   *Journey of a Novel*, p. 123. The entry is dated 11 June 1951.

I have about 600 pages of my book done and about 3 or 400 to go. At last I have a title for it which I like. See if you do. It is east of Eden. It is perfect for the book and it sounds like a very soft title until you read the first 16 verses of the 4th chapter of Genesis. The title comes from the 16th verse but the whole passage is applicable.[1]

He even wanted to have the crucial verse from Gen. 4.16 printed on the title page of the novel just to make sure that there was no doubt about the biblical allusion. Steinbeck goes on to explain that he is using the story of Cain and Abel in Genesis precisely because of its universality, the fact that it is instantly adaptable to the human situation; the story retains its mythical power and there is a strong element of cross-cultural application within it. The novel *East of Eden* is, he says, 'using the Biblical story as a measure of ourselves'.[2] In particular, the key character Cal within the novel is, in Steinbeck's words, 'the Everyman, the battleground between good and evil, the most human of all, the sorry man'.[3] *East of Eden* is an entirely appropriate title given the questions of morality and the struggle between right and wrong which Steinbeck continually addresses within the novel, a story which above all seeks to demonstrate that, in the words of the author/narrator (34:1), 'humans are caught...in a net of good and evil'. As John H. Timmerman puts it,

The symbolism of the title is internally consistent with the story. The great quest of Adam Trask is not to find an Eden but to learn to live east of it— in a fallen world of mortal evil.[4]

1. E. Steinbeck and R. Wallstein (eds.), *Steinbeck: A Life in Letters* (London: Heinemann, 1975), p. 425. The letter is dated 30 July 1951.

2. Steinbeck and Wallstein, *Steinbeck*, p. 123. The entry is dated 12 June 1951.

3. Steinbeck and Wallstein, *Steinbeck*, p. 429. The 'Everyman' motif is extended by Steinbeck to include a positive figure as well. In a moving letter to Mrs John F. Kennedy dated 28 February 1964, shortly after the President's assassination on 22 November 1963, Steinbeck wrote, 'As we all do—I have need, and consider the New Testament many times. And it has seemed to me that Jesus lived a singularly undramatic life—a straight line without deviation or doubt. And then we come to that heart-breaking moment on the cross when He cried "Lama sabachthani". In that one moment of doubt we are all related to him. And when you said you had questions to ask, please remember that terrible question Jesus asked: "My Lord, wherefore hast thou forsaken me?" In that moment He was everyone—Everyone!' (Steinbeck and Wallstein, *Steinbeck*, pp. 795-96).

4. *John Steinbeck's Fiction: The Aesthetics of the Road Taken* (Norman: University of Oklahoma Press, 1986), p. 38. Similarly, J. Fontenrose (*John*

Thus, it is a novel about the complexities of the ongoing struggle of human existence itself—life in the land of Nod.

2. *The Biblical Sub-Plot in* East of Eden

At one point in *East of Eden* (in 24:2) the loveable character Samuel Hamilton offers his opinion on the mysterious nature of the Bible. He describes it as a 'divine book written by the inky finger of God'; an evocative way of emphasizing the mystery, not to say the inscrutability, of the biblical narrative. By this definition the story of Cain and Abel would clearly stand as one of the 'inkiest' recorded, for it is without doubt among the most difficult in the whole of the Old Testament to interpret. All the more reason, therefore, that an attempt like Steinbeck's *East of Eden* should be recognized as a valuable means whereby we can engage the story afresh and attempt to extract some of the richness of the Genesis myth. As John Clark Pratt has commented:

> Discovering that this mixture of crossed biblical allusions is consciously designed to function in the novel, the reader begins to perceive the complex magnitude of Steinbeck's plan. This carefully contrived, complicated relationship of fictional character to biblical antecedent contributes significantly to Steinbeck's overall purpose.[1]

Pratt's point is accurate, even though it is not made in connection with the story of Cain and Abel, but is about Steinbeck's use of the Bible in general, and his use of Genesis in particular.[2] Indeed, one of the best examples of Steinbeck's direct use of the Genesis background occurs in

---

Steinbeck: An Introduction and Interpretation [New York: Holt, Rinehart & Winston, 1963], p. 6) describes 'myth as a palimpsest upon which Steinbeck has inscribed a realistic tale of contemporary men'. However, not all critics have been as positive of the symbolism within the novel. M. Seymour-Smith (*Guide to Modern World Literature* [London: Macmillan Press, 1975], p. 101) describes *East of Eden* as 'pretentiously symbolic'.

1.   *John Steinbeck: A Critical Essay* (CWCPS; Grand Rapids: Eerdmans, 1970), p. 28.

2.   *The Grapes of Wrath* has usually received the bulk of the scholarly discussion concerning Steinbeck's use of biblical imagery within his novels. For an interesting introduction to this subject, see, E. Klammer, '*The Grapes of Wrath*: A Modern Exodus Account', *Cresset* 25 (1962), pp. 8-11.

15:3 where Adam Trask discusses with Samuel Hamilton his intention to
build a new Eden on his property in California and raise his family on it:

> 'Look, Samuel, I mean to make a garden of my land. Remember my
> name is Adam. So far I've had no Eden, let alone been driven out.'
> 'It's the best reason I ever heard for making a garden,' Samuel
> exclaimed. He chuckled. 'Where will the orchard be?'
> Adam said, 'I won't plant apples. That would be looking for accidents.'
> 'What does Eve say to that? She has a say, you remember. And Eves
> delight in apples.'

The story of Adam and Eve and the Fall in the Garden of Eden in
Genesis 2–3 is used here by Steinbeck in an almost cavalier fashion. Yet
the exchange between Adam and Samuel also has an ominous ring to it,
for it hints at the disaster which is to come to the Trask family through
the actions of the Eve-like Cathy Trask. Nevertheless, it is, as I have
already stated, the story of the *children* of Adam and Eve which is an
even more significant focal point for the novel as a whole. Indeed, so
central to Steinbeck's purposes is the story of Cain and Abel from Gen.
4.1-16 that the passage is quoted in its entirety in 22:4 and fully
discussed again in 24:2. But what of the biblical passage itself? In what
ways is it so significant to Steinbeck's artistic purposes? What is it within
the story which lends itself to such explication? It is worth summarizing
some of the scholarly debate revolving around the passage as a
preliminary to my discussion of Steinbeck's use of it.

Gen. 4.1-16, usually assigned by Old Testament scholars to the J
source of the Pentateuch, has received much scholarly discussion and
has, understandably, been subject to an extraordinary amount of theological debate.[1] The crucial couplet of 4.6-7 is particularly important,
given the fact that it somewhat disrupts the narrative and contains some
very unusual Hebrew phrases. No wonder that Claus Westermann has
described 4.6-7 as something of a 'foreign body' and has remarked that
'No satisfactory explanation of these two verses has been proposed as
yet'.[2] The fact that these verses contain so many odd features has led
many scholars to suggest that they are a later addition to a traditional

---

1. E. van Wolde, 'The Story of Cain and Abel: A Narrative Study', *JSOT* 52
(1991), pp. 25-41, discusses the close connection that the story of Cain and Abel in
Gen. 4.1-16 has with the earlier section of Gen. 2–3 and offers an interpretation
focusing on the narrative techniques used by the author in relating the story.

2. *Genesis 1–11: A Commentary* (London: SPCK, 1984), p. 298.

story about Cain and his brother Abel, the archetypal farmer and shepherd.

The technical issues under consideration are many. There are scholarly debates about the place that vv. 6-7 have within the larger story. There are also differences of opinion about how much the similar declaration of Gen. 3.16 has influenced the couplet.[1] Questions have been raised about the precise reading of most of the phrases contained within v. 7, so unusual and obscure are they. For instance, in what sense should the conditional clauses of 7ab be taken? Even more problematic is the curious reference to 'sin, lying in wait at the door' in v. 7; many scholars point to this as being linguistically based upon Assyrian descriptions of demons as personifications of sin.[2] Of special note is 7c, with its many possibilities of Hebrew pointing and the ambiguous reference as to what must be mastered; is it sin? is it desire? or, is it, as some have argued and some modern translations suggest, Cain's brother Abel? In short, not only is Gen. 4.1-16 filled with a host of theological and interpretative difficulties, but the verse crucial to Steinbeck's purposes within *East of Eden*, v. 7, is an exegetical minefield. Let us set forth the couplet of 4.6-7 as it is translated within the RSV:

6a	The Lord said to Cain,
6b	'Why are you angry,
6c	and why has your countenance fallen?
7a	If you do well, will you not be accepted?
7b	And if you do not do well, sin is couching at the door.
7c	Its desire is for you, but you must master it.'

The many difficulties presented by 7c are reflected in the variety of translations which are offered for the concluding phrase:

1. S.T. Foh, 'What is the Woman's Desire?', *WTJ* 37 (1974–75), pp. 376-83, offers an illuminating discussion of the parallels between Gen. 3.16 and 4.7. She interprets the woman's 'urge' in 3.16 as a desire to be independent from the man and to contend with him for leadership in their relationship. Also see J.J. Schmitt, 'Like Eve, Like Adam: *mšl* in Gen. 3, 16', *Bib* 72 (1991), pp. 1-22 for a discussion.

2. Westermann disagrees, primarily because he feels that personification of sin in this manner is a late development and not appropriate for a story as early as that of Cain and Abel. Instead, Westermann suggests that the original form of the story at this point is that Cain here is warned by the ghost of the one whom he murdered (Abel) that he will haunt him. For theological reasons, Westermann conjectures, this proved problematic for subsequent editors and hence the textual and linguistic difficulties of the couplet arise.

KJV	thou shalt rule over him.
NEB	you will be mastered by it.
Moffatt	you ought to master it.
NASB, NRSV and NIV	you must master it.
JB	which you must master.
GNB	you can be his master.
Knox	thou canst have thy way with him.

The meaning of this unusual phrase at the end of Gen. 4.7, notably the Hebrew verb תִּמְשָׁל ('timshol')[1] of which Steinbeck later was to make so much, has also been the subject of considerable discussion amongst Old Testament scholars. Gerhard von Rad remarked on 4.7,

> The statement does not actually speak of an inner emotion, but it shows sin to be an objective power which, as it were, is outside the man and over him waiting eagerly to take possession of him. The man, however, ought to master it and curb it. Man's responsibility with regard to sin is not in the least annulled; on the contrary, this final imperative imposes upon him the whole responsibility.[2]

E.A. Speiser appears to agree with the potential human freedom implied within the verse by translating the crucial phrase as 'yet you can be his master',[3] and U. Cassuto similarly paraphrases the verse as 'you are not delivered into its (sin's) power, and if you only have the desire, you can oppose it and overcome it and free yourself from its influence'.[4] Perhaps the most interesting interpretation is that of G.R. Castellino, which attempts to solve some of the difficult textual considerations by postulating that the contentious verse be taken as a question put to Cain by God. The crucial sentence then becomes, 'Sin will be lying in wait for you, and are you sure, you shall be able to master it?' Castellino goes on to remark that

---

1.   Steinbeck consistently (and wrongly!) transliterates the Hebrew as 'timshel'. In discussing Steinbeck's work I shall, for the sake of convenience, adopt his spelling.
2.   *Genesis* (OTL; London: SCM Press, rev. edn, 1972), p. 105.
3.   *Genesis* (AB, 1; Garden City, NY: Doubleday, 1964), p. 29.
4.   *A Commentary on the Book of Genesis: Part 1 From Adam to Noah (Genesis I–VI:8)* (Jerusalem: Magnes, 1961), p. 212. R.B. Coote and D.R. Ord (*The Bible's First History* [Philadelphia: Fortress Press, 1989], p. 70) say, 'In J, sin is not a universal condition or a general set of undesirable behaviors but a specific act of injustice to be warded off. Sin is resistible.'

Interpreted as an interrogation the last clause eases the text and makes it perfectly plausible. The process of man's liability to sin, that can become an actual temptation, difficult to resist, entangling man and pulling him gradually down into the worst of crimes, is thus described with a psychological insight that makes it valuable for all times, being true to man's nature.[1]

The beauty of the interpretation offered by Castellino is that it allows the possibility of both success and failure within the response of Cain, and by implication, within each of us as we face similar decisions in life. In this way the perennial issue of human responsibility is properly highlighted and made a focal point within the biblical story.

Indeed, it is precisely the timeless quality of the Genesis story which Steinbeck attempts to address within *East of Eden*, lifting the story, as it were, from the mists of prehistory and transplanting it into the contemporary world. Steinbeck builds upon the story of Cain and Abel throughout the novel, cleverly weaving together echoes of the biblical story within his narrative, often at an almost unconscious level. To illustrate: it surely is not without significance that Steinbeck alliterates the names of many of the main characters in the Trask family so as to confirm to the Cain-Abel motif. Thus the Cain-like figures are Cyrus, Charles and Cal (one could perhaps add Cathy Ames) and the Abel-like figures are Alice, Adam and Aron.[2] Beyond the obvious allusion in the title, this is the first internal clue to the importance of the Genesis story as the narrative sub-structure to the novel. Steinbeck pursues his aim of retelling the Cain and Abel story in several ways, mainly through the relationships that the various characters have with one another. He does this by selecting the two main relational encounters within the story in Genesis 4, that of the clash between the two brothers Cain and Abel, and the struggle of Cain to win God's approval, and building his own narrative versions of them. At the heart is an exploration of the theme of jealousy between two brothers as well as an examination of the tension between father and son(s) wherein the son(s) attempt(s) to gain the love of the father in some way. It is not difficult to see that the two motifs overlap, even as they do within the biblical story, and within *East of*

---

1. 'Genesis IV 7', *VT* 10 (1960), p. 445.
2. The alliteration scheme of the novel is discussed at some length in J. Ditsky, *Essays on East of Eden* (Steinbeck Monograph Series, 7; Muncie, IN: Ball State University, 1977), pp. 44-46.

Eden it is impossible to disentangle the two as subplots. A third obvious connection to the Genesis story is the 'mark of Cain' motif, which Steinbeck uses throughout the novel, identifying Cain-like figures within the narrative by means of facial scars.

Let us examine these three particular ways in which Steinbeck recasts the biblical story within *East of Eden* before moving on to consider how the film adaptations of the novel treat the same three themes.

a. *The Clash of Brother against Brother: Charles and Adam Trask; Cal and Aron Trask*

Perhaps the clearest example of the jealous rivalry of brothers, reminiscent of the struggle between Cain and Abel, is that between Charles and Adam Trask which occupies centre stage of the first part of the novel (chapters 1–11). The two brothers are in fact half-brothers, having the same father, Cyrus, but different mothers. Even here we see the roots of a rivalry developed within the story line, for Adam's mother commits suicide very early in the novel (3:1) and his father quickly remarries and sires a second son (Charles) by his new wife Alice (the two boys are thus a year apart in age). Despite the fact that Adam's real mother died before he was old enough to remember her, and Alice became for all practical purposes his mother, there remains in the relationship between the two boys and their parents a tension, a mutual suspicion of favouritism. Charles suspects that his father does not love him, or at least loves Adam more, and he harbours jealousy against his brother for it—a clear echo of the sibling rivalry recorded in the Genesis story. The tension between the two brothers reaches a climax over the gifts that the two boys present to their father on his birthday. The story is strikingly reminiscent of the gifts of sacrifice that Cain and Abel offer to God in Gen. 4.3-5, only to find that God (inexplicably) accepts Abel's offer of a lamb while rejecting Cain's offer of grain. Steinbeck creatively reworks the story, altering the gifts, of course, but keeping their symbolic nature intact (Adam offers an animal as did Abel, while Charles offers a knife, a mechanical instrument of harvest in keeping with the gift of Cain). Thus in 3:4 we have Charles confront Adam about the gifts in the midst of a violent rage:

> 'Look at his birthday!' Charles shouted. 'I took six bits and I bought him a knife made in Germany—three blades and a corkscrew, pearl-handled. Where's that knife? Do you ever see him use it? Did he give it to you? I never even saw him hone it. Have you got that knife in your pocket? What

did he do with it? "Thanks," he said, like that. And that's the last I heard
of a pearl-handled German knife that cost six bits.'...'What did you do
on his birthday? You think I didn't see? Did you spend six bits or even
four bits? You brought him a mongrel pup you had picked up in a wood-
lot. He laughed like a fool and said it would make a good bird dog. That
dog sleeps in his room. He plays with it while he's reading. He's got it all
trained. And where's the knife? "Thanks," he said, just "Thanks".'

Charles is filled with such anger and jealousy that he proceeds to beat
Adam so severely that he almost kills him (not quite emulating his
predecessor Cain). Their father finds out about the beating from Adam
and goes looking for the wayward Charles with a shotgun; fortunately
for Charles his father does not find him before his anger cools. After
some weeks an uneasy truce is arrived at and life takes on some degree
of normality again. The beating over the knife remains a key event in
the relationship between Charles and Adam and is mentioned in several
subsequent passages (including 4:2; 7:2; 7:3). In a subsequent conversation between the two brothers (7:3) the episode is explicitly described by
Adam as Charles's attempt to win the love of his father. 'I didn't know
then, but I know now—you were fighting for your love.'

The Cain-Abel motif is also contained in the second half of the novel
(chapters 22–55) where the twin sons of Adam, Cal and Aron, extend
the motif of brotherly conflict into the next generation. As was the case
with Adam and Charles, there is some irregularity concerning the
familial connection between the two. Some doubts are raised about the
paternity of the two brothers, given Cathy Trask's adulterous affair with
her brother-in-law Charles on her wedding night (11:6). Much is made
of the fact that the twins are born with separate amniotic sacs
(suggesting that Adam is the father of Aron and Charles the father of
Cal). The two (half-)brothers are locked in the struggle from infancy; as
Samuel Hamilton is made to remark (in 17:2) their entry into the world
was 'much more like a bitter, deadly combat than a birth'.

Continuing to illustrate the point of brotherly conflict, Steinbeck gives
several other glimpses of their rivalry as they grow up together. Later,
one of the focal points of the conflict is the struggle between the two
young men for the love of the beautiful young Abra Bacon. In the end
the clash between the two is interwoven with their attempts to please
their father Adam. It concludes tragically with Cal 'killing' his brother
(in true Cain-like fashion) by revealing news about their prostitute
mother. This revelation is too much for the sensitive Aron and he

escapes by enlisting in the army. He is sent to France with the American forces and is killed in battle.

b. *The Struggle of Father and Son: Adam and Cal Trask*

The Genesis story of Cain and Abel making offerings to gain the approval of God is communicated in *East of Eden* primarily by means of the relationships between Cyrus Trask and his two sons (Adam and Charles Trask), and Adam Trask and his two sons (Cal and Aron). The latter father–son tension occupies central position within Part 4 of the novel (chapters 34–55) and will be our focal point, although there are many important passages which set up the clash. Clearly Steinbeck was reliant within the novel upon some of the Old Testament background stories about the dealings of Jehovah with his people Israel. Many of the best-constructed passages of the novel make use of the Old Testament imagery when dealing with the central theme of humankind's relationship to God. At several points within *East of Eden* Steinbeck makes it clear that father figures often stand as symbols of God himself. For example, in 14:1 Steinbeck suggestively describes his mother, Olive Hamilton, with the sentence, 'Her theology was a curious mixture of Irish fairies and an Old Testament Jehovah whom in her later life she confused with her father'. More to the point, in 7:3 Adam and Charles Trask discuss their father and whether he was trustworthy since he has managed to accumulate a fortune while on a meagre government salary. Adam asserts that he believes in his father, despite seeming evidence to the contrary, and equates this belief as an equivalent to belief in the existence of God. Similarly, in 47:3 Aron is made to think of his father Adam Trask as 'the cool, dependable figure of godhead'.

As a character Adam Trask ties the two halves of the novel together. He is one of the few characters who survives for most of the novel, his birth being recorded in 3:1 and his death being related as the last line in the book. Perhaps the most important episode depicting the struggle between Adam and his son Cal involves the son's desire to please his father with a gift, as we read in 39:1: 'He wanted to serve his father, to give him some great gift, to perform some huge good task in honour of his father'. Eventually Cal concocts a scheme whereby he can speculate on crop prices and manages to earn a considerable sum of money as a windfall. He decides to give his father a gift of $15,000, as a repayment for all that had been lost in a disastrous lettuce-refrigeration gamble. This

Adam refuses, setting up a tension which becomes all the more tragic when it is remembered that Adam was himself one who, in his own way, sought to gain his father's love and approval and found in the end that he had nothing but contempt for his father. The final chapters of the novel reveal the terrible cost of the father–son struggle; after Aron is killed in battle in World War I Adam is fatally stricken with a cerebral haemorrhage. It is in this final chapter that the 'Timshel!' theme is brought to centre stage and used to resolve the struggle between father and (surviving) son.

c. *The 'Mark of Cain' Motif*

Another motif which Steinbeck uses to link the story of Charles and Adam to the Cain and Abel story is the image of the 'mark of Cain'; in *East of Eden* this first comes in the form of a large scar on Charles's forehead. The scar is caused by a farming accident in which Charles is clearing rocks from a field in the family farm with a long iron bar. He loses his temper over a particularly large stone and the bar slips out from under the stone and strikes him a wicked blow on the forehead (6:1). The wound produces a scar which stays with him for the rest of his life, gradually growing darker in skin tone. It stands as a symbol of his violent temper, the same temper which caused him to attempt to kill Adam. It is the equivalent of the 'mark of Cain' in Gen. 4.15 and surfaces from time to time within the story, often within the context of conflict between the two Trask brothers (as in 6:2; 7:3; 13:2; 28:3).

The motif of Charles's scar has an important literary counterpoint within the novel. It is also applied to the character of 'monster' Cathy Ames, who in 9:3 is beaten to the point of death by her whoremaster and is left with a scar on her forehead. Indeed, the connection between Charles's 'mark of Cain' and Cathy's is made explicit in 11:2 where Charles is in the Trask house at the bedside of the savaged Cathy:

> When the brothers were in her room, and it took two of them to help her on the bed-pan without hurting her, she studied Charles' dark sullenness. He had something in his face that she recognised, that made her uneasy. She saw that he touched the scar on his forehead very often, rubbed it, and drew its outline with his fingers. Charles said brutally, 'Don't you worry. You're going to have one like it, maybe even a better one.'

Again, the scar is a symbol of Cathy's thoroughgoing wickedness and appears at several points in the story (including 11:1; 11:4; 15:1; 15:4; 17:3; 17:4; 18:1; 18:2; 19:3; 20:2; 25:3). It is a recurrent reminder of her potential destructiveness and heightens the suspense of the narrative, making the reader wonder when the wicked Cathy is going to strike next, and against whom. Without a doubt Cathy/Kate is the most demonic character in the novel[1] and Steinbeck's portrayal of her has been one of the most discussed issues among students of his work.[2] The scar motif certainly adds to the malignant colours in which Steinbeck paints her, perhaps as an intentional allusion to the description of Eve bruising the serpent's head (Gen. 3.15).[3] In a revealing comment about the symbol in *Journey of a Novel*, Steinbeck explains to his editor Covici,

> I hope the incident of the scarred forehead does not throw you. It is going to be a kind of recurring symbol in various forms. And what does it mean? Oh I could tell you, the maimed, the marked, the guilty—all such things, the imperfect. It is a haunting thing. But there are a great many haunting things in this book.[4]

3. *The Film Adaptations of* East of Eden

Although John Steinbeck's *East of Eden* has not enjoyed the praise of critics as much as his *The Grapes of Wrath*, it nevertheless stands as one of the best known works of the Pulitzer Prize- and Nobel Prize-winning author. If he had never written anything else, either work would have been sufficient to grant Steinbeck a place as one of America's greatest twentieth-century novelists. In addition, both novels have been firmly

1. R.E. Morsberger ('Steinbeck's Happy Hookers', *SQ* 9 [1976], p. 111) describes her as 'Steinbeck's one wholly evil character'. Timmerman (*John Steinbeck's Fiction*, pp. 218-47) describes Cathy Ames as the 'central character' of the novel and as the 'pivot of Steinbeck's moral vision'.

2. The literature on this topic is vast. Of note are: R. Demott, 'Cathy Ames and Lady Godiva: A Contribution to *East of Eden's* Background', *SQ* 14 (1981), pp. 72-83; B. Everest and J. Wedeles, 'The Neglected Rib: Women in *East of Eden*', *SQ* 21 (1988), pp. 13-23; M.R. Gladstein, 'The Strong Female Principle of Good or Evil: The Women of *East of Eden*', *SQ* 24 (1991), pp. 30-40; L. Owens, 'The Mirror and the Vamp: Invention, Reflection, and Bad, Bad Cathy Trask in *East of Eden*', in Barbour and Quirk (eds.), *Writing the American Classics*, pp. 235-57.

3. Timmerman, *John Steinbeck's Fiction*, p. 220-22, offers some intriguing parallels between the Genesis story and *East of Eden* with respect to the portrayal of Cathy Ames as a symbol of the evil snake of Gen. 3.

4. *Journey of a Novel*, p. 41.

placed within the public domain by means of the classic film adaptations of them, John Ford's *The Grapes of Wrath* in 1940 and Elia Kazan's *East of Eden* in 1955. Both films were deservedly Oscar winners; Henry Fonda won the Best Actor Oscar for his portrayal of Tom Joad and Jo Van Fleet won Best Supporting Actress for her portrayal of Kate Trask. Indeed, almost all of Steinbeck's major works were made into films, making him one of the most cinematically represented authors in the history of the silver screen. Let us examine the two major attempts to portray *East of Eden* on film, paying particular attention to how faithful the films are to Steinbeck's original and how some of the underlying biblical themes of the novel I have identified are expressed.[1]

a. *Elia Kazan's Version (1955)*

The first attempt to translate Steinbeck's *East of Eden* onto the screen was made by Elia Kazan, who had worked with the author on several earlier projects. Kazan felt instinctively that the whole of the novel was too long and too diffuse to be made into a film and chose instead to concentrate on the last third of the book (from chapter 37 onwards). The focus is thus on the relationship between Adam Trask and his two sons, and on the twin brothers Cal and Aron as they both vie for the love of Abra. Kazan hired the well-known playwright Paul Osborn to do the film screenplay. This was a fortuitous move and Osborn produced a wonderful script, eventually earning an Academy Award nomination for his effort. Indeed, many Steinbeck scholars feel that this film version of *East of Eden* is superior as a piece of art to the novel on which it was based.[2] The film was shot for Warner Brothers in the summer and autumn of 1954 on various locations in California and made its premiere in the USA in April of the following year.

The casting of the theretofore unknown James Dean as the troubled

---

1. A good summary of both films is found in R.E. Morsberger, '*East of Eden* on Film', *SQ* 25 (1992), pp. 28-42.

2. A good example is J.R. Millichap, *Steinbeck on Film* (New York: Frederic Ungar, 1983), p. 140. D. Rathgab ('Kazan as *Auteur*: The Undiscovered *East of Eden*', *LFQ* 16 [1988], pp. 31-38) ascribes the artistic achievement to Kazan's creativity. Kazan discusses how much of the film was autobiographical in nature in *Kazan on Kazan* (ed. M. Ciment; London: Sacker & Warburg, 1973), p. 122.

Cal Trask was also a fortuitous move by Kazan.[1] It was Dean's film debut, but he was enthusiastically embraced by the movie-going public and quickly became a matinee idol. He went on to make only two other films (*Rebel without a Cause* and *Giant*) before dying in a car crash in September of 1955. There is little doubt that Dean's untimely death, at the age of twenty-four, helped to make him the legend that he is today, and his status as the archetypal guilt-ridden youth eager to please was based largely on his role in *East of Eden*.[2] Partly on the strength of his performance *East of Eden* has become a cult classic, portraying the agonies of the younger generation which is misunderstood and rejected by its parents. It is an age-old theme which carries a perennial appeal and there seems little sign of Dean's popularity as a symbol of the teenage rebel waning.

Osborn's screenplay focused the story around the figure of Cal, carefully plotting out the struggles he has with his father and with his brother Aron. A strong note of rejection and alienation is brought to his character and this forms the emotional core of Kazan's film. Indeed, Kazan did everything he could to fuel a conflict between Raymond Massey and James Dean (the actors portraying Adam and Cal Trask) in order to have the tension between them carry over into the film.[3]

As far as the clash between father and son, and indeed between the two brothers, is concerned the film retains a fairly close connection with both Steinbeck's novel and the Genesis story which provides its inspiration. The most obvious illustration of the Cain and Abel motif concerns the gifts that the two sons bring to their father Adam. The dramatic focus of this struggle is Cal's attempt to win his father's love by giving him a birthday present of money lost in his failed business venture. Callously Adam Trask rejects the money, feeling it is war-

---

1. Kazan describes this in his autobiography *A Life* (London: Pan Books, 1989), pp. 574-79.

2. Dean's performance in the film is often absorbed within the mythology which has surfaced around him. It is easy to forget that he was actually nominated for a Best Actor Oscar for his role in the film, eventually losing to Ernest Borgnine's performance in the title role of the film *Marty*.

3. Some of the details of the conflict between the two actors is discussed within Raymond Massey's *A Hundred Different Lives* (London: Robson Books, 1979), pp. 375-80. Also worth consulting on the matter is G. McCann, *Rebel Males: Cliff, Brando and Dean* (London: Hamish Hamilton, 1991), pp. 125-65.

profiteering, and berates Cal to provide him with a birthday present more in keeping with that of his brother Aron (who gave as his birthday gift news of his engagement to Abra, albeit without her knowledge or prior consent). Thus, the struggle of Cal to win his father's love and approval is woven together with the clash between the brothers over the kind-hearted but hapless Abra. In a powerfully emotional scene, arguably one of the best in the film, Cal confronts his father and begs him to accept the gift and love him. When this is refused Cal lashes out in anger against Aron and takes him to the brothel in Monterey run by their long-lost mother, effecting a meeting between them. The Cain-like 'murder' of Aron by Cal is here dramatically portrayed. Just to make it clear that there is a deliberate equation between Cal and Cain, the sheriff of Salinas, Sam Cooper, quotes the critical verse from Genesis at Cal (this takes place following the departure of Aron to the military and the collapse of Adam from his stroke). The sheriff rounds off the quotation with a harsh word of advice to Cal:

> 'Cain rose up against his brother Abel and slew him. And Cain went away and dwelt in the land of Nod, on the east of Eden.' Now why don't you go away someplace?[1]

This speech, the most deliberate reference to the underlying Cain-Abel story within the film, is not found in Steinbeck's original novel. In many other important respects the connection with both Steinbeck's novel and the underlying myth of Cain and Abel is not carried through, and subtle but significant shifts in focus are made. The most obvious of these adaptations is the complete absence of any reference to the 'Timshel!' within the film. Indeed, the character of Lee, so crucial for the 'Timshel!' theme within the novel, is completely written out of Osborn's screenplay. The closest that we come to it are indirect declarations of freedom of choice. For instance, note this exchange between Adam and Cal early in the film, following the son's fit of anger in throwing blocks of ice down the chute and Adam's rebuke of Cal by forcing him to read from Psalm 32 at the dinner table. Cal insists on reading the verse numbers, to the intense annoyance of his father.

---

1.   Other less direct allusions to Genesis have been detected within the film. For example, Rathgab ('Kazan as *Auteur*', pp. 33) discusses Kazan's prominent use of trees in the film and suggests that this is the director's deliberate use of the 'Tree of the Knowledge of Good and Evil' motif in Gen. 3.

Adam:	You have no repentance! You're bad! Through and through, bad!
Cal:	You're right, I am bad. I knew that for a long time.
Adam:	(*apologetically*) I didn't mean that Cal. I spoke in anger.
Cal:	Well, it's true. Aron's the good one. I guess there's just a certain amount of good and bad you get from your parents, and I just got the bad.
Adam:	That's not true! Cal, listen to me! You can make of yourself anything you want, it's up to you. A man has a choice, that's where he's different from an animal.

The theme of freedom of choice is picked up once more at the conclusion of the film where Cal is at the bedside of his dying father. Cal bends over the bedside, bringing his face close to that of Adam. He is reflecting about the earlier conversation between himself and his father, offering on the basis of it an explanation of his actions over the years:

> I tried to believe it was born in me and that I couldn't help it, but that's not so. A man has a choice. You used to say that was where he differed from an animal. You see, I remember! A man has a choice and it's the choice that makes him a man. You see, I do remember!

The absence of any direct reference to 'Timshel' is a significant divergence from Steinbeck's original, despite the fact that the theme is covered by these brief references to freedom of choice. Also altered in Osborn's screenplay is the presentation of the moral character of Cathy/Kate; her role as a prostitute and sexual blackmailer is severely downplayed in the rewriting of the story. Her suicide following her encounter with Aron is completely ignored, as is her murderous past prior to life in the Monterey whorehouse. She is drawn into the centre of the struggle between Cal and Adam by her lending of $5000 to Cal for his financial gamble (in the novel it is Lee who lends the money).

Even the scar motif is carried through in the film, although it is ascribed to Adam and not to Charles. At one point Cal does ask his father where he got the scar on his shoulder, but beyond this passing reference to the scar, this wonderfully evocative image of Steinbeck's is omitted.

b. *Harvey Hart's TV Mini-series (1981)*
Director Harvey Hart's adaptation of Steinbeck's *East of Eden* is much more comprehensive than Kazan's film, attempting to present the earlier portions of the novel which were neglected within Osborn's screenplay. The screenplay for this eight-hour long version was written by Richard

Shapiro and was first broadcast in the USA in three parts by the American Broadcasting Corporation (ABC) network on 8, 9 and 11 February 1981. In the United Kingdom the series is available on two videocassettes from Braveworld Ltd (1990). Unfortunately the mini-series was cut down to four hours for the commercially available videocassettes, which means that many of the most important scenes for the Cain-Abel subplot are lost. Inevitably the story line suffers as a result with allusions to some of the edited portions being made by the characters and discontinuities abounding. For example, the videocassette version completely cuts the beating of Adam by Charles over their respective gifts to their father Cyrus. Yet the incident is later alluded to in several scenes which are retained in the edited version. It is hinted at in a scene where Charles and Adam are reunited following the latter's return from the army; Charles clenches his fists as if to strike again at Adam, who steels himself for the charge (eventually they clasp each other in an embrace). Even more to the point, Cathy Ames alludes to the boyhood fight in a conversation with Charles, claiming that Adam is the source of her information about the incident. Many other key elements of Steinbeck's novel are not contained within this edited version of Hart's mini-series. Notable among them is the complete loss of any of the background of Cathy Ames. The first time we encounter her is when she applies to Mr. Edwards for a job within his brothel; we learn nothing of her murderous past and consequently fail to recognize her as the dramatic counterpoint to Cal when it comes to working out the freedom inherent in the 'Timshel' theme.

However, the scar motif is carried through in the shortened film, albeit in very vague terms. We are never told how it is that Charles has come to bear the 'mark of Cain', although there is a short exchange between him and Cathy over their mutual forehead marks. Charles lightly touches the scar of the recovering Cathy as he says,

> I know your sort. Because we're the same me and you. Why we're even marked the same. The devil is in our veins, both of us, tempting us all the time to do what's mean and rotten.

Although the forehead scar of Cathy/Kate tends to fade in and out of scene depending on the make-up of actress Jane Seymour, it is at least an attempt to be faithful to what is a very important motif within Steinbeck's novel, one which, as I have noted, is neglected within Kazan's version.

The conflict between the brothers Cal and Aron Trask is very much muted within the mini-series, although Aron's ascetic attitude toward sexuality (a dominant matter in Steinbeck's original) is brought out as the main reason for Abra's disaffection with him and her eventual move to Cal as the love interest of her life. This is a significant departure from Kazan's film version which completely downplays the celibacy of Aron as a potential cause of friction between the two brothers.

However, there are scenes which attempt to highlight the struggle of brother against brother. Much more is made in this adaptation of Cal's Thanksgiving Day gift to his father, the $15,000 to recompense the loss for the refrigerated lettuce venture. The rejection of the gift is handled lovingly, but firmly, by father Adam, who (closely following Steinbeck's original) says to Cal,

> You could have made me so happy if you'd just have given me something like what your brother has. Pride in the thing's he's doing, gladness in his progress. Money, even clean money, could never stack up to that.

The influence of Kazan's earlier film version is particularly evident in the portrayal of Cal and Aron's visit to their mother's brothel in Monterey. The layout and dialogue within many of the scenes are taken from Kazan's 1955 version, virtually reproducing it frame for frame.

The 'Timshel!' theme itself does find expression within the miniseries, appearing in two key places within the edited version. The first scene involves Lee whispering the word 'Timshel!' over the coffin of the dead Samuel Hamilton. At the graveside Lee is questioned about the incident by Adam:

Adam: What was it you said to Samuel back there in the church?
Lee: 'Timshel!'
Adam: What?
Lee: 'Thou mayest!' You remember back that day when we were naming the twins we read the story of Cain and Abel and none of us really understood it?
Adam: What has that got to do with ?
Lee: In the King James version we read Jehovah says; 'And thou shalt rule over him'; it was a promise that Cain would conquer sin.
Adam: And you weren't satisfied with that translation.
Lee: I conferred with some Chinese scholars of my acquaintance in San Francisco. Together these four old men and I approached a learned rabbi. I used to go up there every couple of weeks on my days off and study Hebrew, comparing translations.

Adam: That's where you were, the days I needed you?

Lee: Until, after two years, we finally felt, all six of us, that we had a proper translation of the Hebrew word 'timshel'. Not 'Thou shalt' or 'Thou must'; but 'Thou mayest.' 'Thou mayest rule over sin!'

Adam: Two years! One word? Don't you think that's just a bit of ecclesiastical hair-splitting?

Lee: No! No, no, no! Don't you see? It may be the single most important word in the history of the world, because it gives man the right to choose between good and evil, between right and wrong.

Adam: 'Timshel', is it? 'Thou mayest!'

Lee: Gift of free will in a single word.

The second scene is the conclusion of the film as a whole, where Lee, Cal and Abra are gathered at the bedside of the dying Adam. In many ways this is the most dramatically satisfying part of the whole miniseries, largely through the acting of Soon-Tek Oh in the role of Lee.

Lee: [*kneeling by the bedside and whispering to Adam*] Here is your son Caleb. Your only son. Look at him, Adam. I don't know how long you are going to live. Maybe a long time, maybe an hour. But your son will live! He will marry and his children will be the only remnant left of you. He did a thing in anger, Adam, because he thought you had rejected him. And the result of the anger is that his brother is dead. Your son is marked with guilt, almost more than he can bear. Don't leave him with his guilt. Adam, can you hear me? Give him your blessing. Help him, Adam! Give him his chance. Give him your blessing.

[*With great effort Adam extends his hand toward Cal, who makes a move to the bedside as Lee begins to cry.*]

Lee: Thank you, Adam! Thank you, my friend!

[*Cal and Lee exchange positions at the bedside.*]

Lee: Can you move your lips, Adam? Make your lips form his name!

Adam: 'Timshel!'

It would be fair to say that Harvey Hart's adaptation is more faithful to Steinbeck's original, even though the acting within the mini-series is rather stilted at times and the overall dramatic effect is much less powerful than Kazan's version.

4. The Philosophical Core of East of Eden:
'Thou Mayest' (Genesis 4.7c)

As noted above, Steinbeck focuses much attention in *East of Eden* on the Hebrew word תִּמְשָׁל in the verse from Genesis. In 24:2 he takes great pains to point out how the verb is variously rendered in English translations (as 'Thou shalt' in the KJV, and 'Do thou rule over him' in the American Standard version) and weaves the discussion about this within the narrative framework of the novel. This chapter is really the heart of what Steinbeck is attempting within *East of Eden*, and it is no wonder that it has been described as 'the dramatic apex'[1] of the work. The philosophical and theological implications of the word 'Timshel!' have been among the most frequently discussed issues in critical assessments of Steinbeck's work.[2] Not surprisingly, Steinbeck's understanding of the nature of the human being is closely tied to the meaning of the Hebrew term.[3]

The preoccupation with the meaning of the Hebrew word is evidenced within *Journey of a Novel*, where, in a long passage, Steinbeck discusses with Pascal Covici what he feels to be the significance of the verb:

1.   Everest and Wedeles, 'The Neglected Rib', p. 18. Similarly, W. French (*20th Century American Literature* [London: Macmillan, 1980], p. 559) describes East of Eden as 'a laboured fictional pursuit of the Hebrew word "Timshel"'.

2.   See, for example: L.J. Marks, '*East of Eden*: "Thou Mayest"', *SQ* 4 (1971), pp. 3-18; J.L. Gribben, 'Steinbeck's *East of Eden* and Milton's *Paradise Lost*: A Discussion of *Timshel*', *SQ* 5 (1972), pp. 35-43; J.H. Timmermann, 'John Steinbeck's Use of the Bible: A Descriptive Bibliography of the Critical Tradition', *SQ* 21 (1988), pp. 24-39; H. Levant, *The Novels of John Steinbeck: A Critical Appraisal* (Columbia: University of Missouri Press, 1974), pp. 243-46. One scholar, P. Lisca (*John Steinbeck: Nature and Myth* [New York: Thomas Y. Crowell, 1978], p. 710), describes *East of Eden* as a literary failure, arguing that the translation of תִּמְשָׁל as 'Thou mayest' is incorrect and that it does 'grammatical violence' to the Hebrew text. J.C. Pratt (*John Steinbeck*, p. 44) remarks that from a theological point of view Steinbeck's interpretation 'is unassailable except on linguistic grounds'. Also worth consulting on this point is P. Lisca, *The Wide World of John Steinbeck* (New Brunswick, NJ: Rutgers University Press, 1958), pp. 261-75.

3.   As P. Lisca ('Steinbeck's Image of Man and his Decline as a Writer', *MFS* 11 [1965], pp. 3-10) notes. Steinbeck's concept of man as a non-teleological being is discussed in S. Jain, 'The Concept of Man in the Novels of John Steinbeck', *JSL* 3 (1975), pp. 98-102. Steinbeck's *Sea of Cortez* (1941) contains some of his most interesting discussion on the matter.

Your new translation of the story has one most important change. It is the third version. The King James says of sin crouching at the door, 'Thou shalt rule over it.' The American Standard says, 'Do thou rule over it.' Now this new translation says, 'Thou mayest rule over it.' This is the most vital difference. The first two are 1, a prophecy and 2, an order, but 3 is the offering of free will. Here is the individual responsibility and the invention of conscience. You can if you will but it is up to you. I would like to check that phrase over. Will you do it for me? The exact word—because if it is incontrovertibly, 'thou mayest' I must put this in my discussion, because it will turn out to be one of the most important mistranslations in the Old Testament.[1]

Covici had discovered a translation of the passage which rendered the crucial verb in Gen. 4.7 as 'thou mayest' and Steinbeck was interested in exploiting the translation for his artistic purposes within the novel.[2] He even had Covici approach Dr Louis Ginzberg of the Jewish Theological Seminary in New York to inquire about the accuracy of the proposed alternative translation. Apparently Dr Ginzberg was not very supportive of the direction that Steinbeck was heading with his interpretation of the verb and offered what Steinbeck dismissed as a theological rather than an etymological answer.[3] After the publication of *East of Eden* Steinbeck was criticized for adopting this new translation as a true rendering, not only by experts within the biblical field but by literary

1.   *Journey of a Novel*, p. 127.

2.   The translation in question was the Manchester edition of the Douay version of 1812 based upon the Latin Vulgate. The correspondence on this matter is discussed fully within T. Fench, *Steinbeck and Covici: The Story of a Friendship* (Middlebury, VT: Paul S. Eriksson, 1979), pp. 151-65. Also see J.J. Benson, *The True Adventures of John Steinbeck, Writer* (London: Heinemann Press, 1984), pp. 686-87.

3.   *Journey of a Novel*, p. 144. Ginzberg had suggested to Covici in his replying letter that 'timshel' should be translated as a pure future tense. The Hebrew verb which so fascinated Steinbeck is generally taken to be the *qal* imperfect, second person masculine singular form of the verb משל usually translated as 'to rule, have dominion or reign'. With a human being as its subject, the verb occurs in five other places within the book of Genesis: in 3.16 (where man is said to 'rule over' woman), in 24.2 (where Abraham's servant is said to 'rule over' his household), in 37.8 (where Joseph's brothers ask if he is going to 'rule over' them), and in 45.8, 26 (where Joseph is said to 'rule over' Egypt). Many scholars, following Ginzberg, take the imperfect verb to have imperatival force, yielding a sense of the future within the translation, 'thou shalt rule'.

scholars as well.[1] Nevertheless, the difficult reading of the verb תִּמְשָׁל in Gen. 4.7c did lend itself to Steinbeck's purposes and its importance is demonstrated by the place that the word has within the finished novel.

Another incidental indication of the importance of the Hebrew term within the production of the novel is the fact that Steinbeck, who prided himself on being something of a craftsman, made a box to hold the manuscript out of a piece of solid mahogany and carved the title of the book together with the Hebrew characters תִּמְשָׁל into the top. The manuscript of *East of Eden* was eventually presented to Pascal Covici within this wooden container together with a specially written note to his friend and publisher which was eventually published as the dedication of the novel.[2]

Steinbeck returns to the key Hebrew verb at several points within the novel, including 47:2 and, most significantly, in 55:3, the conclusion of the work as a whole. The final reference is the most interesting in that it summarizes the reconciliation, or at least the potential reconciliation, between father and son. Here we have Adam Trask's last word to his son Cal as he lies on his death bed, 'Timshel!'[3] Adam's challenge is for Cal to overcome the rejection and guilt he feels and accept a share of responsibility in the death of his brother Aron. Cal thereby recognizes the value of his own existence and learns to live with his conscience. In a striking way, Steinbeck is able to contrast Cal's free moral agency, as well as his acceptance of responsibility, with that of his mother Cathy/Kate Trask, who is so thoroughly under the dominion of evil that she never has a choice in what she does.[4] Indeed, as Steinbeck presents her,

---

1. Notably Fontenrose, *John Steinbeck*, pp. 118-27.
2. Steinbeck and Wallstein (eds.), *Steinbeck*, p. 433, gives the text of the letter. A photograph of the mahogany box was published with the first edition of *East of Eden*. The box is now in the possession of Pascal Covici, Jr.
3. M.W. Govini ('Symbols for the Wordlessness: The Original Manuscript of *East of Eden*', *SQ* 14 [1981], p. 16) notes that the *timshel* reference at the end of the novel was not part of the original manuscript, but was added by Steinbeck as the work was revised for publication.
4. At one point, Adam Trask is also described in deterministic terms by the character Lee: 'That's his nature. It was the only way he knew. He didn't have any choice.' On the basis of this (and other instances) J. Fontenrose (*John Steinbeck*, pp. 124-25) suggests that Steinbeck presents four inconsistent explanations of the relationship between good and evil in the novel: (1) Good is opposed to evil; (2) Good and evil are complementary; (3) Evil is the source of good and may even be necessary to good; (4) Good and evil are relative terms.

Cathy/Kate seems predestined to evil; doing something good and for the benefit of others is simply not possible in her case for she is, as Steinbeck describes her, a 'monster', a 'malformed soul'. Cal can also be contrasted with his uncle Charles, another Cain-like figure, who never managed to free himself from the terrible circle of rejection-guilt-alienation and ended up with his life collapsing in upon itself. The optimistic note of 'Timshel!' in the final lines of the novel also stands in stark contrast to the conclusion of Part 3 of the book where Tom Hamilton is unable to accept his guilt in playing a part in the death of his beloved sister Dessie. Far from discovering the responsibility and freedom implied in 'Thou mayest!', Tom is crushed under its weight and commits suicide.[1] In contrast, Cal is set free by his father with the utterance of the mysterious Hebrew word, fulfilling his destiny as a human being. In this sense Cal is engaged in a real moral struggle, wrestling with the good and evil aspects of his character he has within him, aspects which he (wrongly) assumes he has inherited from his mother. In the end Cal manages to overcome the pull to wickedness and breaks free from the feeling of determinism with which he has wrestled all his life; he learns that he is not a victim of heredity. As Steinbeck reveals through a conversation Cal has with his mother (39:2):

> Cal said, 'I was afraid I had you in me.'
> 'You have,' said Kate.
> 'No, I haven't, I'm my own. I don't have to be you.'
> 'How do you know that?' she demanded.
> 'I just know. It comes to me whole. If I'm mean, it's my own mean.'

Above, I suggested that the translation of Gen. 4.7c as an interrogative has much to commend it, creating, as it were, an important theological bridge between Steinbeck's understanding of human freedom and the biblical teaching. In terms of the narration of the biblical story, such a translation also allows the phrase in 4.7c to be linked naturally to the other major question uttered by Cain within the chapter, that addressed to God in v. 9: 'Am I my brother's keeper?' The story is then a fine balance of rhetorical questions, divine and human. God asks a question,

---

1.   Marks (*'East of Eden'*, pp. 3-18) discusses this at some length and argues from it that here, contrary to many critical assessments of the novel which assert that *East of Eden* is a confused to-ing and fro-ing between the two family stories, Steinbeck was deliberately juxtaposing the Hamilton and Trask sections of the novel.

the answer to which he (presumably) already knows; Cain replies first with a lie and then with his own question, the answer to which he, too, already knows. He thereby attempts to throw the burden of responsibility back upon God himself, who is, in the final analysis, the only keeper of humankind.[1] In short, the double interrogative not only highlights the nature of human responsibility within the narrative but sets it within proper boundaries.

Interestingly, in 51:1 Steinbeck has his own version of this rhetorical question which Cain puts to God; here Adam Trask interrogates his son Cal about the fate of his brother Aron (who has that very day enlisted in the army):

> Adam asked, 'Do you know where your brother is?'
> 'No, I don't,' said Cal.
> 'Weren't you with him at all?'
> 'No.'
> 'He hasn't been home for two nights. Where is he?'
> 'How do I know?' said Cal. 'Am I supposed to look after him?'

There is a version of this in Kazan's film *East of Eden* following Cal's journey to Monterey to introduce his brother Aron to their mother. Cal returns to the family house and we have an exchange between him and his father which is clearly based upon the biblical story:

> Adam: Where's Aron?
> Cal: I don't know. I am not my brother's keeper.
> Adam: Where did you go?
> Cal: For a ride.
> Adam: What did you quarrel about?
> Cal: You!

The reference to 'brother's keeper' is actually closer to the KJV text of Gen. 4.9 than is Steinbeck's original narrative. In Steinbeck's novel the reference was somewhat oblique; in Kazan's film it is direct and unambiguous. At the same time, Cal's reply in the film is an assertion, rather more forceful than the biblical reply which comes in the form of a rhetorical question. This is to make the struggle between father and son much stronger in dramatic impact.

The TV mini-series also has its own version of this 'brother's keeper' episode, where Adam confronts Cal concerning the whereabouts of his

---

1. As P.A. Reimann ('Am I my Brother's Keeper?', *Int* 24 [1970], pp. 482-91) argues.

brother Aron. Characteristically, this version closely follows Steinbeck's original:

Adam:	Do you know where your brother is?
Cal:	No, I don't.
Adam:	Weren't you with him at all?
Cal:	No!
Adam:	He hasn't been home all night. Where is he?
Cal:	How do I know? Am I supposed to look after him?

Finally, in Genesis this refocus on the figure of Abel within the narrative by means of the interrogatives is perhaps the clue to one of the most perplexing linguistic features of 4.7. The fact that the verse ends with a masculine form בּוֹ has given rise to all sorts of interpretations as to its referent. The problem is exacerbated when it is recalled that the most logical referent (the Hebrew word חַטָּאת, translated as 'sin' in the RSV) is grammatically feminine in gender. Given the grammatical incompatibility of the two words it is perhaps understandable that many interpreters have taken the masculine form בּוֹ to refer to Abel and translate accordingly, 'you shall rule over *him*'. In terms of the narrative this helps bind the story together and highlights the struggle between two brothers. Dramatically, it also makes for a much more powerful story, anticipating the blood-lust and murder which is to follow. Effectively Abel is given a greater role within the story than he might otherwise have had.

In terms of cinematic interpretations of the Cain and Abel story, an interesting expression of precisely this approach is found in John Huston's film *The Bible* (1966), produced by Dino De Laurentiis. This film attempts to present the major stories contained within Gen. 1.1–22.18 and includes the story of the struggle between Adam's two sons. Despite the histrionic gestures of Richard Harris (in the role of Cain) the sequence has several interesting features within it. Within the short Cain-Abel section of film (only 10 minutes in duration) a clever means of highlighting Abel's role within the drama of the narrative is used by Christopher Fry (who wrote the screenplay for the film). Fry dramatically heightens the clash between Cain and Abel by his presentation of the brothers' sacrifices to God, noting God's curious reaction to them. As Fry explains in a Foreword to the published screenplay:

> Do we try to explain why God favoured Abel's sacrifice and rejected Cain's? To do this we should have had to comment on the traditions of the early days of Israel, to make clear, for instance, the distinction in the social order between the shepherd and the farmer, and this would certainly have

spoiled the simplicity and directness of the story. It was better to limit ourselves to the story as it is told in the Bible, with one slight addition, an indication of the human difference between Cain and Abel: that Cain made his offering grudgingly, because it was expected of him and it was safer to stick to 'the rules', while Abel made his with his whole heart and out of his love of God. Thus there is a difference between the words they use at the sacrifice. Abel says: 'Lord, hear and receive my prayer and my offering.' While Cain says brusquely, 'God of the world, take my gift.'[1]

Abel is brought to the fore in one other significant way within this film. Fry has part of the crucial dialogue of Gen. 4.6-7 (which in the biblical narrative is voiced by God) spoken by Abel to his jealous brother Cain. After God has accepted Abel's sacrifice and rejected Cain's, the disaffected brother kicks over his sacrificial altar in a fit of anger. In an attempt to soothe his brother's wounded pride, Abel confronts Cain and says, 'Why art thou angry? if thou doest well, shall thou not be accepted?' Within the dramatic presentation of the story this veiled rebuke is the trigger for Cain's murder of Abel. Cain immediately picks up a jawbone and proceeds to strike his brother on the head from behind, violently beating him to death. One of the most striking images within the film sequence is how the 'mark of Cain' is presented. Following the pronouncement of judgment by God upon the murderer we are presented with a close-up shot of Cain's mark, the image of a tree emblazoned upon his forehead (brought about by a Frankenstein-like lightning bolt!) A connection with the knowledge brought by tasting the fruit of the 'Tree of the Knowledge of Good and Evil' seems implied. It is as if to say that the first act of disobedience is working itself out in the next generation, that Cain's wilful act of murder is but a reflection of that initial act of rebellion against God by Adam and Eve. Cain here is made to bear a physical mark, a sign, recalling the first act of disobedience within the garden of Eden; at the same time it is, paradoxically, a mark of God's protection of Cain.[2]

The way in which the 'mark of Cain' is handled within the film entitled *The Bible: Genesis* (1979) is also worth mentioning briefly. This is a four-part adaptation released by The Genesis Project which attempts to depict the stories contained in the first book of the Bible alongside a

---

1. C. Fry, *The Bible: The Screenplay* (New York: Bantam Books, 1966), pp. 7-8.
2. T.R. Wright (*Theology and Literature*, p. 68) describes the 'mark of Cain' as ambiguous, noting that it is a 'stigma of sinfulness but also a badge of belonging'.

narrator's reading of selections from the AV of the text.[1] The story of Cain and Abel takes some fifteen minutes to relate and culminates in Cain's killing of his brother Abel following their offering of representative gifts to God. Once the murder is done we are given a scene in which Cain runs across the desert, seeking to escape from his guilt, until he falls face down into a pool of water. Here the description of the 'mark' that is put upon him is read (Gen. 4.15), accompanied with a striking visual representation of a glowing, red dot which arises mysteriously from the waters and eventually settles on his forehead. This is yet another attempt at portraying visually what the 'mark of Cain' might mean, although it has to be said that the result is not quite as dramatic, or nearly as suggestive, as that contained within John Huston's film *The Bible*.

All in all, the 'mark of Cain' as something physically seen on Cain's body (namely his forehead!) is a striking idea; Steinbeck's use of it in the novel is a sign of his creative genius. And yet it is also a striking visual image. Indeed, one might well wonder if the representation of the 'mark of Cain' within Huston's film owes something to the influence of Steinbeck himself in this regard. A literary interpretation of the biblical story seems to have influenced the cinematic interpretation of that same story!

5. *Summary*

I began this study by noting the importance within world literature of the biblical story of Cain and Abel. In particular, we examined the crucial role that Gen. 4.1-16 has as a backdrop for John Steinbeck's *East of Eden*. Not only is the title of the work derived from the passage, but the story of Cain and Abel provides the basis for the exploration of the complex, interpersonal relationships of the characters contained within it. I identified several ways in which the Genesis narrative was creatively adapted by Steinbeck within his novel, especially within the story line of the Trask family. Notable among these are the struggle of brother against brother, the relationship between father(s) and son(s) in which the son attempts to gain the love of the father, and use of the 'mark of Cain' motif. We also examined the two major film adaptations

---

1. The series is available in Britain from Island World Communications Ltd (1992). A companion series of four tapes covering the Gospel of Luke is also available.

of the novel, exploring how faithfully they communicated Steinbeck's central themes of human freedom of choice and responsibility in relationships. These explorations drove me to consider afresh the meaning of the cryptic phrase in Gen. 4.7c, 'you must master it', a phrase upon which Steinbeck relies heavily as the philosophical basis of his novel. Many of the various translations of the phrase were discussed in passing, including the suggestion that the phrase is best translated as a question, 'are you able to master it?' This suggestion has much to commend it, and fits well with the direction in which Steinbeck's novel leads us. In the end, I suggest that a greater understanding of the story of Cain and Abel can be arrived at through the agency of Steinbeck's novel and its cinematic adaptations. Steinbeck's *East of Eden* can certainly be used as a means whereby a modern readership is encouraged to engage the biblical story of Cain and Abel with fresh understanding and new purpose.

Chapter 4

FRANKENSTEIN: 'MALE AND FEMALE SHE CREATED THEM?'

Who would have thought that a young, eighteen-year-old woman could
have produced as her first novel a work so profound that it would earn
her a place in literary history? Yet, that is precisely the case with Mary
Shelley's enduring classic *Frankenstein, or, The Modern Prometheus*,
the first edition of which was published anonymously as a three-volume
work in March of 1818. Even today, over 175 years after its
appearance, the popular imagination still remains captivated by Mary
Shelley's haunting tale, if the continual production of books, plays and
films based on the story is anything to go by. *Frankenstein* was the
subject of a theatrical interest shortly after the novel appeared in
bookshops with the first production, entitled *Presumption: or, The Fate
of Frankenstein*, taking place in London at The English Opera House in
the Strand in 1823.[1] In a very real sense, with the publication of her
novel, Mary Shelley (1797–1851) laid the foundation for what has since
become a modern myth, a myth which Hollywood has over the years
been quick to capitalize upon. Today her rather macabre story has been
the inspiration for more film adaptations than perhaps any other single
piece of literature.[2] The idea of a 'Frankenstein monster' is now so
deeply embedded within our culture, and the expressions of it so
manifest, that it is virtually taken for granted. As a reflection of our
times, cinema, not literature, is *the* major vehicle for popular expression

1.   S.E. Forry, *Hideous Progenies: Dramatizations of Frankenstein from the
Nineteenth Century to the Present* (Philadelphia: University of Pennsylvania Press,
1990), discusses this in depth. Also see A. Lavalley, 'The Stage and Film Children of
Frankenstein: A Survey', in G. Levine and U.C. Knoepflmacher (eds.), *The
Endurance of Frankenstein* (Berkeley: University of California Press, 1979), pp. 243-
89.
2.   D.F. Glut, *The Frankenstein Catalog* (London: McFarland & Co., 1984),
pp. 156-234, lists nearly two hundred films which build upon the story.

of the story. We no longer even give a thought to the 'Frankenstein monster' as being initially a work of literature; the mental picture of Boris Karloff as the Monster in James Whale's 1931 film *Frankenstein* now dominates the popular conception. Indeed, so pervasive is the association of the name of Frankenstein with the Monster that we often forget that the creature is never actually given a name within Shelley's book.[1] Today, the Karloff-inspired image of the Frankenstein Monster is used to sell everything from children's cereal to beer to public electricity.[2]

At the same time Mary Shelley's idea has given rise to its application in a wide variety of disparate fields. The 'Frankenstein monster' has been an important literary image since the middle of the nineteenth century[3] and it has found a fruitful application in the arena of political debate over the years, inspired, no doubt, by Mary Shelley's own conscious attempts to address political matters by means of her story.[4]

The last twenty years or so have witnessed a flood of critical studies about Mary Shelley's *Frankenstein*. Her creativity in producing the work has finally begun to be recognized and the ability of the work to engender a wide amount of critical and theoretical discussion is nothing short of remarkable. How might we categorize the book? A description of the novel as a 'horror story' seems to be accepted by many students of literary genre, and it does account for many of the work's most distinctive features including the examination of psychological terror. Others have attempted to set the work within the Romantic literary tradition,[5] or view the work as an example of late-Gothic romance.

---

1.   He is called 'daemon', 'devil', 'thing', 'wretch', 'fiend' and 'monster' within the book.

2.   F. Botting, *Making Monstrous: Frankenstein, Criticism, Theory* (Manchester: Manchester University Press, 1991), pp. 188-204, gives some details.

3.   On this matter, see C. Baldick, *In Frankenstein's Shadow: Myth, Monstrosity, and Nineteenth-century Writing* (Oxford: Clarendon Press, 1987).

4.   L. Sterrenburg, 'Mary Shelley's Monster: Politics and Psyche in *Frankenstein*', in Levine and Knoepflmacher (eds.), *The Endurance of Frankenstein*, pp. 143-72, discusses this. Also worth consulting is J. Blumberg, *Mary Shelley's Early Novels: 'This Child of Imagination and Misery'* (London: Macmillan, 1993), pp. 30-56.

5.   How closely Mary Shelley can be identified with the Romantics is a matter of considerable debate; it is probable that the tendency to view her as falling within the Romantic tradition is derived from her association with Percy Shelley. However, M. Poovey ('My Hideous Progeny: Mary Shelley and the Feminization of

Northrop Frye called attention to the way in which psychological and philosophical questions are handled within the book and described it as 'a precursor...of the existential thriller',[1] while Anne K. Mellor identifies the quest for identity of being as central to the work and follows a much more promising approach by attempting to ground the interpretation of the book within the life experiences of its author as she sought to deal with her own tragic family circumstances.[2] This contextual approach to Mary Shelley's work has been adopted by so many others in the last few decades that it could now be described as axiomatic to any interpretation of *Frankenstein*. Yet, as rich as the book is with insight into human fears and emotional anxieties, it is hardly surprising that psychoanalytic readings of the book abound, particularly since, as Freud suggests, horror-story monsters are expressions of the id.[3] Some have even pointed to *Frankenstein* as the first faltering steps to the genre of literature we now describe as science-fiction. So Brian W. Aldiss, himself a well-respected science-fiction writer, has described Mary Shelley's

Romanticism', *PMLA* 95 [1980], pp. 332-47) argues that Mary was caught between two prevailing models of social expectation, one of which emphasized the need for her to be an artist who challenged the conventions of the day, and the other of which stressed the need for her to be a conventional wife who put husband and family before her career. Poovey suggests that within *Frankenstein* Shelley challenges the Romantic myth that human maturation occurs through self-consciousness, a notion that she found overly optimistic. Instead, Shelley asserts the need for social relationships to serve as guides in life, because an unchecked ambition, the drive to self-indulgence, leads ultimately to destruction (as Victor Frankenstein discovers within the novel). L. Langebauer, 'Swayed by Contraries: Mary Shelley and the Everyday', in A.A. Fisch, A.K. Mellor and E.H. Schor (eds.), *The other Mary Shelley: Beyond Frankenstein* (Oxford: Oxford University Press, 1993), pp. 185-203, contains some relevant discussion on this issue.

1.   *A Study of English Romanticism* (New York: Random House, 1968), p. 44.

2.   *Mary Shelley: Her Life, her Fiction, her Monsters* (New York: Routledge, 1988).

3.   P. Sherwin, '*Frankenstein*: Creation as Chaos', *PMLA* 96 (1981), pp. 883-903, follows this suggestion through, offering what is in effect a Freudian analysis of the novel and noting how *Frankenstein* can be read as a re-enactment of the oedipal drama so central to Freud's thought. Also worth consulting are: G.D. Hirsch, 'The Monster was a Lady: On the Psychology of Mary Shelley's *Frankenstein*', *HSL* 7 (1978), pp. 116-53; M. Jacobus, 'Is there a Woman in this Text?', *NLH* 14 (1982-83), pp. 117-41.

Frankenstein as 'The Origin of the Species'.[1] In the end, however, it must be recognized that Shelley's novel simply defies easy categorization; it cuts across the boundaries of many literary genres, refusing to be contained within one. Perhaps that is why it remains one of the world's literary classics, and why it continues to capture the imagination of film-makers the world over.

My primary concern within this chapter will be a consideration of how Mary Shelley's novel, as well as some select cinematic interpretations of it, make use of the biblical ideas of the creation of man and woman. It is important to appreciate this background, for occasionally both *Frankenstein* and the film interpretations of it allude to and even cite the relevant biblical passages concerned. In keeping with the aims of this book we will examine the creation motif in the *Frankenstein* materials for what they might teach us about the nature of the two stories of human creation in Genesis 1–2, stories which are generally acknowledged to offer two different perspectives on the issue.

I shall pursue this study in four parts: (1) The Writing of *Frankenstein*; (2) The Creation of Adam and Eve in Genesis; (3) The Creation of the Monster and his Mate in Mary Shelley's *Frankenstein*; (4) The Creation of the Monster and his Mate in Film Versions of *Frankenstein*.

1. *The Writing of* Frankenstein

Mary Shelley was the daughter of two of England's most illustrious figures of the late eighteenth century, both of whom produced literary works of considerable merit. Her father William Godwin had distinguished himself as a progressive political thinker, primarily through the publication of his work *An Enquiry concerning Political Justice* (1793). Her mother Mary Wollstonecraft was best known as the authoress of *A*

---

1.   *Trillion Year Spree: The History of Science Fiction* (London: Gollancz, 1986), p. 25. Aldiss contends that science-fiction is a development of the Gothic literary form and that a decisive step is taken by Mary Shelley with the publication of the novel. Also on this point, see: S.S. Prawer, *Caligari's Children: The Film as Tale of Terror* (Oxford: Oxford University Press, 1980), pp. 8-47; D.F. Glut, *The Frankenstein Catalog* (London: McFarland & Co., 1984), pp. 1-27; S. Boyd, Y*ork Notes on Frankenstein* (Harlow, Essex: Longman, 1984), pp. 51-52. An interesting theoretical discussion of the relationship between horror and science fiction as film genres is B. Kawin, 'The Mummy's Pool', in G. Mast and M. Cohen (eds.), *Film Theory and Criticism: Introductory Reading* (Oxford: Oxford University Press, 3rd edn, 1985), pp. 466-81.

Vindication of the Rights of Women (1791), a foundational work in its field. Mary Wollstonecraft Shelley (as she was to become) was thus the product of a most unusual union of two creative minds, each of which helped contribute to her own subsequent development as an author. Her parents had something of a reputation as social rebels, marrying only five months before the birth of their daughter, which took place on 30 August 1797. Sadly, Mary Wollstonecraft Godwin died shortly after giving birth to her daughter, a victim of puerperal fever.[1] This situation was one which caused her father to resent her terribly and which marked her psychologically for the rest of her life; young Mary never got over the fact that her own existence directly caused the death of her mother and there is much to be said for the suggestion that her writing of *Frankenstein* is linked to this fact. In turn she was something of a *cause célèbre* when, at the age of sixteen, she ran away to Switzerland with the young poet Percy Bysshe Shelley, who was married and had two children by his wife at the time. The scandal was made complete when Mary herself gave birth to an illegitimate daughter on 22 February 1815, a child who, tragically, died less than two weeks later. This was to set the pattern for much of Mary Shelley's life; she gave birth to four of Percy's children and once suffered a near-fatal miscarriage; only one of the children survived beyond childhood. In the summer of 1822, after a brief eight years of being with Shelley, Mary was also to suffer his loss when the young poet died in a boating accident on the Bay of Lerici. This backdrop of death and loss, which seemed to characterize her life, is generally thought to have helped contribute to the production of her most famous literary effort, the novel *Frankenstein*.

The circumstances surrounding the writing of *Frankenstein* make an interesting tale in their own right. How the seventeen-year-old Mary Godwin came in June of 1816 to spend a rainy holiday with Percy Bysshe Shelley, her step-sister Claire Clairmont, Dr John Polidori and Lord Byron in Byron's retreat on Lake Léman near Geneva, and begin to write what was to become one of the most famous horror stories of all time, is itself the subject of several recent films. Ken Russell's *Gothic* (1986) and Ivan Passer's *Haunted Summer* (1988)[2] are both given over

---

1.   Details of Mary's birth and the death of her mother are given in C. Tomalin, *The Life and Death of Mary Wollstonecraft* (London: Penguin Books, 1985), pp. 275-83.

2.   Based upon the Anne Edwards novel of the same name (London: Hodder & Stoughton, 1973).

to exploring this theme, as is the more cryptic film by Gonzalo Suarez entitled *Rowing with the Wind*, which portrays the Monster as a dream-like projection of Mary whose intermittent presence always portends disaster for her. We should perhaps not forget that James Whale's classic *The Bride of Frankenstein* (1935) opens with a five-minute prologue which depicts Mary Shelley together with Percy Bysshe Shelley and Lord Byron at Byron's residence in Villa Diodati.[1]

In recent years a number of important biographical studies on the life of Mary Shelley have been produced, most of them giving special attention to the writing of her most famous book, *Frankenstein*.[2] The authoress herself gives details of how the story came to be written within the Introduction to the 1831 edition of the work. She claimed that the inspiration for the novel came to her in the form of a 'waking dream', and that it was prompted by Lord Byron's suggestion that each member of the party write a ghost story for the entertainment of the others.[3] The extent to which her (later) husband Percy Bysshe Shelley contributed to the production of *Frankenstein* has long been a bone of contention among scholars, although most agree that the character of

1.   Brian Aldiss's *Frankenstein Unbound* (London: Panther Books, 1982) might also qualify as dealing with the subject, weaving together as it does a science-fiction story with an interest in the historical circumstances surrounding the writing of *Frankenstein*. This book was made into a film directed by Roger Corman in 1990. A good discussion of the book, detailing its connection with Shelley's *Frankenstein*, is found in P.G. Macleod, '*Frankenstein*: Unbound and Otherwise', *Extrapolation* 21 (1980), pp. 158-66.

2.   For example, see: J. Dunn, *Moon in Eclipse: A Life of Mary Shelley* (London: Weidenfeld & Nicolson, 1978), pp. 124-43; M. Spark, *Mary Shelley* (London: Constable, 1988), pp. 50-54 and 153-78; E.W. Sunstein, *Mary Shelley: Romance and Reality* (Baltimore: The Johns Hopkins University Press, 1989), pp. 121-32. The impetus that both Percy Shelley and Lord Byron gave to Mary in the production of the story is discussed in most of these biographies, although the article by E.J. Lovell, Jr ('Byron and Mary Shelley', *K-SJ* 2 [1953], pp. 35-49) is of special note.

3.   See M. Shelley, *Frankenstein, or, The Modern Prometheus: The 1818 Text* (ed. J. Reiger; Chicago: University of Chicago Press, 1982), pp. 222-29 and 260-87 for further details. The 1831 edition was the third edition of the book (the second appeared in 1823 and was the first to bear the name of the authoress). The textual changes between the editions of 1818 and 1831 have led to considerable scholarly discussion about the shift in perspective that they imply to have taken place within Mary Shelley herself, a movement characterized by a more fatalistic bent of mind.

Frankenstein is modelled, to some degree, on her flamboyant and energetic partner in life.[1]

With regard to the form of the novel itself, it is worth noting that *Frankenstein* is a highly structured tale of 24 chapters, prefaced by four letters which serve as a prologue. The story is related through a series of three concentric narrators (Captain Walton, Victor Frankenstein and the Monster), providing the novel with a simple but powerful chiastic structure which contains a veritable maze of narrative arrangements.[2]

2. *The Creation of Adam and Eve in Genesis*

The differences in theological tone and expression between the accounts of the story of the creation of humankind in Genesis 1–2 have long been recognized by Old Testament scholars. These differences are sometimes explained as due to the use of two separate sources by the final editor(s) of Genesis, with 1.1–2.4a being attributed to the Priestly (P) source and 2.4b-25 being attributed to the Yahwist (J) source. It is generally agreed that the Priestly source is much later than the Yahwist source.[3] In other words, Genesis 1–2 as it now stands contains an older version of the creation of humankind within the larger creation stories contained in Genesis 1–6; in effect Genesis 1–2 contains a double narrative of humankind's origin on earth, two competing accounts detailing how the human race came into being. The theological tensions between the two sources of the book, and in particular how they present the creation of both Adam and Eve, have proven to be matters of continuing scholarly debate. The fluctuation between singular and plural forms in the stories

1.   C. Small, *Ariel Like a Harpy: Shelley, Mary and Frankenstein* (London: Gollancz, 1972), pp. 100-121 pursues this matter.

2.   Walton narrates the introductory letters and the second half of chapter 24; Frankenstein narrates chapters 1–10 and the first half of chapter 24; and the Monster narrates chapters 11–16. All the narration is done in the first-person, something which Mary Poovey ('My Hideous Progeny', p. 339) suggests serves as one of the means whereby the authoress challenges the Romantic suppositions of some of her literary contemporaries, including her husband Percy. A good introduction to the complex narrative technique employed by Shelley throughout the novel is found in K. Newey, *Mary Shelley's Frankenstein* (Horizon Studies in Literature; Sydney: University of Sydney Press, 1993), pp. 1-9.

3.   The Priestly source (P) can be dated to about the 6th–5th century BCE and the Yahwist source (J) to about the 10th–9th century BCE.

of the creation of the first human beings is of special interest, both with respect to the divine plurals used ('Let *us* make man in *our* image') and with respect to the anthropological plurals used ('He blessed *them* and called *them* Man'). The key point for our purposes is the fact that in Gen. 1.26-27 the creation of male and female takes place at the same time, while in 2.21-22 the creation of the female is recorded as being distinct from the creation of the male (and *after* the creation of the beasts of the earth). In this second couplet the creation of woman is temporally distanced from the creation of man—she is a separate creation in her own right, albeit extracted from the man. Note the two relevant passages which set the boundaries of what we might describe as the divide over '*simultaneous* creation' versus '*separate* creation':

> Then God said, 'Let us make man in our image, after our likeness; and let them have dominion over the fish of the sea, and over the birds of the air, and over the cattle, and over all the earth, and over every creeping thing that creeps upon the earth.' So God created man in his own image, in the image of God he created him; male and female he created them. (Gen. 1.26-27)

> So the LORD God caused a deep sleep to fall upon the man, and while he slept took one of his ribs and closed up its place with flesh; and the rib which the LORD God had taken from the man he made into a woman and brought her to the man. (Gen. 2.21-22)

We should perhaps add another passage to the equation, namely 5.1-2, again from the Priestly source, possibly even the passage that originally followed on from 1.1–2.4a.[1] This is a summary statement, maintaining the fluctuation between singular and plural forms which we noted in connection with 1.26-27:

> When God created man, he made him in the likeness of God.
> Male and female he created them, and he blessed them and named them
> Man when they were created. (Gen. 5.1-2)

The main point to note here is how intimately connected are the creation of male and female within the Priestly materials. The creation of humankind in the image of God is accomplished only when both male *and female* are created; it is as if the one cannot exist without the other and both are viewed as a unity, both become expressive of what it

---

1. As suggested by both von Rad (*Genesis*, p. 68) and Westermann (*Genesis 1–11*, p. 347) among others.

means to be 'in the image of God'.[1] We could even go so far as to suggest that the Priestly writer holds a more developed viewpoint than does the Yahwist on the matter, or that he is offering an alternative vision of the creation of human beings. By *more developed* I mean one that is more acceptable to our modern minds which have the benefit of feminist perspectives to draw upon.[2] In the main, I think it fair to say that most modern people would say that a creation which emphasizes the *simultaneous* creation of male and female lends itself to a vision of equality which the *separate* creation (of Eve *from a rib of Adam*) need not. There is something inherently unequal about a vision of the creation of the female as biologically dependent upon, or extracted from, the male. As Robert Alter puts the point, describing the Yahwist's account, '(J) imagines woman as a kind of divine afterthought, made to fill a need of man, and made, besides, out of one of man's spare parts'.[3] It is perhaps worth noting in this connection the recent cinematic interpretation of Genesis issued under the auspices of *The Genesis Project* (1979), a rather conservative attempt to put the book on film complete with narration from the King James translation of the text.[4] Here the two sources of the creation stories are visually hinted at by the fact that the

1.   As P. Trible (*God and the Rhetoric of Sexuality* [Philadelphia: Fortress Press, 1978], pp. 16-21) persuasively argues, pointing out how the Hebrew poetic style of Gen. 1.27 points to a structural equation of 'male and female' with 'the image of God' and sets up a semantic correspondence between them. Her discussion of the need to interpret Gen. 1.27 as a metaphor opens up exciting new avenues of understanding the verse. P.A. Bird ('"Male and Female he Created them": Genesis 1:27b in the Context of the Priestly Account of Creation', *HTR* 74 [1981], pp. 129-159) criticizes Trible's interpretation for isolating v. 27 from its immediate context. She insists that Gen. 1.26-28 must be interpreted as a unit and attempts to reconstruct the theology of the writer of P, which she suggests undercuts the labelling of him as an equal-rights theologian. C. Meyers (*Discovering Eve: Ancient Israelite Women in Context* [Oxford: Oxford University Press, 1988], pp. 78-86) also offers some useful discussion.

2.   See, P. Joyce, 'Feminist Exegesis of the Old Testament: Some Critical Reflections', in J.M. Soskice (ed.), *After Eve: Women, Theology and the Christian Tradition* (London: Marshall Pickering, 1990), pp. 1-10, for a helpful introduction to this.

3.   *The Art of Biblical Narrative*, p. 141. An interesting discussion of this passage from J is found in Coote and Ord, *The Bible's First History*, pp. 55-58.

4.   This is now available in Britain in a boxed set of four videos from Island World Video (1992).

actor and actress portraying the male and female characters of
Gen. 1.26-27 are different from the actor and actress portraying the
characters of Adam and Eve of Genesis 2–3. It must be admitted that
although the presentation of Gen. 1.26-27 is clearly male-centred (it is a
man's image which dominates the visual images with a female figure
only coming in at the end of the film sequence), it does offer a cinematic
interpretation that attempts to acknowledge the differences between the
two sources contained in Genesis 1–3.

Do we detect a minute, but all-important difference of intent between
the Yahwist and the Priestly writer on this score? Most would agree
with this as a suggestion, but how much further does that take us? Does
recognition of this difference help us to grapple with the Old Testament
passages any better? Or, even more importantly, is there any way in
which we can approach the Genesis stories, fully acknowledging the
differences between the J and P accounts, and yet not feel compelled to
jettison the ability of the biblical text to speak to our situation today?

In recent years a number of Old Testament scholars with a more
literary orientation have challenged the need for such source-critical
analyses to dominate our interpretations. Why, they ask, can we not
leave the text intact, accept that there are these inconsistencies in form,
admit that there are thematic contradictions, acknowledge that there are
wide differences in language, and yet venture an interpretation which
accommodates them? Instead of concentrating our attention on the
differences and tensions between the two accounts of the creation of
Adam and Eve, can we not approach the text with a view to discovering
how the (final) author intends us to see the unity of the story as it now
stands? What difference might it make if we view Genesis 1–2 as a
whole? Might we gain a different perspective, one which emphasizes the
dynamic way in which meaning and language relate with one another?
Alter thinks that this is the way forward (and his view is representative
of a number of other Old Testament scholars on this particular point).[1]

1.   Also see M. Bal, *Lethal Love: Feminist Literary Readings of Biblical Love
Stories* (Bloomington: Indiana University Press, 1987), pp. 104-30. Similarly, R.
Salmon and G. Elata-Alster ('Retracing a Writerly Text: In the Footsteps of a
Midrashic Sequence on the Creation of the Male and the Female', in A. Loades and
M. McLain [eds.], *Hermeneutics, the Bible and Literary Criticism* [London:
Macmillan, 1992], pp. 177-97) have recently put forward the case that this is precisely
the sort of interpretation that occurs within certain Jewish midrashic texts with regard

However, he does not think that the recognition of a difference in emphasis should be simply dismissed as contradictory accounts between the two sources. Rather, the two creation accounts need to be viewed as *complementary*, each serving to demonstrate its author's particular theological emphases and each providing its own sense of the movement of the creation. As Robert Alter continues, focusing on the 'notorious contradiction' about the creation of woman in the accounts:

> It may make no logical sense to have Eve created after Adam and inferior to him when we have already been told that she was created at the same time and in the same manner as he, but it makes perfect sense as an account of the contradictory facts of woman's role in the post-edenic scheme of things.[1]

There is much to be said for the suggestion that within Mary Shelley's *Frankenstein* there is precisely the same sort of attention to the nature of the creative act that I suggest is maintained on the part of the Priestly writer and the Yahwist. All three writers seek to assert, each in his and her own way, the complementarity of male and female as part of created humankind. At the same time, the quest for wholeness in the form of companionship with another is very much in evidence; how that unity is expressed is, of course, different in each case. Some, such as William Veeder in his influential book *Mary Shelley and Frankenstein*, have attempted to explain the relationship between the biblical materials and Shelley's novel through the use of the idea of androgyny (the idea that human creation was originally that of an androgynous being, both male and female).[2] However, this does not seem to do justice to the biblical

to these accounts of the creation of humankind in Genesis. They have in mind such texts as *Genesis Rabbah* and *Midrash Tehillim*, both of which contribute to what is described as an 'intertextual web' illustrating how complex the interplay is between the various passages detailing the creation of man and woman. In a sense the Midrash here keeps the reader continually engaging the text, never allowing the meaning either to be reduced to a particular interpretation, nor allowing the reader to fail to search for one. A full study of how Gen. 1–2 has contributed to Jewish and Christian thought concerning creation in the image of God is found in M.C. Horowitz, 'The Image of God in Man—Is Woman Included?', *HTR* 72 (1979), pp. 169-206.

1.   *The Art of Biblical Narrative*, pp. 145-46. He usefully goes on to compare the decision to place two divergent accounts of the creation of humankind to the technique of post-Cubist painting in which more than one perspective of a subject can be presented at the same time.

2.   W. Veeder (*Mary Shelley and Frankenstein: The Fate of Androgyny* [Chicago: University of Chicago Press, 1986], p. 23) associates Gen. 1.27 with both

materials which many Old Testament scholars would argue are reacting against precisely just such a pagan mythology. As Phyllis Trible puts it, commenting on the language of Gen. 1.26-27,

> (The) shifts from singular to plural disallow an androgynous interpretation of *hā-'ādām*. From the beginning humankind exists as two creatures, not as one creature with double sex.[1]

The androgynous ideal does seem to have been influential at points in the history of Christian thought, but almost invariably this is as a result of contact with the influence of Gnostic thought in the second and third centuries which is heavily Platonic in nature.[2] However, the relationship between Shelley's *Frankenstein* and the creation accounts of Genesis is much more subtle than this; the androgynous ideal is not a sufficient basis for comparison. On one level, we could say that a driving feature of the plot of *Frankenstein* might be simply summarized as the desire of the Monster for his mate; in this sense the male–female dynamic is present. The creature is in search of the wholeness of simultaneous creation which he has been denied by Victor—this dream of human sexual complementarity is not dissimilar to that expressed by the Priestly writer. On the other hand, the actual *experience* of the Monster, the aching loneliness and sharp sense of alienation he feels, is reminiscent of a motif which appears prominently in the Yahwist account of Eve's creation—the fact that she was made as a companion to Adam and brings an end to his loneliness and isolation (Gen. 2.18). In short, there is much to suggest that the Genesis stories of the creation of humankind and Mary Shelley's *Frankenstein* have a great deal in common. We may

Plato's *Symposium* and with the *Upanishads* on this point saying, 'Myths have consistently seen God as the supreme male-female, whose first creations were comparably androgynous'. This is the only reference to the biblical materials from Genesis found within the book—no mention is made anywhere of the *separate* creation of Eve described in Gen. 2.

1.   Trible, *Rhetoric*, p. 18.

2.   See W.A. Meeks, 'The Image of the Androgyne: Some Use of a Symbol in Earliest Christianity', *HistRel* 13 (1974), pp. 165-208, for a well-documented discussion. Meeks addresses the whole question in light of Pauline passages, such as Gal. 3.28, which he feels contain language suggestive of a theology of baptismal reunification which is remarkably similar to how other ancient documents discuss the androgyne myths.

well discover that the kind of approach suggested by Robert Alter in approaching the Genesis stories is vindicated by a careful study of how Mary Shelley deals creatively with similar themes in her own novel. Let us explore this theme more closely within *Frankenstein*. We shall want to pay particular attention to the allusions to Adam and Eve which appear in the story, as well as noting how their complementarity as created beings is handled. Of special concern is the importance of the demand by the Monster that Frankenstein make a mate for him—an obvious allusion to the story of the creation of Eve.

3. *The Creation of The Monster and His Mate in Mary Shelley's* Frankenstein

The place that the motif of creation has within Mary Shelley's *Frankenstein* has long been noted and commented upon. Indeed, the creation of the unnamed Monster can be described as the focus of the novel as a whole, the motif which runs through the whole of the story and stitches the narrative together.[1] It is hardly surprising, therefore, that the influence which the story of the creation of Adam and Eve (recorded in Gen. 1–2) had upon that motif within the book is widely recognized. It is, after all, difficult to get around the fact that Victor Frankenstein functions as a God-like figure as he fashions the unnamed creature and brings him to life. Nor should we forget that the title of 'creator' is applied to Frankenstein, and the corresponding title of 'creature' or 'creation' to the Monster, regularly throughout the book.

Yet, there remains considerable room for a more detailed look at this 'creation' motif within *Frankenstein*, particularly as it leads us not only

---

1.   Aldiss, *Trillion Year Spree*, p. 43, describes *Frankenstein* as a 'diseased creation myth'. G. Levine ('The Ambiguous Heritage of Frankenstein', in Levine and Knoepflmacher [eds.], *Frankenstein*, pp. 3-30) argues that the novel represents a secularization of the creation myth. P.A. Cantor (*Creature and Creator: Myth-making and English Romanticism* [Cambridge: Cambridge University Press, 1984]) discusses the larger issue of how the Romantic tradition offered a new conception of human nature based upon a reworking of the biblical creation myths, which effectively parallels the work of the Gnostics in the 2nd–3rd century CE and brings Rosseau's views about human nature (as contained in his *Second Discourse*) into the heart of the discussion. Cantor includes an important discussion of Mary Shelley's *Frankenstein* as part of his argument (pp. 103-32).

to discover something about the literary genius of its composer, but also something about the life of Mary Shelley herself. Indeed, *Frankenstein* has even been described as 'a parable of motherhood',[1] the suggestion being that the authoress is dealing with her own personal life circumstances through the myth of procreation detailed within the story. It is perhaps no accident that recognition of the maternal imagery contained within the book is now a well-established facet of critical studies of the work, no doubt reflective of a healthy consciousness-raising which has come about in light of the modern feminist movement.[2] Two particular points are worth noting in this connection.

The first concerns the image of birth/creation which lies at the heart of the novel. This birth/creation motif has given rise to a seemingly endless stream of critical evaluation of *Frankenstein*, much of it focusing on the complexity of sexual innuendoes contained within the book. As is often pointed out, Frankenstein, in creating the Monster in the manner that he does, is usurping the natural place of the female within the birth process, eliminating the female's main biological function through bypassing the womb. In this sense Victor's creation is unnatural; it is fatherhood without motherhood, a breaking of the natural order of things.[3] This 'birthing' image can be creatively applied to *Frankenstein* at several levels. Indeed, there is much to be said for characterizing the process of

1. M.A. Rubenstein, '"My Accursed Origin": The Search for Mother in *Frankenstein*', *StudRom* 15 (1976), p. 165. Three biographical facts are of special relevance to an interpretative approach such as that of Rubenstein: the first is that Mary's own mother, Mary Wollstonecraft, died giving birth to her; the second is that Mary Shelley had herself given birth to an unnamed daughter in February of 1815 who died when only a few days old; the third is that she also had a son, named William, born in January of 1816 only six months before she began work on the novel.

2. The book by E. Moers, *Literary Women* (Garden City, NY: Doubleday, 1976), is a foundational work in this area, describing *Frankenstein* as a 'birth myth' (p. 92).

3. Mellor (*Mary Shelley*, pp. 115-26) discusses this. The way in which the women characters are portrayed in the novel has engendered a great deal of discussion, particularly as Elizabeth is made to serve Victor in a way that could hardly be described as enlightened; she is the preserver of the social order. S. Bowerbank ('The Social Order *vs* the Wretch: Mary Shelley's Contradictory-Mindedness in *Frankenstein*', *ELH* 46 [1979], pp. 418-31) attempts to set this issue within Shelley's own circumstances.

the writing of the novel itself in such child-bearing terms, with Shelley herself describing *Frankenstein* (in a celebrated phrase from the 1831 Introduction) as 'my hideous progeny'.[1] Perhaps the most telling piece of evidence which supports this contention is the fact that the relating of the story of *Frankenstein* takes exactly nine months, calculating from the dates provided in Captain Robert Walton's letters to his sister; an obvious allusion to the normal gestation period for a woman. It is as if the chronological parameters of the novel's plot are meant to symbolize the process of birth itself—a clever technique which invites speculation that the circumstances of Mary's own life are dictating the novel's narrative structure.[2] Similarly, it has been argued that the way in which the Monster is portrayed within the narrative itself, as one who was isolated and alone, rejected by those with whom he desired a fulfilling life, again arises out of Mary Shelley's own life circumstances. This is especially true, so Marcia Tillotson argues, when it is remembered how Mary Shelley was treated as a female by the males in her life at the time of *Frankenstein's* composition.[3] In the emotional descriptions placed upon the lips of the Monster (so the argument goes) we detect something of how the authoress herself was feeling.

The tension between male and female roles, especially between the main characters of the story, helps carry the book along. At the same time the centrality of the female perspective has been the focus of a number of interpretations of the book, despite the fact that females do not play prominent roles in the narrative. In the words of Sandra Gilbert and Susan Gubar,

> Though it has been disguised, buried, or miniaturized, femaleness—the gender definition of mothers and daughters, orphans and beggars, monsters and false creators—is at the heart of this apparently masculine book.[4]

1. D. Ketterer (*Frankenstein's Creation: The Book, the Monster, and Human Reality* [English Literary Studies, 16; Victoria, BC: University of Victoria, 1979]) puts forward a powerful case for the analogy between the literary creation of Shelley's book and Frankenstein's creation of the Monster which occupies central position within its story line.

2. Mellor (*Mary Shelley*, pp. 54-55) offers a discussion of this.

3. M. Tillotson, '"A Forced Solitude": Mary Shelley and the Creation of Frankenstein's Monster', in J.E. Fleenor (ed.), *Female Gothic* (London: Eden Press, 1983), pp. 167-75.

4. *The Madwoman in the Attic: The Woman Writer and the Nineteenth-Century Literary Imagination* (New Brunswick, CT: Yale University Press, 1979), p. 232. The authors suggest that Mary Shelley's *Frankenstein* is ultimately a rewriting of

The dichotomy of male and female roles within the work has been the subject of an immense amount of scholarly interest, especially in the last dozen years or so.[1]

Secondly, we need to consider the way in which the Genesis story is used, particularly in helping to cast the character of Victor Frankenstein. As Anthony D. York puts it,

> Mary Shelley's classic *Frankenstein* echoes the biblical story with its implication that Frankenstein usurps the knowledge of God in the manner of Adam.[2]

That Shelley intends a connection between Frankenstein and Adam seems a correct interpretation, but there is also a clear association between Adam and the creature himself within the novel. Another way of putting this is to say that Frankenstein and his creature are themselves one psychosomatic unit, that the Monster is the mirror-image of his creator, the two are psychic doubles. As Stephen Boyd puts it, 'Victor and his creation are really two parts of one psychological whole'.[3] *Frankenstein* stands as one of the most powerful expressions of the Doppelgänger motif so prominent in Gothic literature, a motif which is usually meant to serve as the harbinger of death. One could go so far as to say that every time we describe the Monster as 'Frankenstein' we acknowledge the degree to which the novel ultimately accomplishes this identity of characters. In fact, it is this intimate connection between Frankenstein and the Monster that allows the book to explore the co-existence of good and evil within them so creatively. Commenting on the fact that the Monster is identified with both Adam and Satan within the book, M.A. Goldberg perceptively remarks,

---

Paradise Lost which overturns all of the masculine dimensions of Milton's classic in favour of feminine ones, notably the fact that Victor Frankenstein (the archetypal Adam-like figure of Milton) is transformed into an Eve-figure by giving birth to the creature. For a helpful introduction to this theme within Milton's great work, see R.M. Schwartz, *Remembering and Repeating: Biblical Creation in Paradise Lost* (Cambridge: Cambridge University Press, 1988).

1. As can be seen in works such as Veeder, *Mary Shelley and Frankenstein*; M.K.P. Thornburg, *The Monster in the Mirror: Gender and the Sentimental/Gothic Myth in Frankenstein* (Ann Arbor, MI: UMI Research Press, 1987).

2. 'Adam', in D. Lyle (ed.), *A Dictionary of Biblical Tradition in English Literature* (Grand Rapids: Eerdmans, 1992), p. 20.

3. *York Notes on Frankenstein*, p. 53.

The confusion apparent in his own consciousness—whether he is an Adam, destined ultimately for eternal grace, or a Satan, doomed to eternal darkness—is a motif crucial to the entire novel.[1]

Moreover, another important way of interpreting the interplay of characterization within the novel is also possible, which again builds on the suggestion that Frankenstein is an Adam-like figure within the book. In the words of Diane Johnson, there is a 'sense in which the Monster is Mary Shelley's Eve',[2] a suggestion which offers an interesting alternative to the generally accepted way of understanding the novel, one which is especially suited to my theme within this study. Yet, another interesting possibility needs also to be considered, one which does not focus on the identification of Frankenstein with Adam, but on the identification of Frankenstein with God. As Michel Parry puts it,

> *Frankenstein* is really nothing less than a reworking of the biblical story of Adam with the monster taking the part of newly-created man and Frankenstein himself playing God...In this case the monstrous Adam never even gets to set foot in the Garden of Eden (human society) and his vacillating god denies him even the companionship of an Eve.[3]

To put the key point in the form of a series of rhetorical questions: When we come to interpreting the novel is Frankenstein meant to be associated with God (the creator), or with Adam, or with his creation (the Monster)? Is the Monster meant to be associated with Frankenstein, or with Adam, or with Eve? Or is the novel capable of supporting *all* of these suggestions? These are but brief demonstrations of the complex duplication (and reduplication!) of roles which persists throughout all the

---

1.   'Moral and Myth in Mrs. Shelley's *Frankenstein*', *K-SJ* 8 (1959), pp. 27-28. Cantor (*Creature and Creator*, pp. 104-107) suggests that this overlap of good and evil in the characterization of both Frankenstein and the Monster is the result of Shelley's reliance upon Milton's *Paradise Lost* and the fact that she chose to condense Milton's three central figures (God, Satan and Adam) into two (Frankenstein and the Monster). Effectively this causes the elimination of Milton's second figure (Satan) and the redistribution of his evil qualities to the other two, making both Frankenstein and Adam bear semi-Satanic qualities in Shelley's story.

2.   In her 'Introduction' to Mary Shelley, *Frankenstein* (New York: Bantam Books, 1981), p. xiii.

3.   'The *Frankenstein* Saga', in R. Davis (ed.), *The Encyclopedia of Horror* (Twickenham: Hamlyn, 1981), p. 45.

characters of the book, making it a veritable paradise for literary critics who can find any number of levels of meaning embedded within it and making it possible to justify virtually any theory imaginable. Yet whatever approach we choose to adopt as our main hermeneutical key to the work as a whole, the biblical background to the story seems certain. Let us turn now to consider some of the specific passages in *Frankenstein* which are reliant upon the biblical imagery of Genesis 1–2.

The first encounter that Frankenstein has with his creation following the Monster's running away from the laboratory in Ingolstadt is related in chapter 10 and takes place on the Mer de Glace.[1] It is there that we have the first direct reference to Adam as a type of the Monster. He says to his creator,

> Remember that I am thy creature; I ought to be thy Adam, but I am rather the fallen angel, whom thou drivest from joy for no misdeed. Everywhere I see bliss, from which I alone am irrevocably excluded. I was benevolent and good; misery made me a fiend. Make me happy, and I shall again be virtuous. (p. 146)[2]

However, it is in the central section of the book (chapters 11–16), which are given over to describing the plight of the creature and are written in the first person (as though Frankenstein was recording the speech of the creature), that we find the most revealing material for our interest. These six chapters are very important in establishing the Old Testament background of *Frankenstein,* for they build upon this imagery from Genesis 1–2, referring to or alluding to the biblical story of the Creation,

1. In her journal entry for 25 July 1816 Mary Shelley describes a journey she made with her husband Percy to this region of the Alps. See M. Shelley, *The Journals of Mary Shelley 1814–1844* (ed. P.R. Feldman and D. Scott-Kilvert; Oxford: Clarendon Press, 1987), I, pp. 118-19 for a discussion.

2. Quotations and page numbers are those of the Penguin edition, edited by M. Hindle (1985). This is based upon the third edition of 1831 which contains substantial differences from both the original edition of 1818 and a copy of the second edition of 1823 which was annotated by Mary Shelley. James Rieger (*Frankenstein: The 1818 Text*, pp. xxi-xxiii) argues that a close comparison of the three versions reveals the mental anguish of Mary following the death of her husband and children and helps account for some of the alterations made to the original. Similarly, M. Poovey ('My Hideous Progeny', pp. 340-46) argues that the changes made in the 1831 edition reflect an important shift in Mary's attitudes about the nature of social responsibility.

and specifically mentioning the figures of both Adam and Eve, at several points. For example, in chapter 15 the Monster describes how he comes to chance upon a copy of Milton's *Paradise Lost* which he reads assuming it to be a work of history rather than fiction.[1] The Monster says of the book,

> It moved every feeling of wonder and awe that the picture of an omnipotent God warring with his creatures was capable of exciting. I often referred the several situations, as their similarity struck me, to my own. Like Adam, I was apparently united by no link to any other being in existence; but his state was far different from mine in every other respect. He had come forth from the hands of God a perfect creature, happy and prosperous, guarded by the especial care of his Creator; he was allowed to converse with and acquire knowledge from beings of a superior nature, but I was wretched, helpless, and alone. Many times I considered Satan as the fitter emblem of my condition; for often, like him, when I viewed the bliss of my protectors, the bitter gall of envy rose within me. (p. 175)[2]

Or again, from the same chapter:

> God, in pity made man beautiful and alluring, after his own image; but my form is a filthy type of yours, more horrid even from the very resemblance. (p. 176)

There is even an allusion to God's creation of Eve to be the companion of Adam within the chapter. Here once again the serenity and

---

1.   Milton's *Paradise Lost* is quoted and alluded to at several points in Shelley's story. On this subject, see: L. Tannenbaum, 'From Filthy Type to Truth: Miltonic Myth in *Frankenstein*', *K-SJ* 26 (1977), pp. 101-13; Gilbert and Gubar, *The Madwoman in the Attic*, pp. 213-47; Baldick, *In Frankenstein's Shadow*, pp. 40-43; J.B. Lamb, 'Mary Shelley's *Frankenstein* and Milton's Monstrous Myth', *NCF* 47 (1992), pp. 303-19. Whether Mary Shelley was attempting to retell the story of Milton's *Paradise Lost* for her own time (effectively constructing a Romantic version of the Milton myth), or attempting to undermine it and challenge its influence, is a matter of some scholarly debate.

2.   The easy shift that the Monster here makes within the passage (from Adam to Satan) is not without significance; it speaks of the struggle that must be undertaken in establishing his (and by implication, Frankenstein's) identity. The Monster wishes to be identified with Adam, but becomes instead identified with Satan. As Baldick (*In Frankenstein's Shadow*, p. 44) says, 'When Victor and his monster refer themselves back to *Paradise Lost*—a guiding text with apparently fixed moral roles—they can no longer be sure whether they correspond to Adam, to God, or to Satan, or to some or all of these figures'. The multivalence of the main characters of the story is one of the features of the book which makes *Frankenstein* a playground of critical studies.

tranquillity of the Genesis story of the pre-fall Garden of Eden is contrasted with the feelings that the creature has about his state:

> I allowed my thoughts, unchecked by reason, to ramble in the fields of Paradise...But it was all a dream; no Eve soothed my sorrows nor shared my thoughts; I was alone. I remembered Adam's supplication to his Creator. But where was mine? He had abandoned me, and in the bitterness of my heart I cursed him. (p. 176)[1]

The section concludes with a paragraph in which the creature lays his demand for a mate before Frankenstein. He has just detailed to his creator how he had strangled William, the younger brother of Frankenstein, and managed to implicate the servant girl Justine in the youngster's murder. Here again we see how the story of the creation of Eve by God informs the ultimatum put to Frankenstein by the Monster:

> We may not part until you have promised to comply with my requisition. I am alone and miserable; man will not associate with me; but one as deformed and horrible as myself would not deny herself to me. My companion must be of the same species and have the same defects. This being you must create. (pp. 188-89)

Chapter 17 continues the dialogue between the creature and Frankenstein with the Monster imploring his creator to make a mate for him and thereby bring some measure of happiness and fulfilment into his life. He puts this to Frankenstein in the form of a demand based upon moral considerations. Note the following passages which the creature addresses to Frankenstein:

> You must create a female for me with whom I can live in the interchange of those sympathies necessary for my being. This alone you can do, and I demand it of you as a right which you must not refuse to concede. (p. 190)

> What I ask of you is reasonable and moderate; I demand a creature of another sex, but as hideous as myself; the gratification is small, but it is all I can receive, and it shall content me. It is true, we shall be monsters, cut off from all the world; but on that account we shall be more attached to one another. (p. 191)

---

1. The reference to 'Adam's supplication to his Creator' is probably derived from Milton's *Paradise Lost* VIII. 379-97 or X. 743-45. The latter passage was used by Shelley on the title page of the first edition of *Frankenstein*: 'Did I request thee, Maker from my clay / To mould me Man? Did I solicit thee / From darkness to promote me?—'.

If I have no ties and no affections, hatred and vice must be my portion; the
love of another will destroy the cause of my crimes, and I shall become a
thing of whose existence every one will be ignorant. My vices are the
children of a forced solitude that I abhor, and my virtues will necessarily
arise when I live in communion with an equal. I shall feel the affections of
a sensitive being and become linked to the chain of existence and events
from which I am now excluded. (pp. 192-93)

Frankenstein finally agrees to the Monster's request although he ago-
nizes long and hard about the implications of doing so. In the end he
recognizes that his own happiness with Elizabeth (his bride-to-be) is
intimately bound up with the happiness of his creature. Indeed, he feels
completely unable to marry Elizabeth and share a marriage bed with her
until the Monster he has created enjoys the same privileges of a
companion. Thus, the destinies of Frankenstein and his creation are
intertwined; both need the companionship of a mate in order to end the
isolation and loneliness which characterize their lives. As David Ketterer
puts it,

Ironically, having removed himself from the sphere of domestic affection,
he [Frankenstein] creates a being who craves companionship and a wife.
Frankenstein's own impending marriage counterpoints and mocks the
monster's desire for a mate.[1]

Thus Frankenstein says to himself,

I must perform my engagement and let the monster depart with his mate
before I allowed myself to enjoy the delight of a union from which I
expected peace. (p. 197)

Frankenstein departs from the security of his family and loved ones in
Switzerland and travels to the remote islands of Scotland where he
engages in the disagreeable task of making a mate for his creature. It has
been three years since he first fashioned the Monster, three years in
which the creature has wreaked havoc on him, both killing his brother
William and engineering the death of the innocent Justine. In the end,
Frankenstein decides that he cannot go through with the task, largely
because he realizes that he has no way to guarantee that the second
being he might create would agree with the promises made by the
Monster. She would have free agency and might prove to be even more

---

1.   *Frankenstein's Creation*, pp. 50-51.

destructive to the world than the first creature he made. He therefore dismembers the corpse of the female, with the Monster watching through the window. Frankenstein's destruction of the female companion of his creature so angers the Monster that he threatens revenge upon his creator. As the creature takes his leave of Frankenstein, he declares ominously, 'I go; but remember, I shall be with you on your wedding-night' (p. 213). The threat by the Monster causes Frankenstein to agonize over his situation, particularly after he receives a letter from his beloved Elizabeth in which she expresses her love for him in no uncertain terms. His feelings after having received her letter provide us with another instance in which the Genesis story of Adam and Eve is alluded to within the narrative. Note how the following passage incorporates the traditional interpretation of the fruit of the forbidden Tree of the Knowledge of Good and Evil (first mentioned in Gen. 2.17) as being an apple:

> Sweet and beloved Elizabeth! I read and reread her letter, and some softened feelings stole into my heart and dared to whisper paradisiacal dreams of love and joy; but the apple was already eaten, and the angel's arm bared to drive me from all hope. (p. 232)

Here Victor views Elizabeth as his Eve, and their life together as a return to the Edenic paradise; unfortunately such dreams have been shattered by the trespass into forbidden knowledge and the creation of the Monster. Ultimately the Monster claims his revenge, fulfilling his vow and strangling Elizabeth on her wedding night.[1] When Frankenstein finds her, he notices that the Monster is watching through the bedroom window, just as he had when he was forced to watch his own mate be

---

1. Mellor (*Mary Shelley*, p. 121) discusses the fact that Shelley's description of Elizabeth's body following her murder by the Monster appears to be based on the painting by Henry Fuseli (a former lover of her mother Mary Wollstonecraft) entitled, 'The Nightmare' (a plate of the painting is provided within this book). Within the painting the woman represents female erotic desire, and is depicted as thrown across the bed with her arms raised and her head hanging down off of the end (a pose which is used in many of the *Frankenstein* films in connection with Elizabeth's death). Mellor comments, 'Invoking this image, Mary Shelley alerts us to what Victor fears most: his bride's sexuality'. It is perhaps worth noting that a version of Fuseli's painting is used as an image associated with Mary Shelley's nightmares within both Ken Russell's film *Gothic* and Ivan Passer's film *Haunted Summer*.

destroyed. The wheel has turned full circle and the two figures, Frankenstein and the Monster, creator and created, are caught up in a macabre dance of death which impedes the full union of either with their intended companions.[1]

I noted above the threat that the Monster makes to Frankenstein about 'being with him on his wedding night'. Within the novel the line is simple, but profound, and is repeated several times. Above all else it highlights how the destiny of Frankenstein and his monster, the creator and the created, are intertwined. It also invites further consideration of how the Monster serves as an alter ego for Frankenstein within the narrative of the book. Let us briefly examine this suggestion one stage further, noting how Shelley takes the biblical imagery (as channelled through Milton) in a slightly different, but altogether harmonious, direction. In chapter 24 both Victor and the Monster compare themselves to Milton's Satan of *Paradise Lost*, echoing lines from that book. Thus, Victor declares himself 'no less than the archangel ruined', noting that 'like the archangel who aspired to omnipotence, I am chained in an eternal hell' (recalling Book I, lines 34-49). Similarly, the Monster summarizes his life by saying that 'evil thenceforth became my good' (recalling Book I, lines 159-68 and, more directly, Book IV, lines 108-10).

We turn now to consider how the creation motif is handled within some of the film versions of Mary Shelley's *Frankenstein*.

4. *The Creation of the Monster and his Mate in Film Versions of* Frankenstein

Virtually all of the *Frankenstein* films expound the cycle of creation and destruction which lies at the heart of the novel. However, *how* that cycle is presented differs considerably from film to film. We shall examine five different film versions of *Frankenstein*, although many others might have been selected and would provide some interesting insights as well. Any number of film versions of *Frankenstein* invite not only a comparison between the film and Shelley's original novel, but also

---

1.   S. Boyd (*York Notes on Frankenstein*, p. 25) notes, 'one does not have to be a trained psychoanalyst to see that in Victor's psyche sexuality and death seem to be horribly intertwined'. The same might be said of the Monster he has created.

provide some fascinating explorations of how the biblical materials are used to support the creation motif within the film. As a case in point, *Frankenstein: The True Story* (1973) is an attempt which pays lip service to Shelley's original novel, but owes as much to the fevered imaginations of its screenwriters as it does to anything else. This version was directed by Jack Smight with the screenplay being written by Christopher Isherwood and Don Bachardy; it was first shown in the USA on the National Broadcasting Corporation (NBC) television network in November of 1973. Isherwood and Bachardy worked hard at incorporating key characters and elements of both Shelley's life and novel, some of which, unfortunately, did not make it into the film version which was aired. For example, the film opens and closes with Victor Frankenstein's encounter with Captain Walton on board a ship trapped in the Arctic ice. The film is set in Victorian England and Scotland and follows the lead taken in *The Bride of Frankenstein* in opening with a prologue depicting the Shelleys and Lord Byron. Another interesting feature of the film (which echoes Shelley's novel) is the presentation of the Monster as a *tabula rasa* who, suggestively, is named Adam. The latest film adaptation of *Frankenstein*, which is currently in production, is that of director Kenneth Branagh. This film promises to be faithful to the story line of the original novel and should provide an interesting opportunity for comparison.

In any event the five adaptations of Mary Shelley's story I have selected are representative of the host of film versions which are readily available and will allow ample scope to explore this theme. The five are:

Frankenstein (1931)	Directed by James Whale (71 minutes B/W)
The Bride of Frankenstein (1935)	Directed by James Whale (80 minutes B/W)
Frankenstein Created Woman (1967)	Directed by Terence Fisher (87 minutes Colour)
The Bride (1985)	Directed by Franc Roddam (114 minutes Colour)
Frankenstein: The True Story (1992)	Directed by David Wickes (111 minutes Colour)

The release of James Whale's *Frankenstein* by Universal Pictures in 1931 marked the beginning of a new era for film-making. Not only has it proven to be one of the most influential films of the time, but it launched the career of one of Hollywood's most enduring legends, Boris

Karloff in the role of the Monster.[1] The film was shot on the Universal Pictures lot in Universal City, California, over a five-week schedule in August–October of 1931[2] and premiered at the RKO Mayfair Theatre in New York City on 4 December 1931. The studio had set the budget for the film at $262,000, which proved to be a wise investment since the film generated $53,000 in its first week alone and went on to be one of the biggest money-makers in Universal's history. James Whale's *Frankenstein* cast the British actor Colin Clive as Henry Frankenstein, Mae Clarke as Elizabeth, with John Boles as Victor Moritz and, of course, Boris Karloff as the Monster. The special effects of the film contributed in large measure to its success. Jack Pierce was responsible for the make-up which transformed Karloff into a believable Monster, and Kenneth Strickfaden created the laboratory equipment which gave the creation scenes an aura of believability.[3]

While acknowledgment of Mary Shelley's novel is made within the film credits, the story line departs from her original at several key points.[4] Even the first names of two of the principal characters are

1. Karloff was a bit-actor who was discovered by director James Whale while eating lunch in the studio commissary. Details of his casting as the Monster are contained in D. Gifford, *A Pictorial History of Horror Movies* (London: Hamlyn, 1973), pp. 86-89; Glut, *The Frankenstein Catalog*, pp. 96-104.

2. The set for the European village scenes had previously been used for the award-winning anti-war film *All Quiet on the Western Front* (1930), directed by Lewis Milestone.

3. The original equipment was used in Mel Brooke's comedy *Young Frankenstein* (1974), which lovingly re-creates the atmosphere of the original *Frankenstein* films and remains perhaps one of the best cinematic tributes available to the work of James Whale.

4. The screenplay for the film was written by Garrett Fort, Francis Faragoh and Robert Florey based upon the stage play adaptation of Shelley's novel by Peggy Webling (which had opened in London in February of 1930). Full details of the film, including the original shooting script, can be found in P.J. Riley (ed.), *Frankenstein* (Universal Filmscripts Series: Classic Horror Films, 1; Absecon, NJ: MagicImage Filmbooks, 1989). Also worth consulting are: J. Stoker, *The Illustrated Frankenstein* (Newton Abbot: Westbridge Books, 1980), pp. 27-32; Glut, *The Frankenstein Legend*, pp. xiv-xviii, 90-120; Glut, *The Frankenstein Catalog*, pp. 200-201; P. Haining (ed.), *The Frankenstein File* (London: New English Library, 1977); R. Behlmer, *Behind the Scenes* (London: Samuel French, 1982), pp. 1-21; D.J. Hogan, *Dark Romance: Sex and Death in the Horror Film* (Wellingborough:

transposed; Victor Frankenstein becomes *Henry* Frankenstein and Henry Clerval becomes *Victor* Moritz in the film. Another major divergence between the novel and the film occurs in the portrayal of the Monster. In the film the Monster is an inarticulate, lurching giant who is barely in control of his limbs, let alone the higher faculties of speech and reason. This is a far cry from the creature of Shelley's novel, who is articulate, well-read and able to conduct a discussion at a very intelligent level; indeed, at times he bests Victor Frankenstein in the cut and thrust of philosophical debate between them.[1] At one or two points the association of Frankenstein with the creator-God, or perhaps even a wilfully disobedient Adam figure, is made. The clearest example of this occurs in the Prologue to the film, made by the actor Edward Van Sloan (who plays Dr Waldman within the film). He summarizes much of what follows when he says of Frankenstein:

> We are about to unfold the story of Frankenstein, a man of science who sought to create life after his own image, without reckoning on God. It is one of the strangest tales ever told. It deals with the two great mysteries of creation—life and death.

Most important for our consideration in this study is the fact that while the creation motif is retained as far as the Monster is concerned, it is completely missing as far as the creation of a mate for the Monster by Frankenstein is concerned. Nowhere within the film is there ever any mention of the Monster's loneliness or of his desire to have a companion created for him. The focus of the film, as far as the creature is concerned, is almost entirely on the physical appearance of the Monster and the challenge to the pride of Frankenstein that he represents. The closest thing we get to the all-important wedding motif (wherein the Monster declares to Frankenstein that he will be with him on his

Equation Books, 1986), pp. 1-5; G. Wright, *Horrorshows: The A-to-Z of Horror in Film, TV, Radio and Theatre* (London: David & Charles, 1986), pp. 79-82; L. Halliwell, *The Dead that Walk* (London: Paladin Books, 1988), pp. 102-125; W.K. Everson, *Classics of the Horror Film* (New York: Citadel Press, 1990), pp. 36-61.

1. The fact that the Monster is articulate is important in establishing his humanity; to deny his speech is to render him a dumb beast. The matter of the Monster's speech is discussed in P. Brooks, '"Godlike Science/Unhallowed Arts": Language, Nature, and Monstrosity', in Levine and Knoepflmacher (eds.), *The Endurance of Frankenstein*, pp. 205-20.

wedding night as a revenge for the wilful destruction by Victor of his female companion) is an exchange between Frankenstein and Elizabeth about when their wedding will take place. Frankenstein promises that he will always be with her, but this is something we can hardly believe since we have been led to expect the Monster's intervention. The clearest instance of the importance of the wedding-night motif within the film occurs when Frankenstein declares to his friend Victor Moritz,

> There can be no wedding while this horrible creation of mine is still alive. I made him with these hands and with these hands I'll destroy him. I must find him!

In the end, this is proven right, for the Monster is destroyed so as to allow Frankenstein and his beloved Elizabeth to live happily ever after in marital bliss. This is a far cry from the ending of Mary Shelley's novel in which Elizabeth is killed by the Monster on her wedding night and everyone who comes in contact with the creature, including Frankenstein himself, dies. In conclusion, despite the fact that the 1931 film *Frankenstein* made movie history it is something of a disappointment as far as faithfulness to Shelley's original vision is concerned.

However, James Whale's sequel *The Bride of Frankenstein* (1935) is much more satisfying in this regard. In this film both Colin Clive and Boris Karloff reprised their roles from *Frankenstein*, although Karloff was here given top billing. The film also starred Valerie Hobson as Elizabeth, Ernest Thesinger as Dr Pretorius, and Elsa Lanchester as the Monster's mate. A budget of some $297,000 was authorized by Universal Pictures and shooting took place from January–March 1935. Many of the key elements contained within Shelley's story which had been dropped within the 1931 film find their counterpart within this sequel, including the all-important contact that the Monster has with the blind hermit in the woods and the Monster's doomed attempt to save a drowning girl. It seems that there was a much more deliberate effort on the part of William Hurlbut and John L. Balderston, who wrote the screenplay for the film, to return to Shelley's original novel.[1] A number

---

1. P.J. Riley (ed.), *The Bride of Frankenstein* (Universal Filmscripts Series: Classic Horror Films, 2; Absecon, NJ: MagicImage Filmbooks, 1989), gives full details of the film including the original shooting script. Also worth consulting on the film are: Glut, *The Frankenstein Legend*, pp. xiv-xviii, 121-32; Glut, *The Frankenstein*

of incidental details, clearly derived from the book, are included, such as the Monster's vegetarianism while in the wild, and his initial reaction to seeing his face in the pool of water.[1] Another attempt to give due recognition to the original author of *Frankenstein* is contained in the prologue of the film which depicts the Shelleys together with Lord Byron at his Villa Diodati—a scene obviously based on Mary Shelley's 1831 Introduction to *Frankenstein*. During a severe thunderstorm the three discuss the fact that Mary has written the horror story but left it unfinished. Whatever happened to the Monster? The posing of that question leads to the film sequel, and also affords the showing of some of the final scenes from the 1931 film where the Monster is (presumed) burned to death in a windmill fire.

Despite this very clever technique of linking together the two films, there are nevertheless some major continuity problems between *The Bride of Frankenstein* and the earlier film. For example, the 1931 film has as its conclusion a scene in which Frankenstein is recovering in his bed after the fire with faithful Elizabeth and his father at his bedside. The father even drinks a toast to 'a son of the house of Frankenstein'. It seems obvious that Henry Frankenstein is meant here, but it is not too difficult to see that it could also mean a son which the marriage of Henry and Elizabeth will produce, or perhaps, already *has* produced (it is not entirely clear if the bedside scene is Henry's recovery after the fire, or Elizabeth's after the birth of a child!). In *The Bride of Frankenstein*, however, this is all confused with the story line picking up immediately following the burning of the old mill.[2] The local villagers carry the body of Henry Frankenstein to the house where Elizabeth grieves over him (assuming him to be dead). We then find that this is still the day of their wedding as she (and *not* the Monster!) voices the famous line from the conclusion of the book: 'I was foretold of this. I was told, "Beware of my wedding night!"' In another scene, shortly

---

Catalog, pp. 201-202; Wright, *Horrorshows*, pp. 75-76.

1.   Probably a rewriting of a scene from Milton's *Paradise Lost* Book IV in which Eve first beholds her features in a pool of water in the Garden of Eden on the day of her creation. This may be another indication of Shelley's subtle presentation of the Monster as an Eve-like figure.

2.   The final bedside scene was cut from *Frankenstein* when the two films were re-released together in 1935, no doubt to avoid confusion on this point and allow a smooth transition to the story being told in the sequel.

after Elizabeth makes this prophetic declaration and after she discovers that Henry is still alive, she also remarks that once he has recovered from his illness they are to be married. In short, the wedding of Elizabeth and Frankenstein, such an important means within Shelley's novel of communicating the tension that awaits them in their relationship together, finds an echo within this film which is without parallel in Whale's earlier attempt.

At the same time there are some additional characters added to the story, notably Dr Pretorius, who first proposes to Henry Frankenstein that together they create the Monster's mate. Note this exchange between the two obsessive scientists, each of whom is said to defy deity in his own way:

Pretorius:	What a world-astounding collaboration we should be! You and I together!
Frankenstein:	No! No, no! No!
Pretorius:	Leave the charnel-house and follow the lead of nature—or of God if you like your Bible stories: 'Male *and* female created he them…Be fruitful and multiply.' Create a race, a man-made race upon the face of the earth. Why not?
Frankenstein:	I daren't! I daren't even think of such a thing!
Pretorius:	Our mad dream is only half realized. Alone you have created a man. Now together we will create his mate!
Frankenstein:	You mean…?
Pretorius:	Yes. A woman! That should be *really* interesting!

Pretorius eventually befriends the Monster, teaching him to speak in a very rudimentary fashion, and revealing to him his intention to create a mate for him. They first meet in an underground crypt where Pretorius is gathering body parts to fulfil his ambition of creating a female version of the Monster:

Monster:	You make man? Like me?
Pretorius:	No. Woman. Friend for you.
Monster:	Woman? Friend? Yes! I want friend! Like me!
Pretorius:	I think you can be very useful. And you will add a little force to the argument if necessary. Do you know who Henry Frankenstein is? And who you are?
Monster:	Yes. I know. Made me from dead. I love dead. Hate living.
Pretorius:	You are wise in your estimation. We must have a long talk. And then I have an important call to make.
Monster:	[*looking at a skull and some bones which Pretorius has exhumed from the grave*] Woman. Friend! Wife!

The scene immediately following this one shows the visit of Pretorius to the home of Frankenstein where he congratulates Henry and Elizabeth on their wedding. It is clear that this reference to the wedding is to set the stage for what follows, when the Monster steals Elizabeth from her room so as to blackmail Henry into collaborating with Pretorius on the creation of the mate. The juxtaposition of ideas also harks back to the fateful prophecy which Elizabeth herself voiced earlier in the film: 'Beware of my wedding night!'

When the female Monster is eventually created, and brought to life by means of the obligatory lightning bolt, Pretorius proudly announces to the world, 'The Bride of Frankenstein!' while wedding bells chime forth as background music. But whose 'Bride' is the newly created female Monster? Is it Henry Frankenstein's, or the Monster's? She could be either, for the phrase exclaimed by Pretorius is delightfully ambiguous— and perhaps deliberately so. Maybe this is as it should be, for in an early draft script of the film Frankenstein's bride-to-be, Elizabeth, was killed by the servant Karl to provide the heart necessary for the creation of the female Monster. This suggestion was not allowed by the powers that be at Universal Pictures who felt that such a scene was just not acceptable for the general audience, despite the fact that it may run truer to Mary Shelley's original conception. Instead, we are left with the creation of a female Monster whose existence does not threaten the life of either Frankenstein or Elizabeth, at least not directly.

The first word of the Monster upon seeing his newly created mate comes in the form of a question. He raises his hands to her in a gesture of appeal and asks, 'Friend?' She screams in horror at the sight of the Monster and runs away, causing him to declare, 'She hate me! Like the others!' This sends him on a raging rampage wherein he destroys the laboratory and all of its equipment, deliberately killing Dr Pretorius, as well as his female companion, in the process. Only Frankenstein and Elizabeth are allowed by the Monster to escape in a closing scene in which the Monster shows compassion for his creator, declaring them to be part of the living whereas he is only part of the dead. Or, as the Monster puts it in his final words, 'We belong dead!' Here we see another instance of a typically happy Hollywood ending, even if it does differ markedly from Shelley's original novel. There, we recall the so-called 'Bride of Frankenstein' is never brought to life, but is destroyed by a guilt-ridden Frankenstein.

Still, I suppose that we should not be too critical about how far the film departs from Shelley's book. At least the central idea of a mate for the Monster is interjected, as is the crucial verse from Gen. 1.27 which focuses our attention in this study. Many film lovers now regard *The Bride of Frankenstein* to be the quintessential horror film, the finest example of its kind. So influential have the two *Frankenstein* films by James Whale been that a degree of mythology has developed about them and the circumstances surrounding their production. Indeed, it is difficult to separate fact and fiction in this matter. We now have myth wrapped up in myth.

The third of our films to consider is Terence Fisher's *Frankenstein Created Woman* (1966). This is the fourth in a series of seven films based on the character of Frankenstein which were released by Hammer Film Productions, a British company specializing in horror films.[1] These films were released during the 1950s, 60s and 70s. In a very real way Hammer Films succeeded Universal Pictures, which had released seven *Frankenstein* films in the 1930s and 40s, as the main vehicle for cinematic expression of Shelley's story. The Hammer Films were made in vivid colour, in which red blood flowed freely, and distinguished themselves through their graphic portrayal of sex and violence. A new wave of film-making had been created and Mary Shelley's *Frankenstein*, together with Bram Stoker's *Dracula*, was at the heart of it.

A major shift in emphasis is present within the Hammer Films *Frankenstein* series; instead of concentrating on the Monster himself, the focus is on Baron Frankenstein and his descendants, and their attempts to follow in the tradition of creating life from dead parts. Such a shift was necessary for legal reasons, with the play by Peggy Webling, so influential on the story line contained in James Whale's films, still under protective copyright. In the end, the need to steer clear of breaking copyright law proved to be beneficial for Hammer Films because it meant that variations on the basic plot, together with new and different monsters, could be created. The creation of a female Monster by Baron Victor Frankenstein fitted into this new approach quite nicely. The screenplay for *Frankenstein Created Woman* was written by Anthony

---

1.   A. Eyles, R. Adkinson and N. Fry (eds.), *The House of Horror: The Story of Hammer Films* (London: Lorrimer Publishing, 1973), gives details. The seven Hammer films are discussed in Glut, *The Frankenstein Legend*, pp. 189-202; Glut, *The Frankenstein Catalog*, pp. 211-19.

Hinds (under the pseudonym John Elder). It starred Peter Cushing in the role of the Baron and the former *Playboy* model Susan Denberg as the female Creature (understandably, the term 'Monster' is no longer applied).

The plot of the film revolves around the transference of human souls into different bodies, a slight variation on the theme of the reanimation of dead tissue which is the focus in most *Frankenstein* films. Within *Frankenstein Created Woman* the mind of a deceased servant of Baron Frankenstein, the faithful and obedient Hans, is transferred into the body of a young servant girl with whom Hans was in love, the crippled and disfigured Christina. Hans had been wrongfully executed for the murder of Christina's father and the girl is driven to commit suicide by throwing herself off a bridge. Through an accomplice Baron Frankenstein retrieves her body, commandeering the remains of Hans, and effects a transfer of his soul into her body. The re-created Creature, perfectly restored and cured of her physical ailments, then sets out on a course of revenge against those who have killed her father and implicated her lover Hans. Once this vengeance is completed she once again commits suicide by throwing herself off a cliff into the sea below. The story remains a bit far-fetched, but it is an interesting variation on the *Frankenstein* story with Christina's plaintive pleas, 'Who am I?' echoing the queries of the Monster in Mary Shelley's novel. Most curiously, *Frankenstein Created Woman* maintains an androcentric focus within the animation of the Creature; that is to say that it is still the mind of a *man* which animates and controls the new female creature which Frankenstein makes. As the female creature explains to Baron Frankenstein in the final exchange of the film as the two stand at the edge of a cliff overlooking the sea just before she leaps to her death:

Frankenstein: Christina! Stop there! Now listen to what I have to say. It wasn't you who killed those young men. You didn't know what you were doing. Let me tell you who you really are!

Christina: I know whom I am!

Frankenstein: Please...!

Christina: And what I have to do!

The key point here is that the identity of Christina and Hans is fused within the body of the new creation. The thoughts of the two are shared; indeed, at times the female Creature speaks with the voice of the man Hans whose soul has been infused into her body. *Why* Baron Frankenstein decides that he will infuse the mind of Hans into the dead body of Christina, and not restore her own soul to the corpse is something which is never satisfactorily explained within the plot. But at least there is a recognition here that women too can be created by Frankenstein, and in that alone the film is an important variation on the theme.

Franc Roddam's 1985 production of *The Bride* comes to the story with the creation of the female companion for the Monster as its main focus. It begins where most Frankenstein films end—with the creation of the mate of the Monster. The screenplay for this atmospheric rendering of the *Frankenstein* story was written by Lloyd Fonvielle. It stars the pop-music star Sting as Baron Frankenstein (whose first name is here given as Charles) and Jennifer Beals as the Bride, with Clancy Brown as the Monster. This film begins with an elaborately constructed opening sequence (lasting some eight minutes) which depicts the animation of the female mate during a violent thunder storm. One of the tensions throughout this film is the clash between Baron Frankenstein and the Monster for possession of the female companion (there is no Elizabeth character to occupy Frankenstein's attentions and complicate matters here). Early on in the film, just after the beautiful female companion (and it is significant that she is not mutilated as was her male predecessor) is brought to life, the Monster attempts to claim her from Baron Frankenstein by claiming, 'Mine! She is for me!' The Bride, however, is frightened by the Monster, causing him to feel rejected and heightening his sense of isolation. A fire breaks out in the laboratory, destroying the tower of the house of Frankenstein. In the midst of the chaos surrounding the fire, the Monster escapes, although Baron Frankenstein assumes he has died in the fire. The Monster runs away, befriending a midget named Rinaldo with whom he attempts to begin a life working in a circus outside Budapest. With a clever, but highly symbolic, twist the screenplay has Rinaldo give the Monster the name Victor, probably a deliberate echo of Shelley's novel, and a brilliant way of uniting the identity of the Monster and the Baron.

There are several interesting pieces of dialogue which allude to the biblical creation motif, and the fact that women are equal to men within the created order of things. For example, early in the film there is a conversation between Baron Frankenstein and his friend Clerval. Clerval asks about the presence of the strange new female in the house, and Frankenstein is wary in his answers, afraid that he might give too much away concerning her creation:

Clerval:	You have a guest here, Charles?
Frankenstein:	Not exactly. An interesting medical case referred to my care. A young girl found in the forest near Bruckau. She had apparently been struck by lightning—robbed of all memory. She knows nothing of herself. Not even her own name.
Clerval:	Can you cure her? And if not, is she pretty?
Frankenstein:	She is quite remarkably beautiful. And as for the rest, I wonder if 'curing' is what she needs at all.
Clerval:	You mean…that she might be taught a thing or two?
Frankenstein:	She might be taught everything, Clerval. Think of it! She might be made into anything.
Clerval:	A most pliant mistress!
Frankenstein:	I might make the new woman, Clerval. Independent. Free. As bold and as proud as a man. A woman equal to ourselves!
Clerval:	*[laughing]* Charles! Please!

This is immediately followed by a scene in which Baron Frankenstein is seated in the drawing room, sipping a drink in front of the roaring fire. The Bride enters the room cautiously. She is nude, expressive of her Edenic innocence, and comes to sit on the floor next to the chair upon which Charles Frankenstein is resting. In halting, laboured speech she asks:

The Bride:	Who…are…you?
Frankenstein:	My name is Frankenstein.
The Bride:	Who…am…I?
Frankenstein:	We shall call you after the first woman. Eva.

The Baron falls in love with her, becoming insanely jealous of the attentions that any others direct to her. This puts him on a collision course with the Monster, Victor, who finds himself drawn by time and circumstance to her. The clash between the Baron and the Monster for ultimate possession of the Bride is inevitable; she is just too beautiful and intelligent for the Baron to surrender to a creature so crude as his Monster. This is coupled with her growing sense of independence. She finally goads Frankenstein into revealing how it was that he had a formative hand in her existence:

Eva:	You taught me many things. You fed me and you clothed me. But I can make my own way now. I can pay you back.
Frankenstein:	There are things that you just don't understand, Eva.
Eva:	What things?

Frankenstein:	I've told you enough already! You must trust me, and you must obey me!
Eva:	I will not obey you! I will not!
Frankenstein:	Don't provoke me, Eva.
Eva:	I will provoke you! You lied to me! There was no girl found near Bruckau. You lied!
Frankenstein:	Don't insult me! Because I won't have it!
Eva:	You won't have it! *You* won't have it? Who do you think you are?
Frankenstein:	You continue like this, Eva, and I shall tell you!
Eva:	Tell me then. Tell me! You taught me out of books but I have a life of my own. You didn't create me. You didn't create *me*!
Frankenstein:	As a matter of fact, I did. I sewed you together out of corpses. I brought you to life by means of an electrical charge. I created your body, just as I created your mind.

At this point Baron Frankenstein leads her into his secret laboratory, wherein both she and the Monster were made. He invites her to read his journals which detail the gruesome act of creation. Now burdened with knowledge of the means of her creation Eva asks Baron Frankenstein about the fate of her mate:

Eva:	Where is he?
Frankenstein:	Where is who?
Eva:	The creature I was created for?
Frankenstein:	Oh, he's dead. Perished in the fire, I'm sorry to say.
Eva:	Then I am alone! There's no one in the world like me.
Frankenstein:	Oh, I think you miss the point, Eva. It's true I made you to mate with that abortion. But I quickly saw the foolishness of that! I thought you were fit for finer things.
Eva:	What do you mean?
Frankenstein:	I taught you many things, Eva. I made you my equal in thought and reasoning. The last thing I meant to teach you was to love. But you nearly jumped the gun, except that I caught you! Don't forget I made you out of ashes. I can always reduce you to ashes again.
Eva:	You can do what you like. You can take apart the body you put together and you can take away the life you gave me. But you cannot have *me*! Not ever! Not even if you murder me and raise me up a thousand thousand times! You cannot have me!
Frankenstein:	I made you for a wedding. And the wedding-night has come!

The two struggle, and Frankenstein strikes her angrily. She manages to get away from him and he begins to pursue her through the mansion with the obvious desire for sexual gratification. His attempt to rape her is only thwarted by the intervention of Victor, who bursts through the locked door of her bedroom at the critical moment. The two principals, Frankenstein and Monster, creator and created, engage in a heated chase through the remains of the laboratory and tower before the Baron finally falls to his death from the top of the tower to the ground below. Victor returns to the bedroom of Eva, claiming her as *his* Bride, and we are treated to a montage of closing images designed to suggest that the two live happily ever after. The ending of this film is quite unique among the cinematic adaptations of the *Frankenstein* saga. It is the only film I know of which offers a reversal of the generally accepted way of concluding the story of the creation of the Bride. Here the Bride is not only brought to life, but she is united with the Monster, at the expense of the creator Frankenstein himself. This creative ending alone makes this film one of the most interesting to consider when examining our central theme.

In addition, there are some interesting ways in which the film attempts to establish a unity of identity between Eva and the Monster. For example, in one scene the Monster is talking with his friend Rinaldo who asks for details about his past and wants to know more about the woman he assumes has rejected his gruesome-looking friend. Victor answers that there was 'one like me', emphasizing the fact that the two are beings of a different order from the rest of humankind. At several points the editing of the scenes cuts from one of the two creatures to the other as they are involved in doing similar things (such as experiencing hunger at the same time and eating a chicken meal at the same time). This happens even though they are separated by distance, so strong is the bond between them. Similarly, there is a scene in which Eva is spinning herself around and around, an image of childhood play; this makes the Monster dizzy and almost causes him to stumble and fall just as Eva almost does. Or again, there is a scene where Rinaldo dies in the arms of Victor, causing him to break down in tears, we cut immediately to a scene depicting Eva as she lies crying in her bed—the two are united in heartbreak. Likewise, when Eva cries out in mental anguish after reading the journals of Baron Frankenstein in which he describes her creation, we find her cry countered with a shot of Victor sympathetically crying out in anguish as he stands chained in the town jail. Finally, when Baron Frankenstein attacks Eva, attempting to rape her, again we find intersplicing scenes of Victor who struggles desperately to make his way to her and save her.

The 1992 production *Frankenstein: The True Story*, written and directed by David Wickes, makes a deliberate effort to return to Shelley's original story. It stars Patrick Bergin as Victor Frankenstein and Randy Quaid as the Monster. The film begins and ends with Victor Frankenstein's encounter with Captain Walton on board his ship trapped in the Arctic ice, effectively framing the whole of the film within the same narrative structure which is found within the novel. The story of Frankenstein's creation of the monster, and all that ensues from it, is told in a number of flashbacks set within the conversation between Walton and Victor Frankenstein (the Arctic narrative setting is returned to one other time in the film and a number of narrative voice-overs by Frankenstein also help to carry the framework of the story along). Most of the novel's characters are kept, including Henry Clerval, Justine Moritz, William Frankenstein (the younger son of Victor), Elizabeth Lavenza and the blind hermit De Lacey.

At times Wickes adds novel twists to Shelley's original, some of which develop the story line and take it in new and creative directions. A romance between Clerval and Justine is interjected into the story, paralleling that between Elizabeth and Frankenstein. The creation of the Monster takes place in the city of Ingolstadt, as it does in the book, although, interestingly, the (uncompleted) creation of the female companion of the Monster is also set there and not in the remote Orkney Islands as it appears in Shelley's novel. The essential goodness of both Frankenstein and his Monster is asserted throughout much of the film; Frankenstein is presented as a humanitarian figure, whose main interest in creating the Monster is as a medical advancement in the face of the ravages of cholera which he sees taking life all around him. Likewise, the Monster is essentially good-hearted, whose only crime is that he is ugly and deformed and the recipient of hatred and fear on the part of others. It takes the hostile actions of others to drive him to the point where he becomes a figure of evil. This shift in focus subtly changes key features of Shelley's story which makes a great deal out of the moral ambiguity in the character and actions of both Frankenstein and the Monster. For example, here the death of William is presented as an accident, the result of a chance encounter of the Monster with the younger brother of his creator; in Shelley's story it is a deliberate act of revenge against Frankenstein on the part of the Monster.

The creation of the Monster is handled in a novel way, with the scientific apparatus used by Frankenstein being an electro-magnetic machine which duplicates human parts into a chemical solution held in a large vat. Frankenstein first demonstrates the machinery to his friend Henry Clerval, inserting his arm into the electro-magnetic field and reproducing it within the chemical vat. This is followed by a conversation between the two friends which sets the experimentation within a biblical context:

Frankenstein:	What would you say if I could create a whole body?
Clerval:	What do you mean?
Frankenstein:	What if I could make a living man, Clerval? Stronger than you or I, bigger, more intelligent, perfect in every way? A new kind of man, immune to all diseases, more powerful than any man on earth? Would that be a trick too? Or would it be the greatest gift this world has ever known?
Clerval:	Victor, what are you saying?
Frankenstein:	I've discovered the secret of life, Clerval. Here, in this very room. And I control it!
Clerval:	Blasphemy!
Frankenstein:	Oh, my poor dear poet. Do you still believe all that? Adam and Eve, the Garden of Eden, good and evil? Myths and legends, Clerval! The world moves forward, and science *is* the future! Don't you see?
Clerval:	No, I don't see! You are not God, Victor. You cannot create like God!
Frankenstein:	But you've just seen it! Look outside in the streets. The misery, the sickness…
Clerval:	But you are not God!

One of the most interesting features of this production is the way in which the psychic unity of Frankenstein and the Monster is presented. We get an early hint of this during a conversation between Victor Frankenstein and Captain Walton on board the latter's ship. Frankenstein is adamant that the crew of the ship is in danger of being attacked by the Monster and tries to warn Walton. The Monster has been seen by the crew of the ship, making a fire in the distance as he prepares to bed down for the night. We have the following suggestive exchange between the two:

Walton:	So why is he waiting?
Frankenstein:	For the dawn. We hate the darkness.
Walton:	*We*?
Frankenstein:	We are one, Captain. He and I. I made him, like I made the hand. From me. We are two parts of a single man.

This interconnection between Frankenstein and the Monster is brought out in several key scenes (a technique which is similar to the doubling between Eva and the Monster we noted in *The Bride*). For example, there is a scene (taken from Shelley's original story) in which the Monster rescues from drowning a young girl who has fallen into the lake. A pair of hunters stumble upon the Monster just as he is laying the young girl down on the bank and assume that he is attacking her. One of them shoots the Monster in the shoulder—an act which is immediately felt by Frankenstein as he is sitting with Elizabeth in his home in Geneva (the film quickly cuts from the Monster to Frankenstein to reinforce the connection between the two). For a while thereafter, until the Monster heals from his bullet wound, Frankenstein bears a wound upon his own body in exactly the same place as the Monster.

The first mention of the Monster's desire to have a mate occurs in a confrontation that he has with Frankenstein following the death of William:

Frankenstein: What do you want?
Monster: New woman. A woman like you have a woman.
                You…you will give me a woman!
Frankenstein: I can't.
Monster: You can! You can make me a woman, like you made me.
                Tall and strong, like me! To love me, as I am. As your
                woman loves you! And I will go away from this place, away
                from your horses, and your guns, away from all of you! You
                will see me no more. But first, you *will* give me a woman!
Frankenstein: And what if I refuse?
Monster: Then, you will see me on your wedding-night. On *your*
                wedding-night!

Frankenstein then explains the situation to his bride-to-be, eliciting the following exchange between them, which demonstrates again the psychic identity between Frankenstein and his creation. There is, of course, an interesting suggestion that the psychic identity can be extended to a bond between Elizabeth and the Monster's mate. Elizabeth is puzzled about the Monster's promise to go away and live apart from society once he has been provided with a mate:

Elizabeth: But why does he go away and not come back? It doesn't
                make sense!
Frankenstein: Because that's exactly what I would do.
Elizabeth: You?

Frankenstein:	Elizabeth, listen to me. If the only way I could be with you was to live at the ends of the earth, that is exactly what I would do. So he will do the same. Do you understand?
Elizabeth:	He's you! Isn't he?
Frankenstein:	Yes.
Elizabeth:	[*after a moment's reflection*] Who will you use?
Frankenstein:	I'll find someone.
Elizabeth:	Is it dangerous?
Frankenstein:	It's painful, but it won't kiii. [*Then after realizing that Elizabeth intends to offer herself.*] Oh, no! I won't do it, Elizabeth. I won't do it!
Elizabeth:	Who else would you get?
Frankenstein:	I don't know! I'll find someone.
Elizabeth:	Who? An artist's model? Some unsuspecting maid?
Frankenstein:	I don't know, but not you!
Elizabeth:	You're not thinking! Who will ever agree to it?
Frankenstein:	Elizabeth, you're my whole life!
Elizabeth:	So the creature you make from me will be his! The perfect match! Isn't that what he wants? The perfect match?

The attempt to create a mate for the Monster based on Elizabeth does not succeed, however; Frankenstein aborts it when it proves to be too painful for Elizabeth to take. He empties the chemical vat containing the nearly completed body of the female companion—an act which is seen by the Monster, who is outraged as a result. Here once again an important difference occurs from the original novel; in Shelley's story Frankenstein destroys the female companion as a deliberate act whereas in this production his failure to finish the work is due to his noble concern for his beloved Elizabeth. Indeed, the relationship between Victor and Elizabeth within this film does not contain nearly as much of the tortured agonizing that we see presented in the novel. There is no hint of the anxiety over the physical side of their relationship which is so evident in Shelley's novel and which forms a major vehicle for the tension central to the 'wedding-night' motif of the story. Still, the horror of the wedding night comes to pass, as the Monster kills not only Elizabeth, but Clerval and Victor Frankenstein's father after crashing into the grounds of the house following the wedding reception. This leads to Victor vowing for revenge, promising to the God who made him that he will destroy his own creation. A pursuit of one by the other ensues, culminating in their encounter on board Walton's ship. The following climactic exchange between the two again emphasizes the theme of identity which is so prominent within this adaptation:

Monster:	Now! Now you will pay! Here in this place.
Frankenstein:	What are you going to do? Kill me? Why do that? Why kill me here? You had your chance a hundred times before this. Why lead me here? Why?
Monster:	To make you feel pain. Like me. Fear and pain. Like me!
Frankenstein:	To make me feel your pain? You did all this to make me feel your pain? There was no need. I felt it from the start. Your pain is mine. Is my pain not yours? You haven't understood. Kill me and you will die. We are one. Don't you know it? Can you feel it? We are one!
Monster:	[*beginning to cry*] But...I cannot live in your world.
Frankenstein:	Nor I in yours.
Monster:	[*sobbing*] Please help me! Please, help me! Please! Help me!
Frankenstein:	I will. I will help us both. [*Making the sign of the cross*] I will help us both.

The fate of the two protagonists is brought to its inevitable conclusion when, at the end of this dialogue, Victor rushes forward, grabs the Monster and plunges with him over the side of Walton's ship into the icy waters of the Arctic sea below. The two sink to the bottom, drowning together, locked in a close embrace symbolic of their unity of identity. It makes for a dramatic ending, but unfortunately spoils the ambiguity of the ending given the novel by Shelley, where Victor dies but the Monster is simply 'lost in darkness and distance'.

The five films we have examined have provided us with ample opportunity to pursue this study. I have noted several different ways in which the 'birth/creation' motif is used within these films, occasionally even with direct reference to the stories of the creation of man and woman in Genesis 1–2. At the same time, the way in which the central characters of the novel are identified with Adam and Eve, and indeed, with each other, provides much food for thought. Thus, the cinematic interpretations of *Frankenstein* carry through, in their own way, many of the critical issues we find surfacing within interpretative discussions of the novel itself. More to the point, the way in which several of the films deal with the fact that the Monster demands a mate to complete his existence has proven to be of special interest when considering the biblical background to the story.

One final point worth considering briefly concerns the way in which the female characters of the story of *Frankenstein* are sometimes presented; the most significant feature involves the way in which an interesting association of film characters with Mary Shelley is presented. Here it is worth considering two particular *Frankenstein* films, one of which is a serious effort and the second of which is a humorous one. In particular, I mean the way in which the character of Mary Shelley is identified with that of the female mate in the film *The Bride of Frankenstein*, and the way in which there is a doubling of characterization within Mel Brooks's *Young Frankenstein* (1973). In the former, it is worth noting that the actress who played Mary Shelley in the Prologue of the film, Elsa Lanchester, is actually the same actress who played the Monster's mate in the film (although the film credits do not explicitly reveal this to be so, leaving a question mark at the appropriate place). Perhaps this is as it should be, for many would argue that there is more than a hint of Mary Shelley's own person embodied within the work—she is both creator and created![1] *Frankenstein* is above all else *her* Monster; the fact that the Monster was given life and the mate was not is, in the end, of little importance.[2] In the second film *Young Frankenstein*, a meticulously-presented send-up of James Whale's two *Frankenstein* films, presents us with an insightful interpretation of its own, unusually pairing the central characters of the novel. Here Elizabeth is united not with Frederick Frankenstein (grandson of the famous Baron von Frankenstein), but with the Monster himself, while

1.   In Riley (ed.), *The Bride of Frankenstein*, p. 30, Elsa Lanchester offers an explanation about why director James Whale chose to cast in this fashion: 'James' feeling was that very pretty, sweet people, both men and women, had very wicked insides...evil thoughts. These thoughts could be of dragons, they could be of monsters, they could be of Frankenstein's laboratory. So James wanted the same actress for both parts to show that the Bride of Frankenstein did, after all, come out of sweet Mary Shelley's soul.'

2.   Contrary to the suggestion of Small, *Ariel Like a Harpy*, who argues (p. 50) that in Christian representations of the Promethean myth dating from mediaeval times, creation of the woman is the prerogative of God himself, with creation of man being allocated to the divine Promethean agent. This, he continues, influences Shelley's *Frankenstein* as it consciously builds upon the Promethean mythology. In short, as Small puts it (p. 50), 'to make a female is something he (Frankenstein) just cannot do'. However, this seems to outrun the evidence. There is nothing to suggest within the story itself that Frankenstein is incapable of bringing the female Monster to life in precisely the same way that he has done with the male Monster.

Frederick Frankenstein is mated with his servant girl Inga. In this film the Monster gets his (Frankenstein's) bride, although not at the expense of Frankenstein himself; here there are enough women to go around and everyone is happily wed in the end. The key point here is that the Monster is united with the character of Elizabeth, and the 'brain transference' between Frankenstein and his Monster is made all the more significant as a result. Perhaps director Mel Brooks was nearer the truth of Shelley's intention than he realized in presenting the interpenetration of roles as he does. The relationship between Frankenstein and his Monster is often closer than we realize.

Summary

I have attempted to examine how the stories of the creation of man and woman are expressed in the book of Genesis and compare them with Mary Shelley's *Frankenstein*, a work which relies heavily upon the creation motif within its narrative. In short, the tale is about the wholeness which must be sought within a created being, a wholeness which can be found only within a relationship of complementarity. In a sense we could say that underlying Mary Shelley's *Frankenstein* is an intuitive sense of the nature of humankind which is not dissimilar to that expressed in the thought of the Priestly writer of Genesis in 1.26-27 and 5.1-2; this is a theology which stresses the simultaneous creation of male and female as ideal. And yet, the alternative biblical vision of human creation, that embodied in Gen. 2.21-22 by the Yahwist writer, also finds expression in the novel insofar as the Monster feels a profound sense of loneliness and isolation when he is forced to live without a partner. This leads him to demand that a mate be created for him so that the tension presented by the separate creation of male and female be resolved. The novel's description of this mate as a partner, or a helpmeet, is remarkably reminiscent of the story of the creation of Adam and Eve in Gen. 2.4b-25. The fact that Mary Shelley is able to include in the novel aspects of *both* views of humankind, one stressing the simultaneous creation of male and female and the other stressing their separate creation, is one of the features of *Frankenstein* which makes it so interesting to read. Meanwhile, the fact that both visions can be united so powerfully in one book should encourage us as we seek to understand the message of Genesis, which, as Robert Alter and others have argued, effectively does the same thing.

There is much to suggest, therefore, that within *Frankenstein*, Mary Shelley's most original and enduring literary work, we are confronted with an interesting alternative to the standard way of viewing how male and female relate to one another, need one another, and depend on one another for their very existence. This alternative approach drives us to a fresh appreciation of Genesis 1–2, one which is pregnant with possibilities. We will not go far wrong if we paraphrase the Priestly writer, and cast his creative mantle upon the shoulders of Mary Shelley and declare that within this novel *male and female* she *created them.*

Chapter 5

A FAREWELL TO ARMS:
'A TIME TO GIVE BIRTH AND A TIME TO DIE'

What is it which might be said to characterize the book of Ecclesiastes as
a document expressing human hope? What does Qoheleth,[1] the
preacher, have to say about human existence? James L. Crenshaw has
called attention to what he describes as an 'ambiguity about life and
death' within the book, noting how the author fluctuates in his opinions
about the inevitability of death and the place of hope in the midst of the
meaninglessness, the purposelessness, of life.[2] As Crenshaw elsewhere
puts it,

> The arbitrariness of death troubles Qohelet more than anything else...
> Qohelet denies any pattern at all in death's timing and choice of victims.[3]

In short, Ecclesiastes might rightly be described as a book in which hope
is ambiguously presented, and this as a conscious act on the part of the
author, the mysterious preacher Qoheleth. For many interpreters of
Ecclesiastes this gloomy vision of despair holds the key to interpreting
the book as a whole. They argue that Qoheleth says to his readers,
rather brutally, that the haunting spectre of Death casts its icy shadow
over human existence, rendering any attempt to extract meaning
from life futile. The inability of anyone to predict or control the day of

---

1.   The Hebrew name of the book, usually translated as 'Preacher'. Most scholars use the term to describe not only the work itself but also its author.
2.   'The Shadow of Death in Qoheleth', in J.G. Gammie, W.A. Brueggemann,
W.L. Humphreys and J.M. Ward (eds.), *Israelite Wisdom: Theological and Literary
Essays in Honor of Samuel Terrien* (New York: Scholars Press, 1978), p. 205. F.N.
Jasper, 'Ecclesiastes: A Note for Our Time', *Int* 21 (1967), p. 262, similarly remarks,
'the place and purpose of man, in life and in the face of death, is one of the central
problems of the book'.
3.   *Ecclesiastes* (OTL; London: SCM Press, 1987), p. 25.

his or her death feeds the pessimistic outlook of Qoheleth.

This honest, if depressing, picture of life is what has, in a strange sort of way, made the work stand the test of time and helped make Ecclesiastes acceptable as a work worthy of being included within the canon of Old Testament Scripture.[1] This is despite the fact (or perhaps *because* of the fact) that the 'theological corrective' inserted by a later editor(s) in 12.9-14 certainly helped to tone down the unorthodox material contained within the body of the book in which such a thoroughgoing scepticism is expressed.[2]

Qoheleth's perspective is by no means a unique one, for such ambiguity of hope about human existence remains an enduring theme within literature the world over. Within this study I would like to assess Qoheleth's viewpoint in light of one of this century's most important works of literature, which grapples with the same subject and arrives at a similar declaration about the ambiguous nature of life and death—I speak of Ernest Hemingway's classic novel *A Farewell to Arms*. This book comes at the theme through the tale of a fated romance set against the madness of World War I, rivalling Erich Maria Remarque's *All Quiet on the Western Front* (1929) as *the* anti-war novel of the period. In particular, I would like to concentrate on how both Qoheleth and Hemingway use the motif of birth-death to convey their respective ideas about life's meaning (or the lack of it!). Within Ecclesiastes this birth-death motif is given explicit expression in only one place (3.2a), although it is alluded to in several other places (5.15; 6.3-6; and possibly 7.8). In *A Farewell to Arms* it recurs again and again and can be seen as one of the controlling images upon which the book is based. In effect, the attitude to birth and death within the two books sets the scene for a

---

1. See R.B. Salters, 'Qoheleth and the Canon', *ExpTim* 86 (1974–75), pp. 339-42. R. Davidson (*The Courage to Doubt: Exploring an Old Testament Theme* [London: SCM Press, 1983], p. 201) remarks, 'There is no use trying to make Qoheleth fit neatly into the central theme of Israel's religious traditions. At many points he goes far beyond any other thinker in the Old Testament. He rejects much that lies close to the beating of Israel's faith. But he does so with an honesty and integrity which are refreshing.'

2. Most commentators agree that the Epilogue in 12.9-14 represents a substantial reversal of the radical teaching of the book as a whole and many associate with it several other interpolated passages which alter the tone of the book. C.C. Forman ('The Pessimism of Ecclesiastes', *JSS* 3 [1958], p. 336) mentions the tradition that 'Ecclesiastes was admitted to the canon on the strength of its interpolations!'

larger consideration of how we interpret them as works of literature. I shall use the birth-death motif as a window through which to view both books, noting similarities of scholarly assessment and interpretation.

That Hemingway was familiar with Ecclesiastes is certain. He quite regularly ransacked the Bible for phrases or images he could use as titles for his works,[1] and most agree that Eccl. 1.5 provided the key phrase which is used in the title of his first major novel, *The Sun also Rises* (1926).[2] Even more significant are the manuscripts of the Hemingway archives housed in the John F. Kennedy Library in Boston, Massachusetts which contain lists of a number of titles that Hemingway was considering for the book he eventually called *A Farewell to Arms*. Included is a manuscript page which lists nine different potential titles for the book all drawn from phrases which occur in Ecclesiastes.[3] There is much to sustain the suggestion that Ecclesiastes provided Hemingway with considerable food for thought during the composition of *A Farewell to Arms*; one might even go so far as to suggest that Ecclesiastes provided the prevailing mind set which is expressed in the novel. If there is a modern equivalent to Ecclesiastes, a good case could be made for it to be Hemingway's novel.

In this regard it is also interesting to note that the ancient book of Ecclesiastes and *A Farewell to Arms* have one very striking feature in common; they both have been the subject of widely differing, even conflicting, interpretations. Some see the essential point made within the two works of literature as a profound pessimism; others have interpreted them more optimistically, arguing that there is a ray of hope within them, despite the dark clouds which seem to overshadow their shared message. The similar interpretations made of both Ecclesiastes and *A Farewell to Arms* are an open invitation for an interesting comparative

1.   As some of his letters to Maxwell Perkins and F. Scott Fitzgerald indicate. See C. Baker (ed.), *Ernest Hemingway: Selected Letters (1917–1961)* (New York: Charles Scribner's Sons, 1981), pp. 229, 260 and 547-48 for details.

2.   H. Straumann (*American Literature in the Twentieth Century* [London: Arrow Books, 1962], p. 129) remarks that 'the novel is really an illustration of Ecclesiastes's *Vanitas Vanitatum*'. For a discussion of the matter, see R.W. Lewis, Jr., *Hemingway on Love* (Austin: University of Texas Press, 1965), pp. 29-35; S.A. Cowan, 'Robert Cohn, the Fool of Ecclesiastes in *The Sun Also Rises*', *DR* 63 (1983), pp. 98-106.

3.   P. Smith ('Almost all is Vanity: A Note on Nine Rejected Titles for *A Farewell to Arms*', *HR* 2 [1982], pp. 74-76) discusses the manuscript (Item 76A) and lists the passages from Ecclesiastes as 1.9, 1.18, 2.8, 2.14, 3.19, 2.24, 3.8 and 12.5.

study of them to be undertaken, particularly as they both deal with the twin themes of life and death.

In keeping with the theme of this book we shall examine not only the novel itself, but the cinematic adaptations of *A Farewell to Arms*, paying particular attention to how the two available films handle the central themes of birth and death, optimism and pessimism. This will help sensitize us to how the novel *A Farewell to Arms* might be seen in a new way, carefully balancing pessimism and optimism within its pages. Similarly, this reconsideration of Hemingway's novel will allow us to discuss more intelligently some of the more recent interpretations on offer for this most perplexing of all Old Testament books to comprehend, Ecclesiastes. In particular, we shall look at some of the recent suggestions made by two prominent Old Testament scholars, R.N. Whybray and Michael V. Fox, in this regard.[1]

Thus, I shall pursue the body of this study in four major parts: (1) Ecclesiastes: Vanity and Pessimism; (2) Hemingway's *A Farewell to Arms*: A Masterpiece of Pessimism; (3) Film Adaptations of *A Farewell to Arms*; (4) Ecclesiastes and *A Farewell to Arms*: Is There Any Room for Optimism?

1. *Ecclesiastes: Vanity and Pessimism*

Ecclesiastes has been the subject of a considerable revival of scholarly interest in recent years. Not only has there been a great deal of debate about the book's relationship to the Hebrew wisdom tradition, but many have sought to compare the work to either Babylonian and Egyptian or Greek thought of the day, citing such works such as the *Epic of Gilgamesh* and the writings of Hesiod, Theognis or Euripides as parallels.[2] One of the primary reasons for this exploration in background has been

---

1.   Namely, R.N. Whybray, *Ecclesiastes* (NCB; Grand Rapids: Eerdmans, 1989), and M.V. Fox, *Qohelet and his Contradictions* (BLS, 18; Sheffield: Almond Press, 1989). Fox's highly creative approach to Ecclesiastes incorporates his published articles on Qoheleth and I shall focus on these, noting wherever relevant the way in which he builds on them within his book.

2.   See C.F. Whitley, *Koheleth: His Language and Thought* (Berlin: de Gruyter, 1979), pp. 149-75, for details. E. Horton, Jr ('Koheleth's Concept of Opposites', *Numen* 19 [1972], pp. 1-21) offers an interesting discussion along the same lines but expanding the concern to compare Qoheleth with Far Eastern thought, notably Taoism.

the attempt to explain the rather nihilistic streak which runs through Ecclesiastes.[1] Is there a fatalistic determinism in operation here, generally accepted as uncharacteristic of Hebrew thought? Has Qoheleth been contaminated in his thinking and accepted the Greek thought of his day, effectively abandoning belief in the goodness and justice of Yahweh?[2] It is hardly surprising that Qoheleth's place within the wisdom tradition of Hebrew thought has been one of the main areas of scholarly debate about the book. In the provocative words of Norman K. Gottwald,

> The God of the Preacher is impersonal and incommunicative. The wisdom movement seems to have run into bankruptcy; Hebrew humanism has reached a dead end.[3]

Indeed, there has been a long-standing tradition within Judaism that the *Book of Wisdom* was written in part to counteract the subversive negativism of Qoheleth, and reverse the opinion of the book held by the author of the *Wisdom of Ben Sirah*.[4]

Many interpreters have focused on the numerous passages within Ecclesiastes which display a rather negative mind set and seem to have been born out of a bitterness of heart over the rough experiences of life. R.B.Y. Scott's comment is representative of the views of many others:

1.   Forman ('The Pessimism of Ecclesiastes', pp. 336-43) discusses the suggestion that the influence of Greek thought is responsible for the pessimism of Qoheleth. He concludes that such a suggestion is an inadequate solution to the problem and that it underestimates the Jewishness of the book, failing to recognize the pessimistic tradition in Hebraic thought.

2.   It is often pointed out that Ecclesiastes never uses the name יהוה for the Almighty, preferring always to use אֱלֹהִים when speaking of God. This is usually taken to be indicative of the fact that for the author God is a distant figure and one cannot use the more personal name for Him.

3.   *A Light to the Nations* (New York: Harper & Brothers, 1959), p. 490. G. von Rad (*Wisdom in Israel* [New York: Abingdon Press, 1972], pp. 226-39) makes a similar assessment.

4.   The classic work by G.A. Barton, *The Book of Ecclesiastes* (ICC; Edinburgh: T. & T. ClArk, 1908), pp. 53-58, discusses this at some length. G.T. Sheppard ('The Epilogue to Qoheleth as Theological Commentary', *CBQ* 39 [1977], pp. 182-89) discusses the interesting notion that the redactor of 12.13-14 knew the *Wisdom of Ben Sirah* and brought Qoheleth into line with its teaching about wisdom and the observance of the Law by adding the ending that he did. Also on this point, see R.E. Murphy, *Ecclesiastes* (WBC, 23A; Dallas: Word Books, 1992), pp. 123-55.

The author is a rationalist, an agnostic, a skeptic, a pessimist, and a fatalist (the terms are not used perjoratively!).[1]

The all-too depressing refrain of 1.2 and 12.8, 'vanity of vanities, all is vanity',[2] within which the body of the book is framed, is taken as prime evidence of such an assessment. Similarly, the frequent assertion in Qoheleth that finding meaning and purpose in life is like 'striving after wind' (1.14, 17; 2.11, 17, 26; 4.4, 6; 6.9) is said to typify the author's bleak and sombre outlook on human existence. As is typical of Jewish wisdom literature, nature has a prominent role within the teaching of the book as a whole. However, Qoheleth's is a vision of nature in which even the certainty and predictability of the cycle of the seasons and the harmony of the rivers returning to the seas are viewed with a jaundiced eye. The regularity of the created order is all monotonous and boring, with human beings having little, if any, power to effect meaningful change upon the world in which they find themselves placed. Indeed, the whole of the created order is illustrative of the unfathomability of life. As a result, life itself is portrayed as futile, and death, when it comes, as something to be embraced readily. Thus in 4.2-3 we read a statement typical of his rejection of meaning in life:

2 And I thought the dead who are already dead more fortunate than the living who are still alive; 3 but better than both is he who has not yet been, and has not seen the evil deeds that are done under the sun.

In effect, Ecclesiastes can be read as something of a catalogue of despair and despondency. Frederic Beuchner describes it as 'one long-drawn sigh of disillusion'.[3] The book is often taken to be the negative distillation of the thoughts of a man who has become bitter and twisted as a result of what life has served him up on his plate. Qoheleth states that there is no sense within it all. As he sees it, there is no reason for a man to go through the hard task of accumulating respect and authority and

1. *Proverbs and Ecclesiastes* (AB, 18; Garden City, NY: Doubleday, 1965), p. 192. J.L. Crenshaw ('The Birth of Skepticism in Ancient Israel', in J.L. Crenshaw and S. Sandmel [eds.], *The Divine Helmsman: Studies in God's Control of Human Events, Presented to Lou H. Silberman* [New York: Ktav, 1980], pp. 1-19) argues for a distinction to be made between skepticism, pessimism and cynicism, with a decreasing element of faith being inherent in the three groupings. Qoheleth, he feels, falls within the middle category of pessimism.

2. Forms of the word translated 'vanity' (הֶבֶל) occur some 38 times in the book.

3. *Peculiar Treasures: A Biblical Who's Who* (New York: Harper & Row, 1979), p. 86.

wealth in life when it is going to be used unwisely or simply frittered away by his descendants. As Qoheleth puts it in 1.3-11, a passage which helps to set the tone for the whole of the book that follows,

> 3 What does man gain by all the toil at which he toils under the sun? 4 A generation goes, and a generation comes, but the earth remains for ever. 5 The sun rises and the sun goes down, and hastens to the place where it rises. 6 The wind blows to the south, and goes round to the north; round and round goes the wind, and on its circuits the wind returns. 7 All streams run to the sea, but the sea is not full; to the place where the streams flow, there they flow again. 8 All things are full of weariness; a man cannot utter it; the eye is not satisfied with seeing, nor the ear filled with hearing. 9 What has been is what will be, and what has been done is what will be done; and there is nothing new under the sun. 10 Is there a thing of which it is said, 'See, this is new'? It has been already, in the ages before us. 11 There is no remembrance of former things, nor will there be any remembrance of later things yet to happen among those who come after.[1]

There are two passages from Ecclesiastes which are of special importance for our comparative study with *A Farewell to Arms*. The first is a memorable phrase from 3.2a expressing a theme which is prominently developed within Hemingway's novel. This simple line goes a long way in expressing the heart of what Hemingway accomplishes within the fictional story. The second passage from 9.12 involves the evocative image of life as 'a trap' which is sprung upon the unsuspecting. This image, too, is used to great effect in Hemingway's *A Farewell to Arms* and invites some interesting comparisons.[2]

---

1.   This passage is crucial for the creative interpretation of Ecclesiastes offered by P.S. Fiddes, 'The Hiddenness of Wisdom in the Old Testament and Later Judaism' (unpublished DPhil Thesis, the University of Oxford, 1976). He argues that Qoheleth asserts that there is a profound uncertainty in life, an 'incalculability in patterns of human experience' (p. 240) which severely challenges the traditional Jewish understandings of the value of wisdom as the basis for life. In effect, Fiddes argues, the inability of humankind to arrive at knowledge on the basis of its own observations lies at the heart of the message of Ecclesiastes, a message which proclaims the 'hiddenness of wisdom'. It is important to note, Fiddes continues, that Qoheleth is not teaching that life itself is intrinsically meaningless, but that humankind is incapable of discovering the meaning of life within it.

2.   In this connection, mention should perhaps also be made of 8.6-8 where the author continues in his pessimistic state of mind, denying that even kings have any effective power in life and asserting that all people are equally helpless in the face of death. What is interesting, at least from the standpoint of a comparison between

a. *'A Time for Giving Birth and a Time for Dying' (Ecclesiastes 3.2a)*
Most scholars acknowledge that the author of Ecclesiastes is here presenting a highly poetical section (3.2-8) which is framed by an introduction (3.1) and followed by an explanatory conclusion (3.9-15).[1] Embedded within the passage is one of the most cryptic phrases in the whole of Ecclesiastes. In 3.11 Qoheleth says of God,

> He has made everything beautiful in its time; also he has placed eternity into man's mind, yet so that he cannot find out what God has done from the beginning to the end. (RSV)

What is the meaning of this curious declaration? Does it mean that, as a part of the creation of everything beautiful, God has placed within the human heart a sense of the eternal? Does humankind thereby have an in-built gauge against which all of life's experiences must be measured? Scholars have offered a number of interpretations about this curious statement and no clear consensus has emerged.[2] Most agree, however, that the declaration in 3.11 does stand as a summary of the highly poetic section which precedes it, and it is those verses which demand our attention now.

In 3.2-8 we are presented with a series of fourteen antithetical declarations, each set within a highly structured pattern and knit together with the phrase 'A time to...' The first of these declarations sets the tone for all the statements which follow in that it defines the span of human life during which all the remaining antitheses occur. In 3.2a we read, 'A time to give birth and a time to die' (RSV). This is a fairly literal

---

Ecclesiastes and Hemingway's *A Farewell to Arms*, is the fact that this declaration of helplessness is immediately followed by a statement about soldiers not having release during war. In a strange sort of way, one could even describe Hemingway's novel, at least as far as one interpretation of the ambiguous title is concerned, as dealing with precisely this theme. In other words, *A Farewell to Arms* is preoccupied with explaining how a man can find release from war. In the end, Qoheleth is proved right, for there is no 'farewell to arms' without the accompanying encounter with death which the character Frederic Henry must experience.

1. J.L. Crenshaw, 'The Eternal Gospel (Eccl. 3:11)', in J.L. Crenshaw and J.T. Willis (eds.), *Essays in Old Testament Ethics: J. Philip Hyatt, in Memoriam* (New York: Ktav, 1974), pp. 23-55, argues that both style and content point to the unity of 3.1-15.

2. In addition to the article by Crenshaw, see the discussion in Whybray, *Ecclesiastes*, pp. 72-74.

translation of the Hebrew text which reads, עֵת לָלֶדֶת וְעֵת לָמוּת and the only real question of some debate is the meaning of the verb לֶדֶת, the infinitive construct of the verb ילד normally translated as 'to beget', or 'to give birth', or 'to bear'. The Septuagint translates the passage very woodenly, keeping the birthing image at the centre of the meaning by using the verb τεκεῖν for לֶדֶת: καιρὸς τοῦ τεκεῖν καὶ καιρὸς τοῦ ἀποθανεῖν. Indeed, the image of childbirth may help explain two of the more cryptic phrases later in the poem, those found in v. 5a:

עֵת לְהַשְׁלִיךְ אֲבָנִים וְעֵת כְּנוֹס אֲבָנִים
עֵת לַחֲבוֹק וְעֵת לִרְחֹק מֵחַבֵּק:

The RSV offers the translation:

> A time to cast away stones, and a time to gather stones together;
> A time to embrace, and a time to refrain from embracing.

However, the precise meaning of 3.5a has long been debated, particularly as the use of the stones metaphor is very unusual. Many commentators follow the interpretative lead of the *Midrash Qoheleth Rabbah* and take it to be a euphemism for sexual intercourse. This suggestion makes sense if we assume that the two halves of the verse were intended as a deliberate parallelism.[1] Thus the translation offered by GNB for the two lines is given as:

> The time for making love and the time for not making love,
> the time for kissing and the time for not kissing.

In any event, it seems clear that any joy and satisfaction which might be derived from being born into this life is severely curtailed by its negative counterpart—death. There is indeed a time to be born, but there is also an appointed time to die. Qoheleth's uncompromising message is that one cannot enjoy the ecstasies of the former without having ultimately to undergo the agonies of the latter; this sure and certain knowledge of death evacuates life of much of its meaning and value. Life has a hidden price which must be paid and death cannot be bribed, cheated or bargained with. Perhaps it is not surprising that the body of the book

---

1.   J.A. Loader, *Ecclesiastes: A Practical Commentary* (Text and Interpretation Series; Grand Rapids: Eerdmans, 1986), pp. 36-37, discusses this. Loader's article, 'Qohelet 3:2-8—A "Sonnet" in the Old Testament', *ZAW* 81 (1969), p. 242, offers some additional technical details.

closes with a passage (12.1-7) which has often been interpreted as an elaborate allegory of the physical deterioration of an elderly man as he heads towards death.[1]

b. *The 'Trap' of Life (Ecclesiastes 9.12)*
One other brief observation needs to be made. In 9.12 Qoheleth continues his negative assessment of human existence. Here he uses an image apparently drawn from the royal hunting expeditions, and applies it to life:

> For man does not know his time. Like fish which are taken in a net, and like birds which are caught in a snare, so the sons of men are snared at an evil time, when it suddenly falls upon them.

What is somewhat unusual about this verse is the image of life as a snare, a trap which suddenly springs shut and captures the unsuspecting. What precisely is the 'it' which falls upon the 'sons of men'? Some have taken it to be a natural disaster, or an illness of some sort which befalls human beings. However, the image of the trap which ensnares is almost certainly to be linked to Qoheleth's motif of death, in just the same way that the net and the snare become the instruments for the death of the fish and birds respectively. Thus, the statement in 9.12 is similar to the declaration contained in 3.18-21 which emphasizes the common fate of both humankind and beasts. In short, life, or at least some features of life, might be described metaphorically as a trap which inevitably leads to death. We shall see below how Hemingway makes use of a similar motif within his novel.

2. *Hemingway's* A Farewell to Arms: *A Masterpiece of Pessimism*

Critical studies of *A Farewell to Arms* were slow to take off and it was not until the late 1940s and early 1950s that scholarship began to take it seriously as a piece of literature. Now, of course, the novel stands as an acknowledged classic and it features regularly in American Literature courses the world over. The novel is typically sharp and direct,

---

1. M.V. Fox, 'Aging and Death in Qohelet 12', *JSOT* 42 (1988), pp. 55-77, offers a good discussion on this passage. Fox notes (p. 61) that Qoheleth has 'an obsession with death, and his gaze most naturally returns to that subject as he brings his teachings to a close'.

maintaining Hemingway's style of a cut-down narrative, devoid of any superfluous description or extravagance of language. It is a perfect illustration of what has come to be known as Hemingway's 'iceberg theory' of literary composition, whereby the text we read is only a small proportion of what is communicated by the author in the work; a vast amount lies hidden beneath the surface of the text.[1] Most scholars now recognize that the simple narrative form of *A Farewell to Arms* belies an exceedingly complex and intricate work.

The secondary literature on Hemingway is now enormous, and fresh interpretations of *A Farewell to Arms* appear every year, a healthy sign of its value as a piece of literature. It has been described as a masterpiece of anti-war literature, a failed romance,[2] and a tragedy in which the two lovers are innocent victims.[3] Certainly love and (the death brought by) war dominate as complementary themes within *A Farewell to Arms*. No wonder that R.W. Lewis, Jr describes the novel as one in which

> Hemingway moves back and forth between those strange but time-honored bed-companions, love and war.[4]

Hemingway interweaves his material in such a way as to contrast the two, love and war, effectively making them the twin pillars upon which the narrative of the novel rests.

a. *The Plot of the Novel*

The story is set in Italy during World War I and takes place over the course of a little less than three years, from the autumn of 1915 through to the spring of 1918. For the most part, Frederic Henry, the main character, narrates the tale after the fact and the bulk of the novel is written in the first person. Henry is an American serving as an

---

1.   Hemingway uses the iceberg image as a description of his work in an interview with George Plimpton published as 'Ernest Hemingway: The Art of Fiction XXI', *Paris Review* 18 (1958), pp. 60-89. The interview is reprinted in 'An Interview with Ernest Hemingway', in Bloom (ed.), *Modern Critical Views*, pp. 119-36.

2.   J. Beversluis, 'Dispelling the Romantic Myth: A Study of *A Farewell to Arms*', *HR* 9 (1989), pp. 18-25.

3.   E. Wilson, 'On Hemingway (1939)', in J. Meyers (ed.), *Hemingway: The Critical Heritage* (London: Routledge & Kegan Paul, 1982), p. 302.

4.   'The Tough Romance', in J. Gellens (ed.), *Twentieth Century Interpretations of A Farewell to Arms: A Collection of Critical Essays* (Englewood Cliffs, NJ: Prentice-Hall, 1970), p. 45.

ambulance driver with the Italian army on the eastern front north of Trieste. He meets an English nurse named Catherine Barkley and begins a game of seduction with her, a courtship which he describes as being played out like moves on a chess board or a hand of bridge. In a mortar attack at the front lines Henry is badly wounded in the legs. He is eventually shipped to the American hospital in Milan for a long period of convalescence and finds himself in the care of nurse Barkley, who has also been transferred to the hospital. Love between the two blossoms, and Henry realizes that he is in love and that Catherine has given him a reason for living. She becomes pregnant, but the two are unable to get married as they might wish, given the situation in war-torn Italy. After recuperating from his wounds Henry returns to the front lines only to find the Italian army in the disastrous retreat from Caporetto. Henry finds himself separated from his unit and in danger of being shot as an officer who has deserted his command. He escapes execution by jumping in an icy river and swims away to hiding. He manages to return to Milan and Catherine, forsaking any further involvement in the war, and the two of them make plans to escape in a small boat across Lake Maggiore to neutral Switzerland. The pair spend some happy months in the Swiss Alps, relishing their time together and their fortunate escape from the ravages of war. However, they soon settle in Lausanne where Catherine goes into labour, delivering a child by an emergency Caesarean section. The baby son dies, as does Catherine soon afterwards, the doctors being unable to stop her from haemorrhaging. Frederic is left alone to contemplate the losses he has endured and to reflect on the tragedy that is his life.

b. *The Thematic Structure of the Novel*

Hemingway is quoted as once saying that 'character is grace under pressure'. A more succinct summary of what the major figures in his literary work exhibit is difficult to imagine. Like most of Hemingway's fiction, *A Farewell to Arms* has the personal character of the main figures progressively revealed through their facing extreme situations. Dignity in the face of death is hailed as the most noble of virtues in Hemingway's moral code of honour and most of the central characters in his fiction demonstrate it. As Robert Penn Warren puts it, the shadow of ruin is behind the typical Hemingway situation. The typical character faces defeat or death. But out of defeat or death the character manages to salvage something.[1]

A Farewell to Arms conforms to this pattern wonderfully. In the end, the main characters of the novel are realistic and engaging precisely because they demonstrate the moral code in operation. Frederic Henry, Catherine Barkley, Rinaldi, and even the unnamed priest all pursue the lofty ideal in their own way.

A Farewell to Arms is one of Ernest Hemingway's best-loved and most widely known stories. Like all great works of literature, it has been variously assessed by critics. Both the structure and the content of the novel have been the focus of critical attention, and studies in both areas have been offered as interpretative keys to the discovery of the depths of the novel. Even the ambiguous title, taken, as Hemingway himself explains, from the title of a chivalrous poem by George Peele (1558–1597) which he found in his copy of *The Oxford Book of English Verse*, is a good indication of the depth of meaning of the novel itself. To what 'arms' is a farewell being offered? Is it the arms of war, or the arms of love?[2] Or are the two intertwined so thoroughly that it is impossible to separate them? Robert O. Stephens associates the title with the spiritual pilgrimage of Frederic Henry in the novel, stating that

> As Frederic becomes aware of the reality of the soul through the death of Catherine's body and as he learns the significance of defeat, he can achieve a meaningful farewell to arms, a turn from the world of military and amatory arms to divine love.[3]

It appears clear that the title of the work is not without significance for the tale that is related within it. But what of the body of *A Farewell to Arms* itself? How and to what end did Hemingway compose the novel in the way that he did? We all know that during his lifetime he was

---

    1. 'Ernest Hemingway', p. 39. Also see the discussion of C. Stetler and G. Locklin, 'De-Coding the Hero in Hemingway's Fiction', *HR* 5 (1979), pp. 2-10.
    2. N.A. Scott, Jr (*Ernest Hemingway: A Critical Essay* [CWCPS; Grand Rapids: Eerdmans, 1966], pp. 33-35) discusses the 'religion of love' which characterizes the relationship between Frederic Henry and Catherine Barkley within the novel as a whole.
    3. 'Hemingway and Stendhal: The Matrix of *A Farewell to Arms*', *PMLA* 88 (1973), p. 277. Stephens argues that Frederic moves toward belief in God when he recognizes that 'divine love is precipitated by the death of secular love' (p. 279).

acclaimed as an extraordinary writer the world over. He was awarded both a Pulitzer Prize in 1952 and the Nobel Prize for Literature in 1954, generally fairly reliable indications of creative genius in the field of literature. But what are some of the indications within this particular novel of Hemingway's legendary skill as a literary artist? There are several which are worth noting briefly; each helps contribute to the central birth-death motif which we are concentrating our attention upon in this study.

Firstly, *A Farewell to Arms* contains forty-one chapters divided into five books of rather uneven length.[1] At first reading it might appear to be simply a straightforward story, but closer inspection reveals that Hemingway had a definite structure in mind for the work as a whole. The five sections of the book have been compared to some of Shakespeare's five-act tragedies, each section ending with a scene of dramatic tension revolving around the character of Frederic Henry.[2] Thus we have highlighted in the five sections of the book Frederic's wounding, his return to his comrades at the front, his threatened execution as a spy, his threatened arrest by the Italian authorities, and his loss of Catherine.

Secondly, most critics of *A Farewell to Arms* agree that Hemingway creatively imposes a geographical framework upon the novel as a whole, juxtaposing the 'plain' and the 'mountain' within the narrative.[3] The 'plain' is the place of discord, of war, of destruction and of death, while the 'mountain' is the place of serenity and peace, of happiness and of life. The supporting characters Rinaldi and the priest, friends and colleagues of Frederic Henry, embody these two opposing descriptions of existence, and claim as their homes appropriate geographical places to match (the towns Amalfi and Abruzzi respectively). It is often suggested that they also represent the two extremes between which Frederic Henry must

1. The sections divide like this: Book One (chapters 1–12); Book Two (chapters 13–24); Book Three (chapters 25–32); Book Four (chapters 33–37); Book Five (chapters 38–41). I shall henceforth identify passages from the book by book and chapter number. Thus, 3:1 means Book Three, chapter 1. The edition cited is that published by Grafton Books: London, 1977.

2. H.K. Russell, 'The Catharsis in *A Farewell to Arms*', *MFS* 1 (1955), pp. 25-30, discusses this.

3. C. Baker, ('The Mountain and the Plain', in Baker [ed.], *Ernest Hemingway*, pp. 47-60) argues this point forcefully. E.M. Halliday ('Hemingway's Ambiguity: Symbolism and Irony', in Baker [ed.], *Ernest Hemingway*, pp. 61-74) qualifies such an interpretation of the overall symbolic organization of the novel.

decide as the novel progresses and he develops as a character. In effect, Rinaldi and the priest represent respectively the carnal and the spiritual approaches to life. In his relationship with Catherine, Frederic moves from a love based on physical desire to a mature love based on self-giving; he thereby discovers the true nature of divine love as opposed to secular love. As the priest explains to him in 1:11, building on an earlier conversation about Frederic's visits to a whorehouse,

> What you tell me about in the nights. That is not love. That is only passion
> and lust. When you love you wish to do things for. You wish to sacrifice
> for. You wish to serve.[1]

Thirdly, most critics of the novel note Hemingway's use of rain as an image of death and despair, coming as it does in several key places within the narrative, almost always as a warning of some disaster which is to come.[2] For example, the very first chapter of the novel concludes with a dramatically understated paragraph which sets the tone for much that follows:

> At the start of the winter came the permanent rain and with the rain came
> the cholera. But it was checked and in the end only seven thousand died of
> it in the army.[3]

---

1.   W.A. Glasser, 'A Farewell to Arms', SR 74 (1966), pp. 453-69, offers a good discussion of this key passage within the context of Frederic Henry's development. P. Messent, *Ernest Hemingway* (Macmillan Modern Novelists; London: Macmillan, 1992), pp. 103-10, also offers some insights into how the sexuality of Frederic Henry and Catherine Barkley is handled by Hemingway within the novel.

2.   D.J. Schneider, 'Hemingway's *A Farewell to Arms*: The Novel as Pure Poetry', in L. Wagner (ed.), *Ernest Hemingway: Five Decades of Criticism* (East Lansing: Michigan State University Press, 1977), pp. 252-66, discusses this at some length, noting how it helps to contribute to the overall impression of desolation and bitterness which is at the heart of the work and helps constitute Hemingway's lyric style. Malcolm Cowley was the first critic to call attention to this rain motif in the novel in his 'Introduction' to *The Portable Hemingway* (New York: The Viking Press, 1945), pp. vii-xxiv. (This essay is reprinted as 'Nightmare and Ritual in Hemingway', in R.P. Weeks [ed.], *Hemingway: A Collection of Critical Essays* [Englewood Cliffs: NJ: Prentice-Hall, 1962], pp. 40-51.) J. Killinger, *Hemingway and the Dead Gods* (Lexington: University of Kentucky Press, 1960), p. 48, offers an alternative interpretation of the rain motif suggesting that it is also a symbol of fertility (as in T.S. Eliot's *The Wasteland*) and that it points to the idea of rebirth for Hemingway's existential hero Frederic Henry.

3.   J. Phelan, 'The Concept of Voice, the Voices of Frederic Henry and the

The irony of the word 'only' stands out as a powerful indictment of the futility and senselessness of wartime. Another good example of this 'rain motif' occurs in 2:19 when Frederic is in his hospital room in Milan and he engages Catherine in a conversation during a rainstorm. The passage blends together rain, love and death in a most ominous fashion, setting the tone for much that is to follow. Catherine begins the dialogue:

> 'Listen to it rain.'
> 'It's raining hard.'
> 'And you'll always love me, won't you?'
> 'Yes.'
> 'And the rain won't make any difference?'
> 'No.'
> 'That's good. Because I'm afraid of the rain.'
> 'Why?' I was sleepy. Outside the rain was falling steadily.
> 'I don't know, darling. I've always been afraid of the rain.'
> 'I like it.'
> 'I like to walk in it. But it's very hard on loving.'
> 'I'll love you always.'
> 'I'll love you in the rain and in the snow and in the hail and—what else is there?'
> 'I don't know. I guess I'm sleepy.'
> 'Go to sleep, darling, and I'll love you no matter how it is.'
> 'You're not really afraid of the rain are you?'
> 'Not when I'm with you.'
> 'Why are you afraid of it?'
> 'I don't know.'
> 'Tell me.'
> 'Don't make me.'
> 'Tell me.'
> 'No.'

Structure of *A Farewell to Arms*', in F. Scafella (ed.), *Hemingway: Essays of Reassessment* (Oxford: Oxford University Press, 1991), pp. 221-22, discusses this paragraph in detail, suggesting that it indicates a tension between the voice of Frederic Henry as narrator and that of Hemingway as author. This tension, Phelan argues, is only resolved in the last sentence of the novel where Frederic's voice is merged with Hemingway's. Also see Phelan's article 'Distance, Voice, and Temporal Perspective in Frederic Henry's Narration: Successes, Problems, and Paradox', in S. Donaldson (ed.), *New Essays on A Farewell to Arms* (Cambridge: Cambridge University Press, 1990), pp. 53-73. The question of narrative voice will be discussed again below (Section D) when we compare how Ecclesiastes and *A Farewell to Arms* are sometimes interpreted as expressing an optimistic viewpoint.

'Tell me.'

'All right. I'm afraid of the rain because sometimes I see me dead in it.'

In contrast, snow is almost always associated with a sense of calm and peace within the novel. It is surely no accident that snow is usually associated with the mountains, and rain with the plains. The two metaphors interlock and mutually reinforce each other, providing structure to the narrative. I could perhaps mention one further use of water as a metaphor within the book, namely, the presence of bodies of water, such as rivers and lakes. It should not be overlooked that Frederic Henry effects his escape twice by means of water, again at key transitional points in the narrative. The first is in 3:30-31 where he jumps into the Tagliamento River, a scene in the book which has been described by Malcolm Cowley as his 'rebirth', or 'a rite of baptism' into another life.[1] The second is in 4:36-37 where Frederic and Catherine escape in the small rowing-boat across Lake Maggiore.[2]

Finally, although *A Farewell to Arms* has been both widely praised and widely criticized from a variety of angles, most critics focus on the relationship between the two principal characters, and see the novel as adhering to the structure and form of a classical tragedy. This is hardly surprising, since Hemingway is said to have seen Frederic Henry and Catherine Barkley as his version of *Romeo and Juliet*.[3] More than any other of his novels *A Farewell to Arms* expresses one of Hemingway's most memorable lines about the traumas of love: 'If two people love each other there can be no happy end to it'.[4] Yet Hemingway's portrayal of the love affair between Frederic Henry and Catherine Barkley has engendered some very heated discussion among critics. It has been described as a '"dialectic" between female faith and male

---

1.   'Nightmare and Ritual', p. 46.

2.   R.B. Pearsall, *The Life and Writings of Ernest Hemingway* (Amsterdam: Rodopi, 1973), pp. 136-38, offers a stimulating discussion of the symbol of water within the novel.

3.   The influence of Shakespeare's *Othello* can also be clearly seen when Henry is modelled after the title character in being a foreigner who has come to help Italy in a time of war. Indeed, in 4:35 Catherine teases her lover about being like 'Othello with his occupation gone' after he has deserted his army unit. Similarly, in 2:21, Shakespeare's *Julius Caesar* is cited by Frederic in a conversation with Catherine about bravery and death: 'The coward dies a thousand deaths, the brave but one'.

4.   From *Death in the Afternoon* (London: Grafton Books, 1977), p. 110. The novel was first published in 1932.

skepticism'.[1] Some critics have roundly condemned the portrayal of romantic love within the story, suggesting that behind the overly sentimental, idyllic portrayal of the affair between the two central characters Hemingway actually intends to demonstrate his contempt for women. Thus, Judith Fetterley, in one of the most vitriolic articles about *A Farewell to Arms* written from a feminist perspective, describes the novel as Hemingway's 'resentful cryptogram'[2] wherein women are often portrayed as sexual objects existing solely for the carnal pleasure of men. Others take a more positive view of the character Catherine Barkley, arguing that she is a model of courage and self-will, someone who is struggling to gain her sense of self-respect and psychological wholeness following the death of her fiancé in the battle of the Somme.[3] She is, after all, voluntarily serving as a nurse in the midst of the debacle of the First World War, and does so competently and professionally. Far from being an insubstantial figure, she conducts her life with the courage of her convictions, even to the point of ultimate self-surrender in dying through childbirth as the result of her commitment to the man she loves. Pursuing such a course of action is hardly the sign of a weak or timid character; on the contrary, it demands a high degree of strength.[4] No wonder that, if anything, some critics have described Catherine as the stronger of the two main characters of the novel.

This leads us to consider briefly how much of the plot of *A Farewell to Arms* arises out of Hemingway's own life, especially since the character Catherine Barkley is frequently said to have been based upon someone he encountered in Milan when recovering from wounds he himself had sustained while serving on the Italian front in World War I.

1. G. Dekker and J. Harris, 'Supernaturalism and the Vernacular Style in *A Farewell to Arms*', *PMLA* 94 (1979), p. 312.

2. '*A Farewell to Arms*: Hemingway's "Resentful Cryptogram"', *JPC* 10 (1976), p. 203. Also note the excellent study by M. Bell, '*A Farewell to Arms*: Pseudoautobiography and Personal Metaphor', in J. Nagel (ed.), *Ernest Hemingway: The Writer in Context* (Madison: University of Wisconsin Press, 1984), pp. 107-28.

3. For a discussion of Hemingway's portrayal of Catherine Barkley, see R. Whitlow, *Cassandra's Daughters: The Women in Hemingway* (London: Greenwood Press, 1984), pp. 17-25.

4. S.W. Spanier, 'Hemingway's Unknown Soldier: Catherine Barkley, the Critics and the Great War', in Donaldson (ed.), *New Essays*, pp. 75-108, offers a recent discussion of the various ways in which Catherine Barkley has been interpreted by critics over the years.

c. *Reflections of Hemingway's Own Life in the Novel*
Since his untimely suicide Ernest Hemingway (1899–1961) has become
something of a larger-than-life figure. He continues to capture the
imagination of the populace at large; several biographies and studies of
his life appear every year.[1] Anyone who has had any connection with
Hemingway has found a ready market for their story.

Hemingway was a writer who drew upon his own rich experience of
life for the substance of his novels. His interest in bullfighting, big game
hunting and blue-marlin fishing are all put to good use within his novels
and short stories, as *The Sun also Rises* (1927), *Death in the Afternoon*
(1932), *The Snows of Kilimanjaro* (1938) and *The Old Man and the
Sea* (1952) all testify. Hemingway's interest in the Spanish Civil War
was deep and abiding and is perhaps best known through his novel *For
Whom the Bell Tolls* (1940) and the play *Fifth Column* (1938). An even
more substantial autobiographical component comes through in *A
Farewell to Arms*, although Hemingway was frequently to insist that the
novel was not an autobiography. However, from the beginning there
was no doubt that the book was creatively shaped by Hemingway's
own experiences in the First World War. Indeed, Ray B. West attempts
to interpret it in light of the wartime setting in which it was written,
describing it as

> a parable of twentieth-century man's disgust and disillusionment at the
> failure of civilization to achieve the ideals it had been promised throughout
> the nineteenth century.[2]

1.   Some of the more substantial biographical studies of recent years include:
S. Donaldson, *By Force of Will: The Life and Art of Ernest Hemingway* (New York:
Viking, 1977); P. Griffin, *Along with Youth: Hemingway, the Early Years* (Oxford:
Oxford University Press, 1985); J. Meyers, *Hemingway: A Biography* (New York:
Harper & Row, 1985); M.S. Reynolds, *The Young Hemingway* (Oxford: Basil
Blackwell, 1986); *idem*, *Hemingway: The Paris Years* (Oxford: Basil Blackwell,
1989); *idem*, *Hemingway: The American Homecoming* (Oxford: Basil Blackwell,
1992); K.S. Lynn, *Hemingway* (London: Cardinal Books, 1987); D. Brian, *The True
Gen: An Intimate Portrayal by those who Knew him* (London: Grove Press, 1988);
J.R. Mellow, *Hemingway: A Life without Consequences* (London: Hodder &
Stoughton, 1992). C.A. Fenton's *The Apprenticeship of Ernest Hemingway* (New
York: Mentor Books, 1954) and C. Baker's *Ernest Hemingway* (Harmondsworth:
Penguin Books, 1972), remain standard studies upon which many of the subsequent
books are based. A good critical review of some of the recent biographies is
R.W. Lewis, Jr, 'Hemingway's Lives: A Review', *HR* 7 (1987), pp. 45-62.
2.   R.B. West, Jr, 'The Biological Trap', in Weeks (ed.), *Hemingway*, p. 139.

Many have sought to trace the influence of other great literary works of war upon Hemingway in his composition of this novel. Included are Stephen Crane's *The Red Badge of Courage* (1895) about the American Civil War and Stendhal's *Charterhouse of Parma* (1839) about the defeat of Napoleon at Waterloo.[1] Such a reliance upon established war classics is especially argued for in connection with Hemingway's description of the retreat from Caporetto. Most of Book 3 is given over to describing the chaotic situation of the war as the Italian front lines are broken by the advancing Austrian and German armies. Chapters 27–30 detail the retreat from Caporetto which begins with some semblance of order but quickly deteriorates into what Frederick J. Hoffman has provocatively described as 'the landscape of unreason'.[2] The Caporetto episode is considered by most historians to be the low point of the Italian army in the war which cost the lives of some 600,000 soldiers, and it is perhaps understandable why Hemingway turned to it within the novel. Hemingway's graphic description of the incident is often published on its own[3] and is certainly one of the best-known

Similarly, R.P. Warren ('Ernest Hemingway', p. 37) remarks that Hemingway 'seemed to typify in his own experience the central experience of his generation'. Warren makes the comment in the midst of a discussion of World War I as the formative background to the novel.

1. Stephens, 'Hemingway and Stendhal', pp. 271-80, discusses this at length. He argues quite strongly that the character of Frederic Henry is modelled on Stendhal's Fabrizio. Also worth consulting on this point is C.D. Lawson, 'Hemingway, Stendhal and War', *HR* 6 (1981), pp. 28-33. On the other hand, Hemingway's own experiences as a soldier and a war correspondent surely provided him with enough material to construct the Caporetto passages in the novel. For instance, good indications of his attention to detail in describing an army's retreat are his articles 'A Silent, Ghastly Procession', *The Toronto Daily Star* (20 October 1922), and 'Refugees from Thrace', *The Toronto Daily Star* (14 November 1922). These pieces are reprinted in E. Hemingway, *By-Line* (London: Grafton Books, 1989), pp. 72-73 and 77-81.

2. 'No Beginning and no End: Hemingway and Death', *EIC* 3 (1953), p. 79. Here, as we noted about Ecclesiastes, everything is in disorder and no rules or certainties are to be found. Frederic Henry is forced to escape probable execution as a collaborator by jumping into a river and deserting the retreating Italian army.

3. As in *The Essential Hemingway* (London: Grafton Books, 1977), pp. 187-237.

sections from the novel. This is, in itself, a remarkable achievement since Hemingway had no first-hand knowledge of the incident at Caporetto, nor had he ever visited the area prior to his writing *A Farewell to Arms*, despite the attention to detail which suggests to the contrary that his description is autobiographical.

A Farewell to Arms was his first major success, selling 80,000 copies in the first four months, and it launched Hemingway on the world scene as a writer of considerable talent. It was written over a lengthy period of time. It was begun in March 1928 while Hemingway was living in Paris and he continued to work on it when he returned to the United States in the summer. Sections were written in Key West, Florida, in Piggot, Arkansas, in Kansas City, Missouri, and in the mountains near Sheridan, Wyoming. The final manuscript was completed at the end of August 1928, although corrections and revisions of proofs were to occupy Hemingway for most of the year. He signed a deal with *Scribner's Magazine* to have the story appear as a six-part serialization. This helped to prepare the way for the publication of the novel itself, which was published by Scribner's on 27 September 1929 with a cover price of $2.50. The awaited novel gained some notoriety by the fact that the city of Boston banned the sale of the second installment of *Scribner's Magazine*, an act which no doubt helped sales of the book considerably.[1]

Following his normal writing style, Hemingway based *A Farewell to Arms* upon his own experience as a Red Cross ambulance driver in World War I.[2] He had joined the Red Cross at the age of 18 after being turned down by the military because of defective vision and was sent to the Italian front in April of 1918. A youthful flush of enthusiasm for

---

1.   S. Donaldson, 'Introduction', in Donaldson (ed.), *New Essays*, pp. 1-25, discusses the Boston ban in detail.

2.   The fullest discussion of this is now M.S. Reynolds, *Hemingway's First War: The Making of A Farewell to Arms* (Princeton, NJ: Princeton University Press, 1976). Reynolds includes some interesting World War I photographs of both Hemingway and other figures who find their way into his fictional tale, including Agnes von Kurowsky. P. Young, *Ernest Hemingway: A Reconsideration* (University Park: Pennsylvania State University Press, 1966), is also an important, if controversial, work on this subject, offering a psychoanalytical interpretation of both Hemingway and his fiction based upon the impact of the wartime experience upon him.

adventure later gave way to a more cynical assessment of the experience. As Hemingway later remarked in 1942,

> I was an awful dope when I went to the last war. I can remember just thinking that we were the home team and the Austrians were the visiting team.[1]

Hemingway was wounded on 8 July 1918, just a few days short of his nineteenth birthday, and only a week after he had been serving in the front-line trenches. He received severe wounds as a result of enemy machine-gun and mortar fire; a reported 227 shell fragments were removed from his legs. In spite of his wounds he managed to carry another wounded soldier on his back to safety, an act for which he was awarded a silver medal for valour from the Italian government.[2] His experience created quite a stir, since he was among the first Americans to be wounded in Italy, and his case was reported in many of the newspapers back home in his native Chicago. He was eventually sent to the American Hospital in Milan for recovery, where he was nursed back to health by, among others, a Red Cross nurse named Agnes von Kurowsky. Hemingway fell head over heels in love with her, despite the fact that she was seven years his senior.

It is not hard to see that this experience is transformed by Hemingway into what happens to Frederic Henry in *A Farewell to Arms*. Here, once again, we see how the facts of life as he knew them are the source for his narrative creativity. The experience of being so badly wounded was a profound one for the young Hemingway, and brought him face to face with death in a way that he had not encountered it before. As he was later to describe the incident,

> I died then. I felt my soul or something coming right out of my body, like you'd pull a silk handkerchief out of a pocket by one corner. It flew around and then came back and went in again and I wasn't dead anymore![3]

1. Cited in Baker, *Ernest Hemingway*, p. 57.
2. Lynn, *Hemingway*, pp. 69-86, discusses Hemingway's wounding and how it becomes intertwined within the narrative of his fictional work.
3. Reported by M. Cowley, 'A Portrait of Mister Papa', in *Life* 26 (10 January 1949), pp. 86-101. (This article is reprinted in J.K.M. McCaffery [ed.], *Ernest Hemingway: The Man and his Work* [New York: The Word Publishing Company, 1950], pp. 26-48.) S. Sanderson, *Hemingway* (London: Oliver & Boyd, 1961), p. 59, describes this as Hemingway's 'almost uncommunicable experience'. Also,

His romantic view of war was altered by the agonies of personal experience.[1] A more realistic view of the traumas involved in war is to be found in some of Hemingway's letters to his family. He writes to his father, in a passage reminiscent of Eccl. 1.1-7 noted above,

> There are no heroes in this war...All the heroes are dead...Dying is a very simple thing. I've looked at death and really I know. If I should have died, it would have been...quite the easiest thing I ever did...And how much better to die in all the happy period of undisillusioned youth, to go out in a blaze of light, than to have your body worn out and old and illusions shattered.[2]

Another key event in Hemingway's life also finds expression in the novel—the agonies of a difficult childbirth in which the life of the mother is threatened. In the novel the trauma of Catherine's prolonged labour, which eventually demands that a Caesarean be performed, is the emotional climax of the story. Here too art was imitating life, for Hemingway's second wife Pauline Pfeiffer gave birth to their first son by Caesarean following a harrowing eighteen-hour long labour. This took place at the end of June 1928 just as Hemingway was working on the novel and the experience clearly helped him compose the final chapter of the book.

Let us now consider how the central motif of birth-death is brought together in the love affair between Catherine Barkley and Frederic Henry.

d. *The Inescapable 'Biological Trap' of Life*

Dewey Ganzel has described the real concern of *A Farewell to Arms* as 'the discovery of death' in which the main character, Frederic Henry,

---

see A. Josephs, 'Hemingway's out of Body Experience', *HR* 2 (1983), pp. 11-17, for an interesting discussion of this incident in Hemingway's life and how it is reflected in his later fiction.

1.   Donaldson, *By Force of Will*, p. 126, describes *A Farewell to Arms* as 'Hemingway's most extended fictional statement of his disillusionment'.

2.   Cited in Baker, *Ernest Hemingway*, p. 79. Yet it would be a mistake to assume that *A Farewell to Arms* was written just so that Hemingway could express his own personal experiences in narrative form. As he explained later to Lillian Ross (*Portrait of Hemingway* [Harmondsworth: Penguin Books, 1962], p. 47) about why he wrote the novel: 'I am not interested in the G.I. who wasn't one...Or in the injustices done to *me*, with a capital M. I am interested in the goddam science of war.'

is forced to recognize the inevitability of death and the concomitant frustration of trying to secure something of value from its onslaught.[1]

Indeed, there is much to be said for reading *A Farewell to Arms* as an exploration of how death actually gives definition to life in precisely the same way that the writer of Ecclesiastes presents death as the great focal point for his views of life's meaning. Thus Ganzel helpfully suggests that the narrative of the novel concerns the inexorable process of the reduction of choices in life. Ultimately everything culminates in death— supremely in *A Farewell to Arms* with the death of Catherine. For Frederic, life itself is defined by the process of death; he learns the meaning of life by falling hopelessly in love with Catherine, only to find that her life is cruelly taken from him. A 'death-in-life' motif is found throughout the novel, and can most clearly be seen in Catherine's death as a result of childbirth.

Normally, childbirth is recognized as the supreme illustration of hope in life. It guarantees that there is value and joy in living, that life has some purpose and meaning. This is not the case in *A Farewell to Arms* and it is through his reversal of expectations normally associated with childbirth that Hemingway takes his most creative step in the novel. There is, in the words of Qoheleth, 'a time to give birth', yes; but there is also 'a time to die' and in this instance, in Hemingway's powerful treatment, the two are one and come at the same time.

The reader is alerted early on as to the disaster that Catherine's unplanned pregnancy will bring to the couple. At times it is alluded to directly, and at times it is couched in metaphor; often the metaphorical instances are more devastating, having what might be described as an 'emotional delayed fuse' within them. In the very first chapter of the book we have a powerful prefiguration of Catherine's death, associating the imagery of pregnancy with the death-dealing soldiers who carry

> under their capes the two leather cartridge-boxes on the front of their belts, great leather boxes heavy with the packs of clips of thin, long 6.5 mm. cartridges, bulged forward under the capes so that the men, passing on the road, marched as though they were six months gone with child.

---

1. '*A Farewell to Arms*: The Danger of Imagination', *SR* 79 (1971), pp. 576-77. Ganzel argues that this thematic concern on the part of Hemingway is perfectly reflected in the narrative structure of the novel. He comments, 'It is Frederic's discovery of death which directs the novel' (p. 591).

In 2:17 we are given a conversation between Frederic and Catherine's fellow nurse, the Scot Helen Ferguson, along these lines:

> 'Will you come to our wedding, Fergie?' I said to her once.
> 'You'll never get married.'
> 'We will.'
> 'No you won't.'
> 'Why not?'
> 'You'll fight before you'll marry.'
> 'We never fight.'
> 'You've time yet.'
> 'We don't fight.'
> 'You'll die then. Fight or die. That's what people do. They don't marry.'
> I reached for her hand. 'Don't take hold of me,' she said. 'I'm not crying. Maybe you'll be all right you two. But watch out you don't get her in trouble.'

However, the inevitable happens and Catherine does become pregnant. In 2:21 she announces her pregnancy to Frederic and there is a touching passage in which they unite to face the reality of the situation. The passage contains a memorable exchange between the two which reveals how Frederic views her pregnancy as a 'trap', recalling Eccl. 9.12 and its declaration that life contains a trap which leads to death:

> We were quiet a while and did not talk. Catherine was sitting on the bed and I was looking at her but we did not touch each other. We were apart as when someone comes into a room and people are self-conscious. She put out her hand and took mine.
> 'You aren't angry are you, darling?'
> 'No.'
> 'And you don't feel trapped?'
> 'Maybe a little. But not by you.'
> 'I didn't mean by me. You mustn't be stupid. I meant trapped at all.'
> 'You always feel trapped biologically.'

In 5:38 Catherine mentions that the doctor had told her that she was rather narrow in the hips—a clear but ominous warning of the disaster that is to come.[1]

One of the most memorable passages in the whole of the book has Frederic think aloud about the cruelty of fate. In 5:41, immediately after

---

1. N. Friedman, 'Small Hips, not War', in J. Gellens (ed.), *Twentieth Century Interpretations of A Farewell to Arms: A Collection of Critical Essays* (Englewood Cliffs, NJ: Prentice-Hall, 1970), pp. 105-108, offers an interesting discussion of this.

he has been told that the baby has died, Frederic gives his assessment of the situation:

> Now Catherine would die. That was what you did. You died. You did not know what it was all about. You never had time to learn. They threw you in and told you the rules and the first time they caught you off base they killed you. Or they killed you gratuitously like Aymo. Or gave you syphilis like Rinaldi. But they killed you in the end. You could count on that. Stay around and they would kill you.[1]

And in Catherine's words, her final ones to Frederic, she similarly gives her opinion about the senselessness of the situation, bemoaning the absurdity of it all: 'I'm not a bit afraid. It's just a dirty trick.' The final words of the novel, in which Henry is made to say his good-byes to Catherine, are among the most moving that Hemingway penned. Henry sends the nurses out of the room in which the dead Catherine lies, and then we read:

> But after I had got them out and shut the door and turned off the light it wasn't any good. It was like saying goodbye to a statue. After a while I went out and left the hospital and walked back to the hotel in the rain.

The passage is absolutely crucial for the establishment of Henry's character and his relationship with Catherine. It is only through her death that Frederic is able to comprehend the true nature of love. Paradoxically, he discovers that he is more in love with her when staring death in the face than he ever was when she was alive. He comes to understand more about her, and at the same time more about himself, than he could ever have imagined possible. As Gwen L. Nagel states,

> Frederic can more closely relate to Catherine in death, for he is now in a position that Catherine was in when they first met: he is alone, and he is shattered by the loss of a lover.[2]

---

1. B. Stolzfus, 'A Sliding Discourse: The Language of *A Farewell to Arms*', in Donaldson (ed.), *New Essays*, pp. 109-36, notes that this is one of only five passages in the novel where Hemingway shifts from his style of first-person to second-person narration.

2. 'A Tessara for Frederic Henry: Imagery and Recurrence in *A Farewell to Arms*', in Wagner (ed.), *Ernest Hemingway*, p. 192. Nagel offers an interesting discussion of how the theme of the search for the identity of Frederic Henry is treated by Hemingway within the novel.

The death of Catherine is without doubt the emotional climax of the book, enduring with the reader long after it is first read.[1] This is partly because the concluding chapter of the book is supported by several sections which lend emotive power to the scene. One of the most powerful passages is inserted at this point by Hemingway to demonstrate the capriciousness of life. It is the celebrated 'ants in the campfire' story, which E.M. Halliday has described as a parable representing 'Hemingway's *Weltanschauung* at its most pessimistic':[2]

> Once in camp I put a log on top of the fire and it was full of ants. As it commenced to burn, the ants swarmed out and went first towards the centre where the fire was; then turned back and ran towards the end. When there were enough on the end they fell off into the fire. Some got out, their bodies burned and flattened, and went off not knowing where they were going. But most of them went towards the fire and then back towards the end and swarmed on the cool end and finally fell into the fire. I remember thinking at the time that it was the end of the world and a splendid chance to be a messiah and lift the log off the fire and throw it out where the ants could get off onto the ground. But I did not do anything but throw a tin cup of water on the log, so that I would have the cup empty to put whisky in before I added water to it. I think the cup of water on the burning log only steamed the ants.

James F. Light offers the interesting thought about this passage that it demonstrates how closely connected are the divine and the human, united, as it were, through a mutually exclusive self-interest. Frederic Henry never denies the existence of God outright. In fact, he turns to God, praying in a desperate effort to have Catherine's life spared as she hovers near death.[3] But God is as distant and uncaring as Frederic himself was when he did not act to save the ants on the campfire log

---

1.   Some commentators suggest that Hemingway makes Catherine responsible for her own death, as well as the death of the child which she struggles to bring to birth. Thus, Fetterley, '*A Farewell to Arms*', p. 205, remarks of Catherine, 'She presents that *reductio ad absurdum* of the female experience: she feels guilty for dying and apologizes to the doctor for taking up his valuable time with her death— "I'm sorry I go on so long".'

2.   'Hemingway's Ambiguity', p. 62.

3.   Donaldson, *By Force of Will*, pp. 228-29, offers an interesting discussion on how Hemingway's own conversion to Catholicism informs his understanding of the nature of true prayer within his fiction.

which he remembers from years ago. In short, the inefficacy of Henry's prayer to God that Catherine's life be spared is taken to be a demonstration of God's selfishness. It is proof that the human being does not benefit from his or her contact with the Divine. As Light puts it,

> For Lt. Henry this lack of reciprocity makes for the image of a God who in his eternal selfishness is the origin of human selfishness, so that man in his selfishness most accurately reflects God.[1]

What is meant here is, of course, that Henry reminisces about the ants on the log and imagines himself as the messiah who could rescue them from the burning fire but who does not; instead, selfishly, he throws his cup of water on the fire. Light goes on to offer the interpretative comment: 'Divinity, however, does not ease the pain of man's existence, and Henry does not save the ants'.[2] No wonder that this passage is often cited as among Hemingway's most pessimistic. After having learned the painful lessons of defeat in war Frederic makes a 'separate peace' and seeks to ease the pain of his existence elsewhere. Ironically, it is here in the security of a safe haven that he will experience total disaster. It is here, in the sanctuary of the Swiss city of Lausanne, that he will come to feel for himself the truth of which Qoheleth spoke: 'There is a time to give birth and a time to die'. Hemingway could hardly have composed a more gut-wretching ending to the novel. He pulls no punches, sparing no thought for the emotions of the reader. How would such a no-holds-barred ending be accepted by the public?

We turn now to consider how Hemingway's novel fared as it was translated into film.

3. *Film Adaptations of* A Farewell to Arms

Hemingway's novels and short stories were the subject of considerable interest on the part of both Hollywood and Broadway, where powerful figures were aware of the popularity of his work and were quick to try and cash in on it. Over a dozen of his works have found their way onto

---

1. J.F. Light, 'The Religion of Death in *A Farewell to Arms*', *MFS* 7 (1961–62), p. 170. This article is reprinted in Baker (ed.), *Ernest Hemingway*, pp. 37-40.
2. Light, 'The Religion of Death', p. 170.

the stage and silver screen.[1] *A Farewell to Arms* was no exception and was converted into theatrical formats soon after its publication in 1929. A stage play based on the novel was written by Laurence Stallings in 1930, opening in New York in September of that year. The play was not a great commercial success and closed after a run of only three weeks. Meanwhile, in 1939 Orson Welles adapted *A Farewell to Arms* for radio as a part of *The Campbell Playhouse* series broadcast by the Columbia Broadcasting System (CBS) in the United States, and this was accepted with critical acclaim. Welles himself took the role of Frederic Henry and Katharine Hepburn played the role of Catherine Barkley in this production.

However, it is through the two film adaptations that *A Farewell to Arms* has had its greatest public exposure and it is to these that we turn. We will concentrate our attention on the ways in which the films deal with the relationship of Catherine Barkley and Frederic Henry, and on how the novel's central theme of 'birth-death' is expressed. By focusing in this way we shall see how the films allow us to discuss the question of whether Hemingway's story contains any elements of optimism within it.

a. *Frank Borzago's Version (1932)*
This film was made with all the hype and promise that Hollywood and Paramount Pictures could muster. Director Frank Borzago, who had won Oscars for his films *Seventh Heaven* (1927) and *Bad Girl* (1931), was hired to make the film. It starred Gary Cooper in the role of Frederic Henry, Helen Hayes in the role of Catherine Barkley and Adolphe Menjou as Rinaldi. The screenplay was a joint effort by Benjamin Glazer and Oliver H.P. Garrett who took considerable liberties in adapting Hemingway's novel for the silver screen. For example, in her initial meeting with Frederic, Catherine's loose moral character is toned down somewhat and he is portrayed as the more aggressive of the two when it comes to their physical relationship. One of the most

---

1.   F.M. Laurence, 'Hollywood Publicity and Hemingway's Popular Reputation', *JPC* 6 (1972), p. 30, lists fourteen films based on Hemingway's work up to 1964. He discusses how Hollywood publicity vulgarized and sensationalized Hemingway's work in order to increase ticket sales at the box-office, inadvertently enhancing the author's own reputation.

revealing changes of the screenplay is that Frederic and Catherine have a marriage (of sorts!) performed by the priest while Henry is in the American hospital in Milan.

This is somewhat at odds with the declaration in the novel at 2:18 made by Catherine to Frederic when he is convalescing in the hospital in Milan: 'What good would it do to marry now? We're really married. I couldn't be any more married.' This conventional adaptation was done, no doubt, to lessen the scandal which might have arisen should Catherine become pregnant by Frederic without being married to him. Hemingway's sympathetic portrayal of an illicit love affair simply could not be allowed to stand unchallenged in the prudish 1930s; the traditional sanctity of marriage, and the happiness that is assumed to accompany it, must be maintained, even at the cost of faithfulness to the original novel.

There are also many subtle alterations to the main story line, including Rinaldi's operating on Frederic's wounded leg, Catherine's escape to Switzerland on her own, as well as Frederic's subsequent escape in a small boat to meet her there (in the novel they escape from Italy together).

However, at several other points the film is quite faithful to the story line of the novel, especially as it moves to its emotional climax—the death of Catherine. Several religious features of Hemingway's story find expression within the film at this point. For instance, as Catherine lies on her deathbed and Frederic eats breakfast across the street in a nearby café, he prays to God that she might be spared:

> Dear God...O, God...Please don't let her die. I'll do anything for you if you don't let her die. You took the baby...that was all right. But please don't let her die. Please...please God, don't let her die.

The rain motif, symbolizing all that is depressing and nasty within life, is kept fairly consistently throughout the film. Indeed at one point Catherine is made to say that she hates the rain because she sees her own death within it, echoing her words in the novel in 2:19. The desertion of Henry from the Italian army is rather poorly portrayed within the film. As Hemingway himself describes it,

> In the first picture version Lt. Henry deserted because he didn't get any mail and then the whole Italian army went along it seems to keep him company.[1]

1. In a letter to Wallace Meyer dated 24 May 1957. The full letter, which details

Perhaps the most striking liberty that is taken with Hemingway's original story is the fact that the Borzago film was made with two endings, one faithful to the novel in that it presented Catherine's death and the other offering an alternative, a much more optimistic vision in that she lives. In the alternative ending of the film, although Catherine appears to die in the arms of her husband/lover Frederic, she revives miraculously and faces the bright, new future together with her greatly relieved husband! The alternative ending of the film has been the focus of considerable comment and criticism. David Shipman offers his opinion in favour of the ending which is faithful to Hemingway's novel when he remarks that the film

> has a poor ending with Death, Wagner's *Liebestod* and the Armistice all fighting for attention—though we should be grateful that they did not use the alternative 'happy' ending which had been shot.[1]

The fact that Paramount studios decided to make the film with two different endings, one in which Catherine dies and the other in which she appears to recover following her collapse in the arms of Frederic, is the greatest single departure from the story line of Hemingway's novel.[2] This adaptation of the novel, where the commercial pressures of Hollywood apparently meant that a 'happy ending' was added to the film, was done much to Hemingway's personal disgust and he fought it vehemently.

Nevertheless, the film was a hit with the public at large, earning more money at the box office than any other film of the year. It was also a critical success, winning Oscars for Cinematography and Sound-Recording. Given its rather short length (a mere 80 minutes), Borzago's effort has much to commend it, despite some of the liberties which were taken with the story line.

Hemingway's dissatisfaction with the later David Selznick adaptation of his novel (namely the 1957 film adaptation), is provided in Baker (ed.), *Ernest Hemingway*, p. 875.

1. *The Story of Cinema* (London: Hodder & Stoughton, 1982), p. 249.

2. The two endings are discussed in G.D. Phillips, *Hemingway and Film* (New York: Frederic Ungar, 1980), pp. 20-25. Phillips notes that movie theatres were able to order which of the two endings they thought would appeal to their audiences. The version available on videocassette through Virgin Records (1990) has the original ending, the one in which Catherine dies. I have been unable to locate a copy of the film which has the alternative ending.

b. *Charles Vidor's Version (1957)*
This film adaptation of Hemingway's novel was produced by the David Selznick Studios with the screenplay written by Ben Hecht based upon both Hemingway's novel and the play adaptation of it by Laurence Stallings. It was marketed as an extravagant remake of Borzago's classic of 25 years earlier, with the additional gimmick that it was shot on location in Italy. The film starred Rock Hudson as Frederic Henry, Selznick's own wife Jennifer Jones as Catherine Barkley, and Vittorio De Sica as Rinaldi. Originally it was to have been directed by John Huston, but a clash of personalities between this talented director and Selznick meant that Huston walked off of the set just as shooting was to begin.[1] He was replaced by Charles Vidor, a lesser known director whom Selznick could control more easily.

In many respects the film is much closer to the original novel than was Borzago's interpretation. The war is given a much more important place in this film than it had in Borzago's film, or for that matter in Hemingway's novel. In fact, the war scenes are so expanded that the delicate balance of the tale as a love story rather than a war story is somewhat lost. This emphasis on the World War I setting is usually said to be due to the influence of producer David Selznick himself, who, riding high on the critical success of his *Gone with the Wind* (1939), tried to portray the Caporetto retreat in similar style to the acclaimed portrayal of the siege of Atlanta in the earlier film. Yet, even here there are significant differences. For instance, Lt Henry's wounding is completely rewritten and made to take place not in a bunker while eating with his fellow ambulancemen, but in the midst of a battle as he seeks to mobilize the ambulances for action. The Italian army surgeon Rinaldi, who drops from the story line when the Italian army begins its retreat, has a much more prominent role in the retreat itself. He is made into the officer executed by a firing squad for being a traitor, the act which finally pushes Frederic over the edge and drives him to desert (in the book it is an unnamed lieutenant-colonel who is executed). The priest is also given a much fuller role than in the novel. He is made to stay behind with the wounded troops when the Italian army begins the retreat at Caporetto. He becomes a true symbol of bravery in

1. Huston, *An Open Book*, pp. 270-73, gives his version of the event. Grobel, *The Hustons*, pp. 443-48, provides additional details.

the film, leading the wounded soldiers in a song as the hospital is shelled by the advancing German and Austrian armies. We are left with the impression that he dies courageously—the film cuts away from him just as a shell hits the wardroom in which he is standing amidst the wounded. Several of the continuities between the film and Hemingway's novel are worth noting, especially as they bring out the importance of the birth-death theme and the main vehicle for expressing it—the rain motif.

Included in the opening sequences is a voice-over by Frederic Henry, taken from the ominous description in 1:1 where the first indication of the birth-death motif is presented. Here the marching soldiers appear like pregnant women:

> The war had slowed down during the winter, but the troops still marched with heavily-loaded cartridge boxes bulging forward under their capes as though they were six months gone with child.

The dialogue between Catherine and Frederic at the horse races in which she first tells him that she is pregnant is preserved, including the provocative image of the 'trap of life':

Catherine:	That's why I didn't tell you before. I didn't want you to feel trapped. Tell me you're not trapped.
Frederic:	You always feel trapped, biologically.
Catherine:	'Always' isn't a pretty word.

The way in which the marriage theme is handled within the film is also quite revealing. While Vidor does not follow the pathway of propriety that Borzago did and actually have Catherine and Frederic marry, he does insert something like a marriage scene into the film which is not contained in the book. Catherine voices her wedding vows to Frederic shortly after revealing her pregnancy to him. Interestingly, Frederic does not reciprocate these vows, which are made using the traditional formulae of the *Book of Common Prayer*:

Catherine:	I, Catherine, take thee, Frederic, for my wedded husband.
Frederic:	To have and to hold. Till death do us part.
Catherine:	Till death do us part.

The childbirth scene is one of the most harrowing ever portrayed on screen, and remains with the viewer for a long time after he or she has seen it—a testimony to the talents of the actress Jennifer Jones. This is quite an accomplishment in itself since the scene does not focus on the medical side of things; it is not filled with blood and gore, but concentrates instead on the facial expressions of Catherine and Frederic and their conversation as she is in labour.

The film recreates the scene of Frederic's visit to the café across the street from the hospital in Lausanne where Catherine has been engaged in her life-and-death struggle with childbirth. The screenplay takes one major liberty in having the obstetrician go with Frederic to the café, shortly after having informed him about the death of the baby son. This helps to heighten the drama of the scene, making the inevitable sledge-hammer of Catherine's death fall even more heavily upon the hapless Frederic. Frederic mutters to himself over his coffee, in words which are taken virtually phrase by phrase from the novel, and deliberately written in the second person so as to draw the reader into the sentiments contained within them:

> You don't know what it's all about. You never had time to learn. They throw you in and tell you the rules, and the first time they catch you off base, they kill you. You can count on that! Stay around and they'll kill you. Poor Cath. Poor dear Cath. This is the price you pay for sleeping together.
> She didn't have a bad time when she was pregnant. She had a good time. She was hardly ever sick. She wasn't even very uncomfortable until... until it was the last. But you never get away with anything. Get away, hell! They get you in the end.

After the climactic death of Catherine, Henry is made to say to her, as he kisses her for the final time and utters words true to the ending of the novel itself,

> Darling, my wonderful darling. You'll never leave me. You're with me till I die, my darling. Till I die. [*He kisses her.*] Cold! Cold! You're so cold, Cath. Like a statue!

While this film version of *A Farewell to Arms* does not go so far as to provide us with a fictional ending completely at odds with Hemingway's original (as did Borzago's alternative ending), it does subtly alter the ending of the novel in several important ways.

First, the final words we hear spoken by Catherine are different in the film from those contained in the book. In the novel her last words are spoken to Frederic as he is at her bedside; these are preserved within the film fairly accurately, broken up into three short sentences: 'I'll come and stay with you nights. I'm not a bit afraid, darling. It's just a dirty trick!' If these were the last words we hear from Catherine in the film we might feel that loyalty to Hemingway's ending of the story had been maintained, and that Catherine's rather pessimistic final sentence in the novel is given its due weight. However, these are not the last words of Catherine which we, as an audience, hear for there is a flashback scene which follows. As Frederic leaves the hospital and walks away along the wet pavement he recalls several things Catherine has said to him during their fated love affair. Three separate sayings are interwoven into this flashback experienced by Frederic, including a fade-in/fade-out clip from an earlier scene when the two lovers are in bed together. The three statements of Catherine are:

> Won't it be fun! There'll be three of us!

> I'm not a bit afraid, darling. I just hate it.

> Darling, you will be good to me, won't you? You will, won't you? Because we're going to have a strange life. But it's the only life I want.

It is interesting that two of the three are rather optimistic declarations, based on the hope of happiness which Catherine anticipates in her life with Frederic. The second, pessimistic statement is from the final death bed scene, although it is a slightly amended declaration by Catherine and does not appear in the original scene as such; it is really a conflation of two separate lines spoken earlier at different times.

Secondly, we note how the rain motif, so important as a thematic thread running throughout the novel, is presented at the ending of the film. In the final chapter of the novel Hemingway mentions three times in the narrative that it is raining during the course of Catherine's difficult labour; this is in addition to the final reference to Frederic walking away in the rain following her death. Similarly, in the film we are given no less than four different scenes which emphasize that it is raining during her trial. The first occurs as she is in the delivery room struggling to give birth and the camera pans back to reveal through the windows above that it is raining outside. The second takes place when Frederic leaves the delivery room under doctor's orders and retreats to a hallway at the end of which is a door to the outside. Through the glass panes of this door we can see again that it is raining. The third scene takes place just after Frederic has given his consent for Catherine to have the Caesarean. He enters her room and the following lines are exchanged between them:

Catherine: Darling, is it raining?
Frederic: No, I don't think so.
Catherine: I think it's raining.

Frederic lies here, telling her that he doesn't think it is raining, even though he knows full well that it is. The fourth scene takes place immediately afterwards as the Caesarean is being performed and Frederic watches from an observation hall above. Here we do not actually see the rain but we can hear the downpour going on outside as the operation takes place; it is raining outside.

Most importantly, following Catherine's death, we are given a scene in which Frederic is seen leaving the hospital where she has died, stepping out into the street, and walking away. But what is striking here is the fact that it is no longer raining! To be fair, the rain has just ended, if the wet pavements and the puddles we see in the street are anything to go on, but the rain is not falling down as Frederic leaves the scene. This is in sharp contrast to the novel itself, in which Hemingway makes a deliberate point of ending the story with the word 'rain', just to highlight the motif he had used so effectively throughout the book.

Finally, it is worth making an observation about the other memorable image of the absurdity of life contained in the final chapter of the book, the so-called 'parable of the ants in the fire'. Neither of the film interpretations of *A Farewell to Arms* include this scene within their adaptations. In some ways this omission is understandable; it would be very difficult to present visually what is, in effect, a memory of Frederic. However, these difficulties are not insurmountable. The story could have been done as a flashback while Frederic is agonizing over his coffee and brioche about Catherine's state of health, or, alternatively, it could have been spoken by Frederic to the doctor as they sat together in the restaurant. One cannot help but lament the fact that such an powerful image was not taken up within either of the two films, since it goes far in expressing the feelings of Frederic about his situation.

4. *Ecclesiastes and* A Farewell to Arms: *Is there Room for Optimism?*

Above I noted how both Ecclesiastes and *A Farewell to Arms* are often interpreted as profoundly pessimistic works of literature; first readings of either of them invariably lead to such conclusions. In the past Ecclesiastes has often been appealed to as the wellspring from which many celebrated pessimists have drunk deeply.[1] The renowned sceptic Ernst Renan, revealing his own prejudices, once described it in deliberately ironical terms as 'a charming book, the only pleasant book that has been composed by a Jew'.[2] But is this the whole story? Is it fair to dismiss the book as having nothing positive to offer? Others see Ecclesiastes, and indeed *A Farewell to Arms*, as containing elements of optimism in the face of the obvious vagaries of life. Northrop Frye offers another opinion on the author of Qoheleth:

> He is not a weary pessimist tired of life; he is a vigorous realist determined to smash his way through every locked door of repression in his mind.[3]

In short, it seems that the book of Ecclesiastes is able to generate quite differing opinions about the basic mind set of its author. At times he appears exceedingly pessimistic; of that there can be no doubt. But there is at the same time something within the content of the book as a whole which militates against such a one-sided assessment of its message. As Graham Ogden remarks,

> The contents of the book appear to be so confusing that two opposite, and not just variant interpretations seem possible. Either Qoheleth contains contradictory statements, or his diverse material forces the interpreter to choose to emphasize one aspect rather than another.[4]

How do we reconcile these two diametrically opposed perspectives: one which sees purpose, meaning and value in life and the other which, apparently, sees life as ultimately empty and void? The various attempts to answer this dilemma are the history of the interpretation of Ecclesiastes in a nutshell. On any reckoning, the question of the ambiguous perspective on value in life remains central to all scholarly investigation of Ecclesiastes.

In recent years a host of new monographs, commentaries and articles have been written in order to try to come to terms with the meaning of

---

1.   C.H.H. Wright, *The Book of Koheleth, Commonly Called Ecclesiastes, Considered in Relation to Modern Criticism and to the Doctrines of Modern Pessimism* (London: Hodder & Stoughton, 1883), pp. 141-84, discusses it in relation to Schopenhauer, von Hartmann and Buddhism.

2.   *L'antichrist* (Paris: M. Lévy Frères, 1873), p. 101. The passage is discussed in Whitley, *Koheleth*, p. 1.

3.   *The Great Code: The Bible and Literature* (London: Ark Paperbacks, 1982), p. 123.

4.   *Qoheleth* (Sheffield: JSOT Press, 1987), p. 10.

the book. A number of interpretations have wrestled with the structure and integrity of the work as a whole, producing a wide range of interesting and complex, if incompatible, solutions to the plan of the book.[1] The essential problem here is the composite nature of Ecclesiastes and the fact that it fails to maintain a consistency of argument in the midst of its teaching. A variety of attempts at 'cracking the code' of Qoheleth have been put forward. Some have attempted to solve the dilemma presented by its conflicting teaching on a source-critical basis; that is to say, maintaining that the two opposing attitudes to life are the result of the uneasy integration of two different sources into the completed work. Others have sought to hold the two viewpoints together by suggesting that they represent different periods of the author's own life, that the earlier more positive attitudes to life are the result of youthful enthusiasm and that this eventually gives way to the cynicism of later life. Yet another means of explaining the inconsistencies of the book is the suggestion that the author is quoting sections from his opponents, and since there was no means whereby the equivalent of quotation marks could be inserted in the Hebrew, the modern reader tends to confuse these particular passages with the genuine thoughts of the author himself. Still others have attempted to solve the puzzle by holding the two perspectives together within the completed work and have seen them as flip sides of the same coin, offering what is in effect a dialectical interpretation of the book. One of the most helpful attempts to pursue this particular line of interpretation is that of Michael V. Fox, who makes a similar observation to that of Ogden in his study of the book. However, Fox is not afraid to label these tensions as out-and-out *contradictions* within Qoheleth, although he does take a slightly different path towards their resolution. Whereas most are content to accept the contradictions as arising out of our conflicting interpretations of Ecclesiastes, Fox sees them in another way. As he explains,

> Qohelet uses contradictions as the lens through which to view life; it is appropriate, then, that we use his contradictions as the angle of approach to his thought.[2]

---

1. Crenshaw, *Ecclesiastes*, pp. 34-49, discusses these. Also worth consulting on this approach is A.G. Wright, 'The Riddle of the Sphinx: The Structure of the Book of Qoheleth', *CBQ* 30 (1968), pp. 313-34.

2. *Qohelet and his Contradictions*, p. 11.

In other words, the front line in the battlefield of interpretation of Ecclesiastes is shifted from the variety of differing assessments about the *true* meaning of the text to a discussion about the flexibility of the mind of the author Qoheleth himself, who is assumed to have embodied contradictions within his work as a means to an end. Little wonder that Fox takes the Epilogue of 12.9-14 as an essential component of the original author's message in the book, and, indeed, turns to that passage as one of the keys to his interpretation of it (see below).

In one sense, we could view the cinematic interpretations of Hemingway's rather depressing novel as adopting precisely the same sort of approach. These films wrestle with what is, on the surface, an extremely gloomy story, filled with death and loss, which readily lends itself to pessimistic interpretations. To neutralize this despair the films each, in their own way, inject an optimistic ingredient to the film, effectively creating a different interpretation of it. In the case of Borzago's 1932 film the possibility of showing a happy ending is offered, at least to theatre owners so minded. In the case of Charles Vidor's 1957 version, a slightly more optimistic ending (in which Hemingway's rain motif, the harbinger of death, is downplayed somewhat) is provided. But what of the two literary works themselves, Ecclesiastes and *A Farewell to Arms*? Is there sufficient material within the books themselves to justify these more optimistic interpretations on offer, especially by the film makers in their adaptations of *A Farewell to Arms*? Let us examine each in turn, noting particular points of interest paralleled within the two books along the way.

a. *The Optimism of Qoheleth*

I noted above how the inevitability of death colours the opinion of Qoheleth about the meaning and purpose of life. Many interpreters feel that for him death sets the boundaries on life, effectively evacuating human life of any significance. Qoheleth seems to say that there is no escaping from the reality of death—it is the ultimate fact of life and has a determined place in the scheme of things in precisely the same way that birth does (as Eccl. 3.2a asserts). One of the most well-known lines from Ecclesiastes is often used at funerals as a declaration of the mortality of humankind and the reality of death itself. The well-known line spoken at graveside interments, 'ashes to ashes, dust to dust', is based upon Eccl. 3.20 (probably echoing Gen. 3.19): 'All go to one place; all are from the dust, and all turn to dust again' (RSV). But how far are Qoheleth's beliefs about death themselves determined by his ideas about the afterlife? Is it possible that he views life beyond the grave in a more positive light? Clearly he does believe in the Jewish idea of Sheol (as 9.10 indicates), but precisely how much is invested in this abode of the dead by Qoheleth is a matter of great speculation. To put the question in another form: Does Qoheleth have a belief in the resurrection of the dead? Might this in some way purge his thoroughly negative view of life? These questions are not as strange as they might first appear. After all, within the mainstream of the Judaeo-Christian tradition the difficulties of life are set over against belief in the resurrection from the dead and the scales of the meaning of human existence adjusted accordingly. Unfortunately, the answer to these questions, at least as far as Qoheleth is concerned, is almost certainly a resounding 'No!' Qoheleth says nothing concrete about his belief in anything beyond the stark reality of the grave. For Qoheleth meaning and purpose does not lie beyond the grave. What meaning there is in human existence must be found within the bounds of this life. As Howard N. Bream puts it, 'His realistic bent of mind led him to accept death as inevitable and final'.[1] Nevertheless, there are a number of passages in Ecclesiastes in which the active pursuit of pleasure and joy within this life is encouraged. At several places the writer of Ecclesiastes goes so far as to suggest that these pleasures of life are gifts from God himself. Indeed, one of the most memorable lines from Ecclesiastes expresses a strikingly hedonistic outlook on life. In 8.15 we read,

> And I commend enjoyment, for man has no good thing under the sun but
> to eat and drink, and enjoy himself, for this will go with him in his toil
> through the days of life which God gives him under the sun.

Perhaps not so surprisingly, this has a parallel in Hemingway's novel. In 3:32, as Frederic seeks to justify his desertion from the Italian army, he says, 'I was not made to think. I was made to eat. My God, yes. Eat and drink and sleep with Catherine.' At several points within the narrative of *A Farewell to Arms* a great deal of attention to detail is given over to just what is eaten and drunk by the various characters. Passages abound

---

1. 'Life without Resurrection: Two Perspectives from Qoheleth', in H.N. Bream, R.D. Heim and C.A. Moore (eds.), *A Light unto my Path: Old Testament Studies in Honor of Jacob M. Myers* (Philadelphia: Temple University Press, 1974), p. 53. Similarly, Murphy, *Ecclesiastes*, p. lxviii, remarks, 'It is abundantly clear that Qoheleth does not hold out any hope for life after death'.

in which descriptions of wines, liqueurs and speciality items from Italian, French and Swiss kitchens are provided, all of which help to provide an example of precisely the kind of attitude to life that Qoheleth commends in his writing. This positive attitude towards the good things in life is worth exploring further, for it does provide the basis for a more positive interpretation of Ecclesiastes. Perhaps the most vocal exponent of this particular approach is R.N. Whybray.[1] In an influential and stimulating article, Whybray identifies seven passages in which the author recommends a whole-hearted pursuit of the joys of life (2.24a; 3.12, 22a; 5.17; 8.15a; 9.7-9a; 11.7–12.1a).[2] For example, we read in 3.10-13 the concluding remarks made on the highly poetic section 3.1-9 (almost certainly an earlier source quoted by the author):

> 10 I have seen the business that God has given to the sons of men to be busy with. 11 He has made everything beautiful in its time; also he has put eternity into man's mind, yet so that he cannot find out what God has done from the beginning to the end. 12 I know that there is nothing better for them than to be happy and enjoy themselves as long as they live; 13 also that it is God's gift to man that every one should eat and drink and take pleasure in all his toil.

In short, we should not overlook the handful of passages which do emphasize the positive side of life. They may indicate that Qoheleth's was a more optimistic message than we often give him credit for. In addition, there is another approach to interpreting Ecclesiastes which needs to be kept in mind. This concerns modern investigations into literary-critical theory and the attempts by scholars and specialists to apply the results to the study of the biblical texts.

Above I mentioned how many of the critical discussions of Hemingway's *A Farewell to Arms* have revolved around his narrative

1. Especially in his *Ecclesiastes*. In addition to the articles by Whybray discussed below, note his succinct summary on 'Ecclesiastes' in R.J. Coggins and J.L. Houlden (eds.), *A Dictionary of Biblical Interpretation* (London: SCM Press, 1990), pp. 183-84. The trend toward more optimistic interpretations of Ecclesiastes is helpfully discussed in R.K. Johnston, '"Confessions of a Workaholic": A Reappraisal of Qoheleth', *CBQ* 38 (1976), pp. 14-28. A. Gianto, 'The Theme of Enjoyment in Qohelet', *Bib* 73 (1992), pp. 528-32 is also worth consulting.

2. 'Qoheleth, Preacher of Joy', *JSOT* 23 (1982), pp. 87-98. In a related article ('Ecclesiastes 1.5-7 and the Wonders of Nature', *JSOT* 41 [1988], pp. 105-112) Whybray challenges the commonly-held assumption that Qoheleth presents a picture of the futility of the natural phenomena mentioned in ch. 1, namely the sun, the winds and the rivers.

technique, particularly the way in which he uses a narrator speaking (for the most part) in the first person as the 'voice' which the reader hears within the novel. An interesting parallel to such a study of Hemingway's use of narrative voice is offered for Ecclesiastes by Fox and is used by him in a creative way to propose a solution to the vexing question of authorship, and in a roundabout way answer some of the questions about the age-old pessimism/optimism debate.[1] In particular, Fox discusses the change in voice found in Eccl. 1.2, 7.27 and 12.8; but he does not, in contrast to many other scholars, feel that this necessarily indicates an editorial hand which is different from that of the author. Instead, he argues forcefully for a single hand in the creation of the book, and identifies this author as using a 'frame-narrator' to carry the story along. According to Fox, this single author is responsible for the book as it stands, including the controversial Epilogue of 12.9-14. Fox's article represents one of the most complex arguments for solitary authorship of Qoheleth available, and offers a very creative way forward for handling the peculiarities of the troublesome book.[2] However, it should be noted that he has to appeal to the insights afforded by modern literary-critical methods to make the case; the 'frame-narrator' solution would not be the most immediate interpretation to spring to mind for the typical reader.

Yet, in the eyes of some even this may be insufficient to redeem Qoheleth from the charge of pessimism. Fox has more than one string to his bow, however, and he has offered supportive arguments to sustain his case. One of the most interesting is an article from 1986 on the key word הֶבֶל.[3] A wide variety of terms have been suggested for this word including 'vanity', 'futility', 'meaninglessness', 'incomprehension', 'irony', 'profitlessness',[4] 'incongruity',[5] and (emphasizing the physical

---

1. M.V. Fox, 'Frame-Narrative and Composition in the Book of Qohelet', *HUCA* 48 (1977), pp. 83-106.

2. Murphy, *Ecclesiastes*, pp. xxxiii-lix and 123-55 offers an extensive discussion of the Epilogue and its place within Ecclesiastes.

3. M.V. Fox, 'The Meaning of Hebel for Qohelet', *JBL* 105 (1986), pp. 409-27. He cites *The Myth of Sisyphus* by Albert Camus as a classic description of the meaning of 'the absurd' in the modern setting and uses the novel to help set the tone for his discussion of Ecclesiastes. Murphy, *Ecclesiastes*, pp. lviii-lix, also discusses this.

4. Crenshaw, 'The Wisdom Literature', p. 379, building upon the way in which הֶבֶל was used in daily commerce.

5. E.M. Good, *Irony in the Old Testament* (London: SPCK, 1965), p. 182.

image underlying the Hebrew) 'vapour'.[1] One commentator even
suggests a modern equivalent for the key phrase in which the term
occurs, offering the rather inelegant, but highly expressive 'everything is
shit'.[2] Fox suggests the English translation 'absurd' more closely
approximates the meaning of the Hebrew word. At heart is an understanding of 'absurdity' as the irrationality of life as a whole, a
fundamental incompatibility between what could be reasonably expected
and what is experienced; the universe does not operate according to the
accepted principle of reward for virtue and punishment for evil. The
result of Fox's study is that many of the perceived incompatibilities of
Ecclesiastes evaporate when the meaning of הֶבֶל is seen in this light. A
strictly rational approach to life, which attempts to reason everything
out, is simply not up to the task and can only understand the realities of
life as 'absurd'. When it comes to the subject of human mortality within
the book, Fox comments that 'death sets the seal on life's absurdity'.[3]
This interpretation also helps to make sense of how it is that the author
can both declare the goodness of God's gifts in life, and plunge into the
most gloomy description of its goal.

In summary, a wholly pessimistic interpretation of Ecclesiastes, which
has characterized so many traditional assessments of the book, may have
to be modified somewhat. As R.N. Whybray has argued powerfully,
there are a number of passages which in themselves run against such a
thoroughly negative assessment of life. In addition, as Michael V. Fox
argues, the key concept of 'absurdity' when properly understood may
demand such a modification. Even more importantly, a sensitivity to the
narrative framework of the book may well be the final piece of evidence
which indicates that a more hopeful message is the one that Qoheleth
ultimately wants us to hear.

1. J.G. Williams, 'What Does it Profit a Man?: The Wisdom of Koheleth', in
J.L. Crenshaw (ed.), *Studies in Ancient Israelite Wisdom* (New York: Ktav, 1976),
pp. 375-89, suggests this, as do Scott, *Proverbs and Ecclesiastes*, and many others.
Scott explains (p. 202): 'The word *hebel*, "vapor", or "breath", connotes what is
visible or recognizable, but unsubstantial, momentary, and profitless'.
2. F. Crüsemann, 'The Unchangeable World: The "Crisis of Wisdom" in
Koheleth', in W. Schottroff and W. Stegemann (eds.), *God of the Lowly: Socio-
Historical Interpretations of the Bible* (New York: Orbis Books, 1984), p. 57.
3. Fox, 'The Meaning of Hebel', p. 425.

b. *The Optimism of* A Farewell to Arms

Hemingway's *A Farewell to Arms* is sometimes described as one of the most depressing works of modern fiction. Indeed, a close friend of mine, who is by no means undiscerning in his literary tastes and is one of the most widely-read people I know, admitted to me recently that he has only read one of Hemingway's books, that being *A Farewell to Arms*. He read it, so he said, about twenty years ago and it so depressed him that he had never been able to bring himself to read anything else by the author. For him it was a profoundly pessimistic work, and had spoiled the development of any interest on his part in Hemingway as a writer.

Are there any grounds for interpreting the work in a more optimistic light? Is it possible to adopt the same sort of approach I noted in the discussion about Ecclesiastes and apply it to a study of *A Farewell to Arms*? Perhaps not everything should be surrendered to the pessimistic camp so quickly. There are, after all, scattered hints of the redemptive nature of human suffering within the novel. To cite one general example, I note a passage which occurs in 3:26 where Henry has a conversation with the priest about the senselessness of the war and the possibility of one or both sides taking the first steps in stopping the fighting. Hemingway gives us this suggestive conversation between Henry and the priest:

Priest:	Then you think it will go on and on?
Henry:	I don't know. I only think the Austrians will not stop when they have won a victory. It is in defeat that we become Christian.
Priest:	The Austrians are Christians—except for the Bosnians.
Henry:	I don't mean technically Christians. I mean like Our Lord.

Indeed, the whole retreat from Caporetto can be seen as an extended metaphor of defeat and the lessons that can be learned from it. Unfortunately, very few of the soldiers involved are able to see reality clearly in the midst of such a situation. In 3:30 the Italian military police at the Tagliamento Bridge do not really appreciate what is happening, declaring officers as unpatriotic and executing them as deserters. The truth is only arrived at through the penetrating question of one of the condemned officers to the battle police: 'Have you ever been in a retreat?' Frederic Henry does grasp what is happening and takes a large step to his own emancipation, and, ironically, his eventual demise, when he flees from the police and begins his long and arduous journey to Catherine. Through the ignominious defeat of Caporetto he is made even more acutely aware of the utter futility of war. He opts instead for the safety, or so he perceives it, of life with Catherine in neutral

Switzerland. That defeat can prove to be a catharsis of the human soul is a theme interwoven into the very fabric of the novel as a war story. The same might also be said about *A Farewell to Arms* as a love story, where hope needs to be seen as arising out of the defeat that is Catherine's death.

I have already noted that the cinematic adaptations of the novel do something akin to this, offering a more hopeful ending to the film than can be justified on the basis of an uncritical reading of the published novel itself. That is to say, neither of the two cinematic adaptations remain entirely faithful to Hemingway's ending; both alter it in their own way. Several features of the body of the work also lend themselves to a more hopeful interpretation of it as a story, including the much-discussed original ending of the book. Let us examine some of these features.

The Original Ending of the Novel. Hemingway agonized over how he would end the novel. He instinctively knew that much critical opinion about the novel as a whole would ride upon its final pages. Consequently he wrote, and rewrote, and re-rewrote the ending, declaring at one stage to have written no less than 39 different conclusions to the novel.[1] As a consequence, the ending of *A Farewell to Arms* has become something of a specialized field of study among students of Hemingway's work and a great deal of ink has been poured out by scholars jockeying for position in the growing ranks of Hemingway specialists.

In 1962 the eminent Hemingway scholar Carlos Baker received permission from Hemingway's widow, Mary, to publish for the first time what he described as 'The Original Conclusion to *A Farewell to Arms*'. This conclusion differs from the published ending in a number of interesting ways. It reads,

> It seems she had one hemorrhage after another. They couldn't stop it. I went into the room and stayed with Catherine until she died. She was unconscious all the time, and it did not take her very long to die.
>
> There are a great many more details, starting with my first meeting with an undertaker, and all the business of burial in a foreign country and going on with the rest of my life—which has gone on and seems likely to go on for a long time.
>
> I could tell how Rinaldi was cured of the syphilis and lived to find that

1. In an interview with George Plimpton published as 'Ernest Hemingway: The Art of Fiction XXI', *Paris Review* 18 (1958), p. 84.

the technic learned in wartime surgery is not of much practical use in peace. I could tell how the priest in our mess lived to be a priest in Italy under Fascism. I could tell how Ettore became a Fascist and the part he took in that organization. I could tell how Piani got to be a taxi-driver in New York and what sort of a singer Simmons became. Many things have happened. Everything blunts and the world keeps on. It never stops. It only stops for you. Some of it stops while you are still alive. The rest goes on and you go on with it.

I could tell you what I have done since March, nineteen hundred and eighteen, when I walked that night in the rain back to the hotel where Catherine and I had lived and went upstairs to our room and undressed and slept finally, because I was so tired—to wake in the morning with the sun shining in the window; then suddenly to realize what had happened. I could tell you what has happened since then, but that is the end of the story.[1]

Perhaps most important for our considerations is the fact that this conclusion is not nearly as pessimistic as the published ending. Frederic Henry does 'wake in the morning with the sun shining in the window'—something decidedly more optimistic than walking away in the rain. He also comes to realize that life 'goes on and you go with it'. However, this alternative ending is not the only extant one among the papers and manuscripts of Hemingway which have survived. Indeed, Bernard Oldsey has made a full-length study of the ending of *A Farewell to Arms* and has suggested that there are between 32 and 41 conclusions to the novel within the papers of the Hemingway Collection housed in the John F. Kennedy Library in Boston, Massachusetts.[2] Oldsey has grouped these into nine different categories, depending on their content and what particular twist they bring to the story as a whole. Some of these are in typescript and some are written by hand; almost all have some deletions and corrections within them. One group is based upon suggestions made by F. Scott Fitzgerald to Hemingway about how to end the novel—suggestions which Hemingway ultimately rejected.[3] Unfortunately, it is impossible to trace a development of

1. The ending is contained in Baker (ed.), *Ernest Hemingway*, p. 75.
2. *Hemingway's Hidden Craft: The Writing of A Farewell to Arms* (University Park: Pennsylvania State University Press, 1979). Oldsey notes that the ending published by Baker in 1962 was the original ending to the *Scribner's Magazine* serialization of the novel, but that it was almost certainly preceded by several other attempts by Hemingway to write a conclusion. Reynolds, *Hemingway's First War*, pp. 45-51, also contains some valuable discussion.
3. Donaldson, *By Force of Will*, pp. 201-15, gives details of the friendship between the two authors.

composition among the various sayings since none of them are dated. About the only consistency among the various endings is the fact of Catherine's death. However a wide variety of interpretations of what her death means for Frederic are explored among the numerous endings Hemingway wrestled to compose. Perhaps the most brutal and pessimistic of the endings is one that Oldsey places in a group he entitles 'The Nada Ending': 'That is all there is to the story. Catherine died and you will die and I will die and that is all I can promise you.' In at least one of the endings Frederic contemplates suicide, before deciding that life must go on regardless of the pain and loss that is sustained in life. At least three of the endings have a religious motif running through them, wherein the death of Catherine drives Frederic to reconsider the wisdom of the priest's faith and reassess his own relationship to God in light of it. Several other endings have the child survive, although one of these has Hemingway philosophically tie together birth and death in a single, concluding sentence which is remarkably reminiscent of Eccl. 3.2a. This particular ending (Oldsey designates it as Version 9) reads,

> I could tell about the boy. He did not seem of any importance then except as trouble and God knows that I was bitter about him. Anyway, he does not belong in this story. He starts a new one [story]. It is not fair to start a new story at the end of an old one but that is the way it happens. *There is no end except death and birth is the only beginning.*[1]

The point of all of this is to suggest that Hemingway himself struggled to find what he felt to be the appropriate conclusion to the novel. At times these endings have a strongly pessimistic tone and at times they are less so, even bordering on the optimistic. As it stands the published ending does seem to fall on the side of pessimism rather than on the side of optimism. But at least the manuscript evidence suggests that Hemingway was having a real battle in concluding the novel in that way. The numerous endings indicate that he was grappling with the dilemma of having the novel end in such a rain-splattered way. The fact that the film-makers seek to modify this concluding note of negativism and interject a more optimistic ending is perfectly understandable. It may even be likened to what the final editor of Ecclesiastes attempts by adding the Epilogue in 12.9-14. However, there is another feature of the novel which must be taken into account when we consider whether there is, in the final analysis, any optimism in *A Farewell to Arms*. Not

---

1.   Oldsey, *Hemingway's Hidden Craft*, p. 108. The italics are mine.

only can the (original?) ending of the story be taken as optimistic, but so too can the narrative stance implied throughout the novel.

The Optimism of Narration. We could focus this particular point by asking a rhetorical question of the novel: Is there life for Frederic Henry after the death of Catherine? In many ways this question is not dissimilar to that which lies unspoken, but fermenting, in the back of the mind of Qoheleth: Is there life after death?

It is sometimes easy to overlook the fact that the narrator of *A Farewell to Arms* is Frederic Henry himself, and that he narrates virtually the whole of the tale some time after it had taken place. In other words, the fact that the story is related at all means that there is something more than Henry's leaving the hospital in the rain to be kept in mind by the reader. Indeed, at several key points within the story itself, Henry acknowledges his vantage point as the narrator who is telling his story long after the events took place, perhaps even years later.[1] This feature of the novel invites us to reconsider the role that narrative style has in connection with the question of an optimistic interpretation of the work.

One of the most important passages to illustrate this point about narrative style appears in 1:3 where Frederic Henry is in conversation with the priest. He is explaining his failure to visit the priest's home region of Abruzzi and how he had gone to the bars and whorehouses in several of the major cities of Italy instead. Frederic then lifts the veil on the conversation for just a moment, allowing us to see that he is relating past events when he says of the priest,

> I tried to tell about the night and the difference between the night and the day and how the night was better unless the day was very clean and cold and I could not tell it; as I cannot tell it now. But if you have had it you know. He had not had it but he understood that I had really wanted to go to the Abruzzi but had not gone and we were still friends, with many tastes alike, but with the difference between us. *He had always known what I did not know and what, when I learned it, I was always able to forget. But I did not know that then, although I learned it later.*[2]

Frederic says this with hindsight, offering an interpretation of his conversation with the priest which arises long after the conversation

---

1. Perhaps this retrospective stance is inevitable given the fact that Hemingway himself began writing the story some ten years after his own wounding in Italy.
2. The italics are mine.

itself had taken place. The comment is narrated with a clarity of insight that only the passing of time brings; even the reader is brought into focus for a moment when Hemingway shifts to the second person in the middle of the passage. The remark is usually taken to indicate that Frederic eventually comes to some sort of faith, or at least an uneasy acceptance of the reality of his situation. As Robert W. Lewis, Jr states,

> While it is true that Catherine's death concludes the novel, her death is really only the end of a beginning as far as Frederic Henry is concerned; he is now ready to reflect on his experiences and to present them to the reader, and he is a very sophisticated narrator. He is not merely recounting events in an objective way...Henry has undergone an initiatory and learning experience that he is now ready to interpret.[1]

Catherine's promise to Frederic on her deathbed in 5:41 that she will come and visit him in the night also hints at his subsequent life, as does her noble declaration that she wants him to have other women. Here Hemingway paints for us a powerfully emotive scene, beginning with a question on the lips of Frederic:

> 'Do you want me to do anything, Cat? Can I get you anything?'
> Catherine smiled. 'No.' Then a little later, 'You won't do our things with another girl, or say the same things, will you?'
> 'Never.'
> 'I want you to have girls though.'
> 'I don't want them.'
> 'You are talking too much,' the doctor said. 'Mr Henry must go out. He can come back later. You are not going to die. You must not be silly.'
> 'All right,' Catherine said. 'I'll come and stay with you nights,' she said.

This passage seems deliberately designed to invoke a connection of thought in the mind of the reader, recalling two earlier passages. First, it harks back to Catherine's words to Frederic in 1:6 where, as part of their courtship, she asks him to act out the role of her deceased fiancé. Frederic remembers the incident:

> She looked at me. 'And you do love me?'
> 'Yes.'
> 'You did say you loved me, didn't you?'
> 'Yes,' I lied. 'I love you.' I had not said it before.

---

1. 'The Tough Romance', p. 41. The article is taken from Lewis's *Hemingway on Love*. Also see: E. Rovit and G. Brenner, *Ernest Hemingway* (Boston: Twayne, rev. edn, 1986), pp. 81-89; J. Nagel, 'Catherine Barkley and Retrospective Narration in *A Farewell to Arms*', in Wagner (ed.), *Ernest Hemingway*, pp. 171-85.

'And you call me Catherine?'
'Catherine.' We walked on a way and were stopped under a tree.
'Say, "I've come back to Catherine in the night."'
'I've come back to you in the night.'
'Oh, darling, you have come back, haven't you?'
'Yes.'
'I love you so and it's been awful. You won't go away?'
'No. I'll always come back.'

The second passage occurs in 3:28 and builds upon this image of 'coming back in the night'. The scene here takes place during the Caporetto retreat, where the exhausted Frederic falls asleep and dreams of Catherine coming to be with him in his dreams. As he falls asleep we have a surreal scene in which Frederic addresses Catherine:

Try and go to sleep, sweet.
I was asleep all the time, she said. You've been talking in your sleep. Are you all right?
Are you really there?
Of course, I'm here. I wouldn't go away. This doesn't make any difference between us.
You're so lovely and sweet. You wouldn't go away in the night, would you?
Of course I wouldn't go away. I'm always here. I come whenever you want me.

In other words, as Frederic sits at the bedside of his beloved Catherine, waiting for her to die, he is now in the position that she was in at the beginning of their relationship together. The dream sequence serves as a reminder of the bond that exists between them, a bond which points beyond her death, and uses the image of 'coming back in the night' to communicate it. Frederic is now the one who has to learn to live with the loss of the one he loved. He must look optimistically to the future for other lovers to take her place in the same way that he stepped in for Catherine's fiancé killed in the Somme. This seems meagre consolation for Frederic considering what he has lost in Catherine, but then such anguish is built within the very nature of true loss. To borrow one of the most evocative phrases in the novel about what life does to you and, even more importantly, what it demands of you, Hemingway drives Frederic to the point that he must realize that 'life breaks us all and afterward many are strong at the broken places'. It is true that the reader can only guess at what Frederic's life is like now that Catherine is dead, but passages such as these are scattered throughout the novel and offer brief glimpses of it. Life has moved on for Frederic Henry, and the fact that he is even telling us the story at all is testimony to that fact. In short, the narrative style of the novel by Frederic Henry is itself a subtle feature of optimism and invites the reader to reconsider the validity of an overly pessimistic reading of it.

Yet, while it may be fair to say that a closer reading of *A Farewell to Arms* might well bear the weight of a more optimistic interpretation of the novel, I would venture to suggest that this is not the kind of initial response that most readers have to it. Like the optimistic readings of Ecclesiastes offered by Whybray and Fox discussed above, such an interpretation must be painfully dug out of the novel, extracted like gold from a deep mine. In both works, the reader must be very careful to pick up all of the nuances of the author's (Qoheleth's and Hemingway's) narrative technique. Attention to detail is the order of the day if an optimistic interpretation is to hold sway. Perhaps it is not surprising that most optimistic interpretations of Ecclesiastes only arise when similar attention to detail and a careful reassessment of Qoheleth's narrative technique are accepted as the basis upon which an interpretation of Ecclesiastes is to proceed.

5. *Summary*

I began this study by noting how Ecclesiastes and Hemingway's *A Farewell to Arms* shared a remarkable history of interpretation: both expressed a certain ambiguity about the meaning of life and death and both have been the subject of pessimistic and optimistic interpretations by competent scholars and critics. I also noted how the two books were obsessed with the idea of the inevitability of death, and examined what implications such a belief had for the attitude to life presented within them. In particular, I noted how the birth-death metaphor of Eccl. 3.2a characterizes the message of the book and how Hemingway made extensive use of the same theme throughout his own novel, linking it to other important metaphors in the book such as those involving rain and geography. Most importantly, I noted how the film adaptations of Hemingway's novel have tended to downplay the pessimism of the ending in favour of a more optimistic ending to the love affair between Frederic Henry and Catherine Barkley. I have also noted how Hemingway himself toyed with a number of more hopeful endings to the novel. Such optimistic readings of *A Farewell to Arms* are also supported by interpretations which pay close attention to the narrative technique employed by Hemingway in the composition of the novel. All of this is to suggest that interpretations of both *A Farewell to Arms* and Ecclesiastes which argue for an inherent optimism may indeed be closer to the truth than we might at first be willing to admit. The interpretations of such Old Testament scholars as R.N. Whybray and Michael V. Fox, neither of whom is willing to accept the traditional interpretation of Ecclesiastes as essentially a work of profound pessimism and leave it at that, offer a different approach to the book. A closer examination of the circumstances surrounding the composition and transmission of *A Farewell to Arms*, as well as the fact that the story is presented with a happier ending in the two cinematic adaptations available, sensitizes us to new possibilities of its interpretation. So, too, could a closer examination of Ecclesiastes yield similar results in the book's interpretation. There is much to be gained from such a comparative study of the two pieces of literature, which seem to have so much in common.

If there is anyone who might be said to embody the perspective of Qoheleth about the ambiguities of life and death it would be Ernest Hemingway. His zest for living might be taken as evidence of someone who has followed the advice of Qoheleth about pursuing pleasure in life seriously. At the same time, there are numerous episodes within his life which indicate that a profound pessimism characterized his thinking. The fact that Hemingway felt himself driven, whether by despair or by madness, to take his own life on 2 July 1961 might itself be interpreted as a demonstration of his adherence to his own moral code—dignity in the face of death. At the same time, from an outsider's point of view, it represents the supreme irony of all that he stood for. In this sense, it is true to what Michael V. Fox has described as central to the meaning of Qoheleth's favourite term הֶבֶל: life is indeed absurd; but it is to be enjoyed nonetheless for it is a gift of God.

CONCLUSION

We come now to the end of this study, five essays of quite a diverse
subject matter but gathered together under one purpose: to investigate
creatively how Scripture, literature and cinema sometimes come together
and mutually enrich our appreciation of human artistic achievement. I
have undertaken an exploration into the ways in which portions of the
Old Testament have been translated onto the cinema screen, sometimes,
as in the case of Cecil B. De Mille's *The Ten Commandments*, as an
attempt to *re-create* ancient history and thereby bring us closer to the
Scriptures themselves. More often, however, the five essays contained
within this volume have called attention to the ways in which the Old
Testament has served as the backdrop against which time-honoured
works of literature have framed their stories and led us to consider how
the cinematic interpretations of those works of literature have sought to
bring them to life. Insofar as I have attempted to suggest that a
profitable way of reading the Old Testament afresh is through the lens
offered by the works of literature (and their cinematic interpretations) I
have been pursuing the task of which the book's subtitle speaks: I have
been reversing the hermeneutical flow within the interpretative process.

Three of the five chapters have dealt with American authors and their
novels, namely Herman Melville's *Moby-Dick*, John Steinbeck's *East of
Eden* and Ernest Hemingway's *A Farewell to Arms*; only one work
discussed is from a British writer, namely Mary Shelley's *Frankenstein*.
The only other European contribution has been the film interpretation of
the Ten Commandments by the Polish director Krzysztof Kieslowski.
Perhaps the overbalance in favour of the United States is somewhat
inevitable given the fact that the most important film-producing centre
in the world is in Hollywood, California, and the film-making industry
is quintessentially American in both its sympathies and financial
infrastructure. Yet there remains something timeless and eternal about
the biblical stories and myths which underlie the works of literature and
their cinematic interpretations discussed here, regardless of their national

origin. I have covered a wide-ranging selection of Old Testament texts in the course of this discussion, everything from the Genesis stories of Adam and Eve and Cain and Abel, to the story from Exodus of the deliverance of the people of Israel from bondage in Egypt, to the message of the prophet Jonah, to the wisdom books of Job and Ecclesiastes. In short, all three major sections of the Old Testament, the Torah, the Prophets and the Writings are included in the discussion, and this by design. At the same time I have tried to present an accurate account of the latest literary-critical discussions of the various works of literature under scrutiny. This has, in itself, been something of an uphill struggle since so much has been written about many of the chosen authors and their literary compositions. One could easily concentrate for a lifetime on any one of the four major literary figures represented here: Shelley, Melville, Hemingway and Steinbeck.

As I suggested in the earlier volume on *The New Testament in Fiction and Film* this is merely an experiment in hermeneutics. My only hope is that others have found their reading of, and appreciation for, the Old Testament documents enhanced by a consideration of them in light of the attempts of literary greats to make the stories contained within them relevant to a contemporary readership. Other explorations of the relationship between biblical materials and classic works of literature hopefully will be forthcoming by others who recognize this as a fruitful field of investigation; this book is only meant to serve as a representation of what is possible by a careful study of how Scripture and modern works of literature and cinema interrelate.

BIBLIOGRAPHY

Aldiss, B.W., *Trillion Year Spree: The History of Science Fiction* (London: Gollancz, 1986).

—*Frankenstein Unbound* (London: Panther Books, 1982).

Alter, R., *The Art of Biblical Narrative* (London: Allen & Unwin, 1981).

Atkinson, D., *The Message of Job* (Leicester: Inter-Varsity Press, 1991).

Auden, W.H., 'The Romantic Use of Symbols', in Gilmore (ed.), *Moby-Dick*, pp. 9-12.

Babington, B. and P.W. Evans, *Biblical Epics: Sacred Narrative in the Hollywood Cinema* (Manchester: Manchester University Press, 1993).

Baker, C., 'The Mountain and the Plain', in C. Baker (ed.), *Ernest Hemingway: Critiques of Four Major Novels* (New York: Charles Scribner's Sons, 1962), pp. 47-60.

—*Ernest Hemingway* (Harmondsworth: Penguin Books, 1972).

Baker, C. (ed.), *Ernest Hemingway: Critiques of Four Major Novels* (New York: Charles Scribner's Sons, 1962).

Baker, J.A., 'The Book of Job: Unity and Meaning', in Livingstone (ed.), *Studia Biblica I*, pp. 17-26.

Bal, M., *Lethal Love: Feminist Literary Readings of Biblical Love Stories* (Bloomington: Indiana University Press, 1987).

Baldick, C., *In Frankenstein's Shadow: Myth, Monstrosity, and Nineteenth-century Writing* (Oxford: Clarendon Press, 1987).

Barbour, J., 'The Composition of *Moby-Dick*', *AL* 47 (1974), pp. 343-60.

—'"All my Books are Botches": Melville's Struggle with *The Whale*', in Barbour and Quirk (eds.), *Writing the American Classics*, pp. 25-52.

Barbour, J., and T. Quirk (eds.), *Writing the American Classics* (London: University of North Carolina Press, 1990).

Barr, J., 'The Book of Job and its Modern Interpreters', *BJRL* 54 (1970–71), pp. 28-46.

—*The Bible in the Modern World* (London: SCM Press, 1973).

Barton, G.A., *The Book of Ecclesiastes* (ICC; Edinburgh: T. & T. Clark, 1908).

Battenfield, D.H., 'The Source of the Hymn in *Moby-Dick*', *AL* 27 (1955), pp. 393-96.

Bedford, R.C., 'Steinbeck's Uses of the Oriental', *SQ* 13 (1980), pp. 5-19.

Behlemr, R., *Behind the Scenes* (London: Samuel French, 1982).

Behnken, E., 'The Joban Theme in *Moby-Dick*', *IR* 33 (1976), pp. 37-48.

Bell, M., '*A Farewell to Arms*: Pseudoautobiography and Personal Metaphor', in J. Nagel (ed.), *Ernest Hemingway: The Writer in Context* (Madison: University of Wisconsin Press, 1984), pp. 107-28.

Benson, J.J., *The True Adventures of John Steinbeck, Writer* (London: Heinemann Press, 1984).

Beuchner, F., *Peculiar Treasures: A Biblical Who's Who* (New York: Harper & Row, 1979).

Beversluis, J., 'Dispelling the Romantic Myth: A Study of *A Farewell to Arms*', *HR* 9 (1989), pp. 18-25.

Bewley, M., 'Melville and the Democratic Experience', in Chase (ed.), *Melville*, pp. 91-115.

Bird, P.A., '"Male and Female he Created them": Genesis 1:27b in the Context of the Priestly Account of Creation', *HTR* 74 (1981), pp. 129-59.

Bloom, H. (ed.), *Modern Critical Views: Ernest Hemingway* (New York: Chelsea House, 1985).

Blumberg, J., *Mary Shelley's Early Novels: 'This Child of Imagination and Misery'* (London: Macmillan, 1993).

Boller, P.F., Jr, and R.L. Davis, *Hollywood Anecdotes* (London: Macmillan, 1987).

Booth, T.Y., '*Moby Dick*: Standing up to God', *NCF* 17 (1962–63), pp. 33-43.

Botting, F., *Making Monstrous: Frankenstein, Criticism, Theory* (Manchester: Manchester University Press, 1991).

Bowerbank, S., 'The Social Order *vs* the Wretch: Mary Shelley's Contradictory-Mindedness in *Frankenstein*', *ELH* 46 (1979), pp. 418-31.

Boyd, S., *York Notes on Frankenstein* (Harlow, Essex: Longman, 1984).

Braswell, W., 'Melville as a Critic of Emerson', *AL* 9 (1937), pp. 317-34.

—*Melville's Religious Thought: An Essay in Interpretation* (Durham, NC: Duke University Press, 1943).

Braude, W.G., 'Melville's *Moby-Dick*', *Exp* 21 (1962–63), n. 23.

Bream, H.N., 'Life without Resurrection: Two Perspectives from Qoheleth', in H.N. Bream, R.D. Heim and C.A. Moore (eds.), *A Light unto my Path: Old Testament Studies in Honor of Jacob M. Myers* (Philadelphia: Temple University Press, 1974), pp. 49-65.

Brenner, A., 'Job the Pious? The Characterization of Job in the Narrative Framework of the Book', *JSOT* 43 (1989), pp. 37-52.

Brenner, G., and E. Rovit, *Ernest Hemingway* (Boston: Twayne Publishers, rev. edn, 1986).

Brian, D., *The True Gen: An Intimate Portrayal by those who Knew him* (New York: Grove Press, 1988).

Brodhead, R.H., 'Trying all Things: An Introduction to *Moby-Dick*', in Brodhead (ed.), *New Essays*, pp. 1-21.

Brodhead, R.H. (ed.), *New Essays on Moby-Dick* (Cambridge: Cambridge University Press, 1986).

Brooks, P., '"Godlike Science/Unhallowed Arts": Language, Nature, and Monstrosity', in Levine and Knoepflmacher (eds.), *The Endurance of Frankenstein*, pp. 205-20.

Brown, R.E., J.A. Fitzmyer and R.E. Murphy (eds.), *The New Jerome Biblical Commentary* (London: Geoffrey Chapman, 1991).

Brueggemann, W., *Genesis* (IC; Atlanta: John Knox Press, 1982).

Buell, L., '*Moby-Dick* as Sacred Text', in Brodhead (ed.), *New Essays*, pp. 53-72.

Camus, A., *The Plague* (Harmondsworth: Penguin Books, 1947).

Cantor, P.A., *Creature and Creator: Myth-making and English Romanticism* (Cambridge: Cambridge University Press, 1984).

Carfield, F.X., '*Moby-Dick* and the Book of Job', *CW* 174 (1952), pp. 254-60.

Carroll, R., 'The Discombobulations of Time and the Diversities of Text: Notes on the *Rezeptionsgeschichte* of the Bible', in Carroll (ed.), *Text as Pretext*, pp. 61-85.

Carroll, R.P (ed.), *Text as Pretext: Essays in Honour of Robert Davidson* (JSOTSup, 138; Sheffield: JSOT Press, 1992).

Cassuto, U., *A Commentary on the Book of Genesis: Part 1 From Adam to Noah (Genesis I–VI:8)* (Jerusalem: Magnes, 1961).

Castellino, G.R., 'Genesis IV 7', *VT* 10 (1960), pp. 442-45.

Chase, R., 'Melville and *Moby-Dick*', in Chase (ed.), *Melville*, pp. 49-61.

Chase, R. (ed.), *Melville: A Collection of Critical Essays* (Englewood Cliffs, NJ: Prentice-Hall, 1962).

Ciment, M. (ed.), *Kazan on Kazan* (London: Sacker & Warburg, 1973).

Clines, D.J.A., *Job: 1–20* (WBC, 17; Waco, TX: Word Books, 1989).

—'Deconstructing the Book of Job', in M. Warner (ed.), *The Bible as Rhetoric: Studies in Biblical Persuasion and Credibility* (London: Routledge, 1990), pp. 65-80.

Cook, R.L., 'Big Medicine in *Moby-Dick*', in Stern (ed.), *Moby-Dick*, pp. 19-24.

Cooper, A., 'Reading and Misreading the Prologue to Job', *JSOT* 46 (1990), pp. 67-79.

Coote, R.B., and D.R. Ord, *The Bible's First History* (Philadelphia: Fortress Press, 1989).

Cowan, S.A., 'Robert Cohn, the Fool of Ecclesiastes in *The Sun Also Rises*', *DR* 63 (1983), pp. 98-106.

Cowley, M., 'Introduction' to *The Portable Hemingway* (New York: Viking, 1945), pp. vii-xxiv.

—'A Portrait of Mister Papa', in *Life* 26 (10 January 1949), pp. 86-101.

—'A Portrait of Mister Papa', in J.K.M McCaffery (ed.), *Ernest Hemingway: The Man and his Work* (New York: The Word Publishing Company, 1950), pp. 26-48.

—'Nightmare and Ritual in Hemingway', in Weeks (ed.), *Hemingway*, pp. 40-51.

Cox, M.H., 'Steinbeck's Family Portraits: The Hamiltons', *SQ* 14 (1981), pp. 23-32.

Crawley, T., *The Steven Spielberg Story* (London: Zomba Books, 1983).

Crenshaw, J.L., 'The Eternal Gospel (Eccl. 3:11)', in J.L. Crenshaw and J.T. Willis (eds.), *Essays in Old Testament Ethics: J. Philip Hyatt, in Memoriam* (New York: Ktav, 1974), pp. 23-55.

—'The Shadow of Death in Qoheleth', in J.G. Gammie, W.A. Brueggemann, W.L. Humphreys and J.M. Ward (eds.), *Israelite Wisdom: Theological and Literary Essays in Honor of Samuel Terrien* (New York: Scholars Press, 1978), pp. 205-16.

—'The Birth of Skepticism in Ancient Israel', in J.L. Crenshaw and S. Sandmel (eds.), *The Divine Helmsman: Studies in God's Control of Human Events, Presented to Lou H. Silberman* (New York: Ktav, 1980), pp. 1-19.

—'The Wisdom Literature', in D.A. Knight and G.M. Tucker (eds.), *The Hebrew Bible and its Modern Interpreters* (Philadelphia: Fortress Press, 1985), pp. 369-407.

—*Ecclesiastes* (OTL; London: SCM Press, 1987).

Crüsemann, F., 'The Unchangeable World: The "Crisis of Wisdom" in Koheleth', in W. Schottroff and W. Stegemann (eds.), *God of the Lowly: Socio-Historical Interpretations of the Bible* (New York: Orbis Books, 1984), pp. 57-77.

Davidson, R., *The Courage to Doubt: Exploring an Old Testament Theme* (London: SCM Press, 1983).

Davies, G.H., 'Ark of the Covenant', *IDB*, I, pp. 222-26.

Davies, W.D., and D.C. Allison, *The Gospel according to Saint Matthew* (ICC; Edinburgh: T. & T. Clark, 1991).

Davis, M., Review of L. Thompson, *Melville's Quarrel with God*, *RES* (July 1954), p. 327.

Davis, R. (ed.), *The Encyclopedia of Horror* (Twickenham: Hamlyn, 1981).

Day, J., *God's Conflict with the Dragon and the Sea* (Cambridge: Cambridge University Press, 1985).

Dekker, G., and J. Harris, 'Supernaturalism and the Vernacular Style in *A Farewell to Arms*', *PMLA* 94 (1979), pp. 311-18.

Delbanco, A., 'Introduction' to Herman Melville's *Moby-Dick or, The Whale* (London: Penguin Books, 1992), pp. xi-xxx.

Demott, R., 'Cathy Ames and Lady Godiva: A Contribution to *East of Eden*'s Background', *SQ* 14 (1981), pp. 72-83.

Ditsky, J., *Essays on East of Eden* (Steinbeck Monograph Series, 7; Muncie, IN: Ball State University, 1977).

Donaldson, S., *By Force of Will: The Life and Art of Ernest Hemingway* (New York: Viking, 1977).

—'Introduction', in Donaldson (ed.), *New Essays*, pp. 1-25.

Donaldson, S. (ed.), *New Essays on A Farewell to Arms* (Cambridge: Cambridge University Press, 1990).

Dunn, J., *Moon in Eclipse: A Life of Mary Shelley* (London: Weidenfeld & Nicolson, 1978).

Eaton, J.H., *Job* (OTG; Sheffield: JSOT Press, 1985).

Edwards, A., *Haunted Summer* (London: Hodder & Stoughton, 1973).

Elata-Alster, G., and R. Salmon, 'Retracing a Writerly Text: In the Footsteps of a Midrashic Sequence on the Creation of the Male and the Female', in A. Loades and M. McLain (eds.), *Hermeneutics, the Bible and Literary Criticism* (London: Macmillan, 1992), pp. 177-97.

Elley, D., *The Epic Film: Myth and History* (London: Routledge & Kegan Paul, 1984).

Everest, B., and J. Wedeles, 'The Neglected Rib: Women in *East of Eden*', *SQ* 21 (1988), pp. 13-23.

Everson, W.K., *Classics of the Horror Film* (New York: Citadel Press, 1990).

Faulkner, W., 'View Points', in Gilmore (ed.), *Moby-Dick*, p. 109.

Fench, T., *Steinbeck and Covici: The Story of a Friendship* (Middlebury, VT: Paul S. Eriksson, 1979).

Fenton, C.A., *The Apprenticeship of Ernest Hemingway* (New York: Mentor Books, 1954).

Fetterley, J., '*A Farewell to Arms*: Hemingway's "Resentful Cryptogram"', *JPC* 10 (1976), pp. 203-14.

Fiddes, P.S., 'The Hiddenness of Wisdom in the Old Testament and Later Judaism' (unpublished DPhil thesis, the University of Oxford, 1976).

Fitzmyer, J.A., *The Gospel according to Luke (X–XXIV)* (AB, 28A; Garden City, NY: Doubleday & Co., 1985).

Foh, S.T., 'What is the Woman's Desire?', *WTJ* 37 (1974–75), pp. 376-83.

Fontenrose, J., *John Steinbeck: An Introduction and Interpretation* (New York: Holt, Rinehart & Winston, 1963).

Forman, C.C., 'The Pessimism of Ecclesiastes', *JSS* 3 (1958), pp. 336-43.

Forry, S.E., *Hideous Progenies: Dramatizations of Frankenstein from the Nineteenth Century to the Present* (Philadelphia: University of Pennsylvania Press, 1990).

Fox, M.V., 'Frame-Narrative and Composition in the Book of Qohelet', *HUCA* 48 (1977), pp. 83-106.

—'The Meaning of Hebel for Qohelet', *JBL* 105 (1986), pp. 409-27.

—'Aging and Death in Qohelet 12', *JSOT* 42 (1988), pp. 55-77.

—*Qohelet and his Contradictions* (BLS, 18; Sheffield: Almond Press, 1989).

Franklin, H.B., *The Wake of the Gods: Melville's Mythology* (Stanford: Stanford University Press, 1963).

French, W., *20th Century American Literature* (London: Macmillan, 1980).

Friedman, M., 'The Modern Job: Melville, Dostoievsky, and Kafka', *Judaism* 12 (1963), pp. 436-55.

Friedman, N., 'Small Hips, not War', in J. Gellens (ed.), *Twentieth Century Interpretations of* A Farewell to Arms: *A Collection of Critical Essays* (Englewood Cliffs, NJ: Prentice-Hall, 1970), pp. 105-108.

Frost, R., 'A Masque of Reason', in I. Hamilton (ed.), *Selected Poems* (London: Penguin Books, 1973), pp. 229-47.

Fry, C., *The Bible: The Screenplay* (New York: Bantam Books, 1966).

Frye, N., *A Study of English Romanticism* (New York: Random House, 1968).

—*The Great Code: The Bible and Literature* (London: Ark Paperbacks, 1982).

Ganzel, D., 'A Farewell to Arms: The Danger of Imagination', *SR* 79 (1971), pp. 576-97.

Geiger, D., 'Melville's Black God: Contrary Evidence in "The *Town-Ho's* Story"', in Stern (ed.), *Moby-Dick*, pp. 93-97.

Gianto, A., 'The Theme of Enjoyment in Qohelet', *Bib* 73 (1992), pp. 258-32.

Gibson, J.C.L., 'A New Look at Job 41.1-4 (English 41.9-12)', in R.P. Carroll (ed.), *Text as Pretext: Essays in Honour of Robert Davidson* (JSOTSup, 138; Sheffield: JSOT Press, 1992), pp. 129-39.

—'On Evil in the Book of Job', in L. Eslinger and G. Taylor (eds.), *Ascribe to the Lord: Biblical and other Essays in Memory of Peter C. Craigie* (JSOTSup, 67; Sheffield: JSOT Press, 1992), pp. 399-419.

Gifford, D., *A Pictorial History of Horror Movies* (London: Hamlyn, 1973).

Gilbert, S., and S. Gubar, *The Madwoman in the Attic: The Woman Writer and the Nineteenth-Century Literary Imagination* (New Haven: Yale University Press, 1979).

Gilmore, M.T., 'Introduction', in Gilmore (ed.), *Moby-Dick*, pp. 1-8.

Gilmore, M.T. (ed.), *Twentieth-Century Interpretations of Moby-Dick: A Collection of Critical Essays* (Englewood Cliffs, NJ: Prentice-Hall, 1977).

Gladstein, M.R., 'The Strong Female Principle of Good or Evil: The Women of *East of Eden*', *SQ* 24 (1991), pp. 30-40.

Glasser, W.A., 'A Farewell to Arms', *SR* 74 (1966), pp. 453-69.

Glut, D.F., *The Frankenstein Legend* (Metuchen, NJ: The Scarecrow Press, 1973).

—*The Frankenstein Catalog* (London: McFarland & Co., 1984).

Goldberg, M.A., 'Moral and Myth in Mrs Shelley's *Frankenstein*', *K-SJ* 8 (1959), pp. 27-28.

Good, E.M., *Irony in the Old Testament* (London: SPCK, 1965).

Gordis, R., 'Wisdom and Job', in S. Sandmel (ed.), *Old Testament Issues* (London: SCM Press, 1969), pp. 213-41.

Gottwald, N.K., *A Light to the Nations* (New York: Harper & Brothers, 1959).

Govini, M.W., '"Symbols for the Wordlessness: The Original Manuscript of *East of Eden*', *SQ* 14 (1981), pp. 14-23.

Graham, L., with N. Nodel, *The Ten Commandments* (Classics Illustrated, 135a; New York: Gilberton Company, 1956).

Gribben, J.L., 'Steinbeck's *East of Eden* and Milton's *Paradise Lost*: A discussion of *Timshel*', *SQ* 5 (1972), pp. 35-43.

Griffin, P., *Along with Youth: Hemingway, the Early Years* (Oxford: Oxford University Press, 1985).

Griggs, J., *The Films of Gregory Peck* (London: Columbus Books, 1984).

Grobel, L., *The Hustons* (London: Bloomsbury, 1990).

Gubar, S., and S. Gilbert, *The Madwoman in the Attic: The Woman Writer and the Nineteenth-Century Literary Imagination* (New Haven: Yale University Press, 1979).

Habel, N.C., *The Book of Job* (OTL; London: SCM Press, 1985).

Haining, P., (ed.), *The Frankenstein File* (London: New English Library, 1977).

Halliday, E.M., 'Hemingway's Ambiguity: Symbolism and Irony', in Baker (ed.), *Ernest Hemingway*, pp. 61-74.

Halliwell, L., *The Dead that Walk* (London: Paladin Books, 1988).

Harris, J., and G. Dekker, 'Supernaturalism and the Vernacular Style in *A Farewell to Arms*', *PMLA* 94 (1979), pp. 311-18.

Heimart, A., '*Moby Dick* and American Political Symbolism', *AQ* 15 (1963), pp. 498-534.

Heinlein, R.A., *Job: A Comedy of Justice* (New York: Ballantine Books, 1984).

Heller, J., *God Knows* (London: Jonathan Cape, 1984).

Hemingway, E., 'A Silent, Ghastly Procession', *The Toronto Daily Star* (20 October 1922).

—'Refugees from Thrace', *The Toronto Daily Star* (14 November 1922).

—'The Original Conclusion to *A Farewell to Arms*', in Baker (ed.), *Ernest Hemingway*, p. 75.

—*A Farewell to Arms* (London: Grafton Books, 1977).

—*Death in the Afternoon* (London: Grafton Books, 1977).

—*The Essential Hemingway* (London: Grafton Books, 1977).

—*Selected Letters (1917–1961)* (ed. C. Baker; New York: Charles Scribner's Sons, 1981).

—*By-Line* (London: Grafton Books, 1989).

Herbert, T.W., Jr, 'Calvinism and Cosmic Evil in *Moby-Dick*', *PMLA* 84 (1969), pp. 1613-19.

—*Moby-Dick and Calvinism: A World Dismantled* (New Brunswick, NJ: Rutgers University Press, 1977).

—'Calvinist Earthquake: *Moby-Dick* and Religious Tradition', in Brodhead (ed.), *Moby-Dick*, pp. 109-140.

Hetherington, H.D., 'Early Reviews of *Moby-Dick*', in Stern (ed.), *Moby-Dick*, pp. 1-18.

Higham, C., *Cecil B. De Mille* (New York: DaCapo Books, 1973).

—*Orson Welles: The Rise and Fall of an American Genius* (London: New English Library, 1985).

Hirsch, G.D., 'The Monster was a Lady: On the Psychology of Mary Shelley's *Frankenstein*', *HSL* 7 (1978), pp. 116-153.

Hoffman, D., '*Moby-Dick*: Jonah's Whale or Job's?', in Gilmore (ed.), *Moby-Dick*, pp. 59-75.

Hoffman, F.J., 'No Beginning and no End: Hemingway and Death', *EIC* 3 (1953), pp. 73-84.

Hoffman, Y., 'The Relation between the Prologue and the Speech-Cycles in Job: A Reconsideration', *VT* 31 (1981), pp. 160-70.

Hogan, D.J., *Dark Romance: Sex and Death in the Horror Film* (Wellingborough: Equation Books, 1986).

Holman, C.H., 'The Reconciliation of Ishmael: *Moby-Dick* and the Book of Job', *SAQ* 57 (1958), pp. 477-90.

Holstein, A., 'Melville's Inversion of Job in *Moby-Dick*', *IR* 35 (1978), pp. 13-19.

Horowitz, M.C., 'The Image of God in Man—Is Woman Included?', *HTR* 72 (1979), pp. 169-206.

Horsford, H.C., 'The Design of the Argument in *Moby-Dick*', *MFS* 8 (1962–63), pp. 233-51.

Horton, E., Jr, 'Koheleth's Concept of Opposites', *Numen* 19 (1972), pp. 1-21.

Huston, J., *An Open Book* (London: Columbus Books, 1988).

Jacobus, M., 'Is there a Woman in this Text?', *NLH* 14 (1982–83), pp. 117-41.

Jain, S., 'The Concept of Man in the Novels of John Steinbeck', *JSL* 3 (1975), pp. 98-102.

Jasper, D., *The New Testament and the Literary Imagination* (London: Macmillan, 1987).

—*The Study of Literature and Religion: An Introduction* (London: Macmillan, 2nd edn, 1992).

Jasper, F.N., 'Ecclesiastes: A Note for Our Time', *Int* 21 (1967), pp. 259-73.

Johnson, D., 'Introduction' to Mary Shelley, *Frankenstein* (New York: Bantam Books, 1981), pp. vii-xix.

Johnson, D.G., *From Chaos to Restoration: An Alternative Reading of Isaiah 24–27* (JSOTSup, 61; Sheffield: JSOT Press, 1988).

Johnston, R.K., ' "Confessions of a Workaholic": A Reappraisal of Qoheleth', *CBQ* 38 (1976), pp. 14-28.

Josephs, A., 'Hemingway's out of Body Experience', *HR* 2 (1983), pp. 11-17.

Josephus, *Jewish Antiquities, Books IX–XI* (trans. R. Marcus: LCL; London: Heinemann, 1937), VI.

Joyce, P., 'Feminist Exegesis of the Old Testament: Some Critical Reflections', in J.M. Soskice (ed.), *After Eve: Women, Theology and the Christian Tradition* (London: Marshall Pickering, 1990), pp. 1-10.

Kale, B., 'The Author', *Saturday Review* 35 (20 September 1952), p. 11.

Kawin, B., 'The Mummy's Pool', in G. Mast and M. Cohen (eds.), *Film Theory and Criticism: Introductory Reading* (Oxford: Oxford University Press, 3rd edn, 1985), pp. 466-81.

Kazan, E., *A Life* (London: Pan Books, 1989),

Keneally, T., *Moses: The Lawgiver* (London: Collins, 1975).

Ketterer, D., *Frankenstein's Creation: The Book, the Monster, and Human Reality* (English Literary Studies, 16; Victoria, BC: University of Victoria, 1979).

Kieslowski, K., *Kieslowski on Kieslowski* (London: Faber & Faber, 1993).

Kieslowski, K., with K. Piesiewicz, *Decalogue: The Ten Commandments* (London: Faber & Faber, 1991).

Killinger, J., *Hemingway and the Dead Gods: A Study in Existentialism* (Lexington: The University of Kentucky Press, 1960).

Klammer, E., 'The Grapes of Wrath: A Modern Exodus Account', *Cresset* 25 (1962), pp. 8-11.

Kreitzer, L.J., *The New Testament in Fiction and Film* (BSS, 17; Sheffield: JSOT Press, 1993).

—'The Cultural Veneer of *Star Trek*', *JPC* (forthcoming).

Lamb, J.B., 'Mary Shelley's *Frankenstein* and Milton's Monstrous Myth', *NCL* 47 (1992), pp. 303-19.

Langebauer, L., 'Swayed by Contraries: Mary Shelley and the Everyday', in A.A. Fisch, A.K. Mellor and E.H. Schor (eds.), *The other Mary Shelley: Beyond Frankenstein* (Oxford: Oxford University Press, 1993), pp. 185-203.

Laurence, F.M., 'Hollywood Publicity and Hemingway's Popular Reputation', *JPC* 6 (1972), pp. 20-31.

Lavalley, A., 'The Stage and Film Children of Frankenstein: A Survey', in Levine and Knoepflmacher (eds.), *The Endurance of Frankenstein*, pp. 243-89.

Lawrence, D.H., 'Moby Dick, or the White Whale', in Stern (ed.), *Moby-Dick*, pp. 35-44.

—'Herman Melville's Typee and Omoo', in Chase (ed.), *Melville*, pp. 11-20.

Lawson, C.D., 'Hemingway, Stendhal and War', *HR* 6 (1981), pp. 28-33.

Letter, L., 'Queequeg's Coffin', *NCF* 13 (1958–59), pp. 249-54.

Levant, H., *The Novels of John Steinbeck: A Critical Appraisal* (Columbia: University of Missouri Press, 1974).

Levine, G., 'The Ambiguous Heritage of Frankenstein', in Levine and Knoepflmacher (eds.), *The Endurance of Frankenstein*, pp. 3-30.

Levine G., and U.C. Knoepflmacher (eds.), *The Endurance of Frankenstein* (Berkeley: University of California Press, 1979).

Lewis, R.W., Jr, *Hemingway on Love* (Austin: University of Texas Press, 1965).

—'The Tough Romance', in J. Gellens (ed.), *Twentieth Century Interpretations of A Farewell to Arms: A Collection of Critical Essays* (Englewood Cliffs, NJ: Prentice-Hall, 1970), pp. 41-53.

—'Hemingway's Lives: A Review', *HR* 7 (1987), pp. 45-62.

Light, J.F., 'The Religion of Death in *A Farewell to Arms*', *MFS* 7 (1961-62), pp. 169-73.

—'The Religion of Death in *A Farewell to Arms*', in Baker (ed.), *Ernest Hemingway*, pp. 37-40.

Lisca, P., *The Wide World of John Steinbeck* (New Brunswick, NJ: Rutgers University Press, 1958).

—'Steinbeck's Image of Man and his Decline as a Writer', *MFS* 11 (1965), pp. 3-10.

—*John Steinbeck: Nature and Myth* (New York: Thomas Y. Crowell, 1978).

Livingstone, E.A. (ed.), *Studia Biblica I (1978)* (JSOTSup, 11; Sheffield: JSOT Press, 1979).

Loader, J.A., 'Qohelet 3:2-8—A "Sonnet" in the Old Testament', *ZAW* 81 (1969), pp. 240-43.

—*Ecclesiastes: A Practical Commentary* (Text and Interpretation Series; Grand Rapids: Eerdmans, 1986).

Loades, A., and M. McLain (eds.), *Hermeneutics, the Bible and Literary Criticism* (London: MacMillan, 1992).

Locklin, G., and C. Stetler, 'De-Coding the Hero in Hemingway's Fiction', *HR* 5 (1979), pp. 2-10.

Lovell, E.J., Jr, 'Byron and Mary Shelley', *K-SJ* 2 (1953), pp. 35-49.

Loving, J.M., 'Melville's Pardonable Sin', *NEQ* 47 (1974), pp. 262-78.

Lynn, K.S., *Hemingway* (London: Cardinal Books, 1987).

MacKenzie, R.A.F., and R.E. Murphy, 'Job', in Brown, Fitzmyer and Murphy (eds.), *Jerome Biblical Commentary*, pp. 466-88.

MacLeish, A., *J.B., a Play in Verse* (Boston: Houghton Mifflin, 1961).

MacLeod, P.G., '*Frankenstein*: Unbound and Otherwise', *Extrapolation* 21 (1980), pp. 158-66.

Marks, L.J., '*East of Eden*: "Thou Mayest"', *SQ* 4 (1971), pp. 3-18.

Mary Ellen, Sister, 'Duplicate Imagery in *Moby-Dick*', *MFS* 8 (1962), pp. 252-64.

Massey, R., *A Hundred Different Lives* (London: Robson Books, 1979).

Mayoux, J.J., *Melville* (New York: Grove Press, 1960).

McCann, G., *Rebel Males: Cliff, Brando and Dean* (London: Hamish Hamilton, 1991).

McClary, B.H., 'Melville's *Moby-Dick*', *Exp* 21 (1962–63), n. 9.

McIntosh, J., 'The Mariner's Multiple Quest', in Brodhead (ed.), *Moby-Dick*, pp. 23-52.

Meeks, W.A., 'The Image of the Androgyne: Some Use of a Symbol in Earliest Christianity', *HistRel* 13 (1974), pp. 165-208.

Mellor, A.K., *Mary Shelley: Her Life, her Fiction, her Monsters* (New York: Routledge, 1988).

Mellow, J.R., *Hemingway: A Life without Consequences* (London: Hodder & Stoughton, 1992).

Melville, H., *The Letters of Herman Melville* (ed. M.R. Davis and W.H. Gilman; New Haven: Yale University Press, 1960).

—*Moby-Dick* (A Norton Critical Edition; ed. H. Hayford and H. Parker; New York: Norton, 1967).

—*Moby-Dick; or, The Whale* (ed. H. Beaver; London: Penguin Books, 1986).

—*Moby-Dick or, The Whale* (ed. T. Quirk; London: Penguin Books, 1992).

Messent, P., *Ernest Hemingway* (Macmillan Modern Novelists; London: Macmillan, 1992).

Meyers, C., *Discovering Eve: Ancient Israelite Women in Context* (Oxford: Oxford University Press, 1988).

Meyers, J., *Hemingway: A Biography* (New York: Harper & Row, 1985).

Millichap, J.R., *Steinbeck on Film* (New York: Frederic Ungar, 1983).

Moers, E., *Literary Women* (Garden City, NY: Doubleday, 1976).

Moore, R.D., 'The Integrity of Job', *CBQ* 45 (1983), pp. 17-31.

Morsberger, R.E., 'Steinbeck's Happy Hookers', *SQ* 9 (1976), pp. 101-15.

—'*East of Eden* on Film', *SQ* 25 (1992), pp. 28-42.

Murphy, R.E., *The Tree of Life: An Exploration of Biblical Wisdom Literature* (AB Reference Library; Garden City, NY: Doubleday, 1990).

—*Ecclesiastes* (WBC, 23A; Dallas: Word Books, 1992).

Murray, H.A., 'In Nomine Diaboli', in Stern (ed.), *Moby-Dick*, pp. 25-34.

Nagel, G.L., 'A Tessara for Frederic Henry: Imagery and Recurrence in *A Farewell to Arms*', in Wagner (ed.), *Ernest Hemingway*, pp. 187-93.

Nagel, J., 'Catherine Barkley and Retrospective Narration in *A Farewell to Arms*', in Wagner (ed.), *Ernest Hemingway*, pp. 171-85.

Newey, K., *Mary Shelley's Frankenstein* (Horizon Studies in Literature; Sydney: University of Sydney Press, 1993).

Ogden, G., *Qoheleth* (Sheffield: JSOT Press, 1987).

Oldsey, B., *Hemingway's Hidden Craft: The Writing of A Farewell to Arms* (University Park: Pennsylvania State University Press, 1979).

Ord, D.R., and R.B. Coote, *The Bible's First History* (Philadelphia: Fortress Press, 1989).

Owens, L., 'The Mirror and the Vamp: Invention, Reflection, and Bad, Bad Cathy Trask in *East of Eden*', in Barbour and Quirk (eds.), *Writing the American Classics*, pp. 235-57.

Paul, S., 'Melville's "The *Town-Ho's* Story"', in Stern (ed.), *Moby-Dick*, pp. 87-92.

Pearsall, R.B., *The Life and Writings of Ernest Hemingway* (Amsterdam: Rodopi, 1973).

Phelan, J., 'Distance, Voice, and Temporal Perspective in Frederic Henry's Narration: Successes, Problems, and Paradox', in Donaldson (ed.), *New Essays*, pp. 53-73.

—'The Concept of Voice, the Voices of Frederic Henry and the Structure of *A Farewell to Arms*', in F. Scafella (ed.), *Hemingway: Essays of Reassessment* (Oxford: Oxford University Press, 1991), pp. 214-32.

Phillips, G.D., *Hemingway and Film* (New York: Frederic Ungar, 1980).

Plimpton, G., 'Ernest Hemingway: The Art of Fiction XXI', *Paris Review* 18 (1958), pp. 60-89.

—'An Interview with Ernest Hemingway', in Bloom (ed.), *Modern Critical Views*, pp. 119-36.

Poovey, M., 'My Hideous Progeny: Mary Shelley and the Feminization of Romanticism', *PMLA* 95 (1980), pp. 332-47.

Powell, D., *The Dilys Powell Film Reader* (Oxford: Oxford University Press, 1992).

Pratt, J.C., *John Steinbeck: A Critical Essay* (CWCPS; Grand Rapids: Eerdmans, 1970).

Prawer, S.S., *Caligari's Children: The Film as Tale of Terror* (Oxford: Oxford University Press, 1980).

Pyper, H., 'The Reader in Pain: Job as Text and Pretext', in Carroll (ed.), *Text as Pretext*, pp. 234-55.

Quinones, R.J., *The Changes of Cain* (Princeton, NJ: Princeton University Press, 1991).

Rad, G. von, *Genesis* (OTL; London: SCM Press, rev. edn, 1972).

—*Wisdom in Israel* (New York: Abingdon Press, 1972).

Rathgab, D., 'Kazan as *Auteur*: The Undiscovered *East of Eden*', *LFQ* 16 (1988), pp. 31-38.

Reed, H., *Moby Dick: A Play for Radio from Herman Melville's Novel* (London: Jonathan Cape, 1947).

Reimann, P.A., 'Am I my Brother's Keeper?', *Int* 24 (1970), pp. 482-91.

Renan, E., *L'antichrist* (Paris: M. Lévy Frères, 1873).

Reynolds, M.S., *Hemingway's First War: The Making of A Farewell to Arms* (Princeton, NJ: Princeton University Press, 1976).

—*The Young Hemingway* (Oxford: Basil Blackwell, 1986).

—*Hemingway: The Paris Years* (Oxford: Basil Blackwell, 1989).

—*Hemingway: The American Homecoming* (Oxford: Basil Blackwell, 1992).

Riley, P.J. (ed.), *Frankenstein* (Universal Filmscripts Series; Classic Horror Films, 1; Absecon, NJ: MagicImage Filmbooks, 1989).

—*The Bride of Frankenstein* (Universal Filmscripts Series; Classic Horror Films, 2; Absecon, NJ: MagicImage Filmbooks, 1989).

Rodd, C.S., 'Which is the Best Commentary?: Job', *ExpTim* 97 (1985–86), pp. 356-60.

—*The Book of Job* (EC; London: Epworth Press, 1990).

Romney, J., 'No End to the Enigma', *The Guardian* (Arts Section, 15 October 1993), p. 6.

Rosenberry, E.H., *Melville* (London: Routledge & Kegan Paul, 1979).

Rosenfeld, W., 'Uncertain Faith: Queequeg's Coffin and Melville's Use of the Bible', *TSLL* 7 (1965), pp. 317-27.

Ross, L., *Portrait of Hemingway* (Harmondsworth: Penguin Books, 1962).

Rovin, J., *The Films of Charlton Heston* (Secaucus, NJ: Citadel Press, 1977).

Rowley, H.H., 'The Book of Job and its Meaning', *BJRL* 41 (1958–59), pp. 167-207.

Rowold, H., 'Leviathan and Job in Job 41:2-3', *JBL* 105 (1986), pp. 104-109.

Rubenstein, M.A., '"My Accursed Origin": The Search for Mother in *Frankenstein*', *StudRom* 15 (1976), p. 165-94.

Russell, H.K., 'The Catharsis in *A Farewell to Arms*', *MFS* 1 (1955), pp. 25-30.

Salmon, R., and G. Elata-Alster, 'Retracing a Writerly Text: In the Footsteps of a Midrashic Sequence on the Creation of the Male and the Female', in Loades and McLain (eds.), *Hermeneutics* , pp. 177-97.

Salters, R.B., 'Qoheleth and the Canon', *ExpTim* 86 (1974–75), pp. 339-42.

Sanderson, S., *Hemingway* (London: Oliver & Boyd, 1961).

Sartre, J.-P., 'Herman Melville's *Moby-Dick*', in Gilmore (ed.), *Moby-Dick*, pp. 94-97.

Sasson, J., *Jonah* (AB, 24B; Garden City, NY: Doubleday, 1990).

Sawyer, J.F.A., 'The Authorship and Structure of the Book of Job', in Livingstone (ed.), *Studia Biblica I*, pp. 253-57.

Schmitt, J.J., 'Like Eve, Like Adam: *mšl* in Gen. 3, 16', *Bib* 72 (1991), pp. 1-22.

Schneider, D.J., 'Hemingway's *A Farewell to Arms*: The Novel as Pure Poetry', in Wagner (ed.), *Ernest Hemingway*, pp. 252-66.

Schwartz, R.M., *Remembering and Repeating: Biblical Creation in Paradise Lost* (Cambridge: Cambridge University Press, 1988).

Scott-Kilver, D., with P.R. Feldman, *The Journals of Mary Shelley 1814–1844* (Oxford: Clarendon Press, 1987), I.

Scott, N.A., Jr, *Ernest Hemingway: A Critical Essay* (CWCPS; Grand Rapids: Eerdmans, 1966).

Scott, R.B.Y., *Proverbs and Ecclesiastes* (AB, 18; Garden City, NY: Doubleday, 1965).

Seed, D., *The Fiction of Joseph Heller: Against the Grain* (London: Macmillan, 1989).

Sewall, R.B., 'The Book of Job', in P.S. Sanders (ed.), *Twentieth-Century Interpretations of the Book of Job* (Englewood Cliffs, NJ: Prentice-Hall, 1968), pp. 21-35.

—'*Moby-Dick*', in Gilmore (ed.), *Moby-Dick*, pp. 42-54.

Seymour-Smith, M., *Guide to Modern World Literature* (London: Macmillan, 1975).

Shelley, M., *Frankenstein, or, The Modern Prometheus: The 1818 Text* (ed. J. Rieger; Chicago: University of Chicago Press, 1982).

—*Frankenstein* (ed. M. Hindle; London: Penguin Books, 1985).

—*The Journals of Mary Shelley 1814–1844* (ed. P.R. Feldman and D. Scott-Kilvert; Oxford: Clarendon Press, 1987), I.

Sheppard, G.T., 'The Epilogue to Qoheleth as Theological Commentary', *CBQ* 39 (1977), pp. 182-89.

Sherwin, P., '*Frankenstein*: Creation as Chaos', *PMLA* 96 (1981), pp. 883-903.

Shipman, D., *The Story of Cinema* (London: Hodder & Stoughton, 1982).

Simon, N., *God's Favourite* (London: Samuel French, 1975).

Slotkin, R., '*Moby-Dick*: The American National Epic', in Gilmore (ed.), *Moby-Dick*, pp. 13-26.

Small, C., *Ariel Like a Harpy: Shelley, Mary and Frankenstein* (London: Gollancz, 1972).

Smith, H.N., 'The Image of Society in *Moby-Dick*', in Gilmore (ed.), *Moby-Dick*, pp. 27-41.

Smith, P., 'Almost all is Vanity: A Note on Nine Rejected Titles for *A Farewell to Arms*', *HR* 2 (1982), pp. 74-76.

Solomon, P.C., *Dickens and Melville in their Time* (New York: Columbia University Press, 1975).

Spanier, S.W., 'Hemingway's Unknown Soldier: Catherine Barkley, the Critics and the Great War', in Donaldson (ed.), *New Essays*, pp. 75-108.

Spark, M., *The Only Problem* (London: Penguin Books, 1984).

—*Mary Shelley* (London: Constable, 1988).

Speiser, E.A., *Genesis* (AB, 1; Garden City, NY: Doubleday, 1964).

Stanonik, J., *Moby Dick: The Myth and the Symbol* (Ljubljana: Ljubljana University Press, 1962).

Steinbeck, E., with R. Wallstein, *Steinbeck: A Life in Letters* (London: Heinemann, 1975).

Steinbeck, J., *East of Eden* (London: Mandarin Books, 1990).

—*Journey of a Novel* (London: Mandarin Books, 1991).

Stephens, R.O., 'Hemingway and Stendhal: The Matrix of *A Farewell to Arms*', *PMLA* 88 (1973), pp. 271-80.

Stern, M.R. (ed.), *Discussions of Moby-Dick* (Boston: D.C. Heath & Co., 1960).

Sterrenburg, L., 'Mary Shelley's Monster: Politics and Psyche in *Frankenstein*', in Levine and Knoepflmacher (eds.), *The Endurance of Frankenstein*, pp. 143-72.

Stetler, C., and G. Locklin, 'De-Coding the Hero in Hemingway's Fiction', *HR* 5 (1979), pp. 2-10.

Stewart, G.R., 'The Two *Moby-Dicks*', *AL* 5 (1954), pp. 417-18.

Stewart, R., 'The Vision of Evil in Hawthorne and Melville', in N.A. Scott, Jr (ed.), *The Tragic Vision and the Christian Faith* (New York: Association Press, 1957), pp. 238-63.

Stoker, J., *The Illustrated Frankenstein* (Newton Abbot: Westbridge Books, 1980).

Stolzfus, B., 'A Sliding Discourse: The Language of *A Farewell to Arms*', in Donaldson (ed.), *New Essays*, pp. 109-36.

Stout, J., 'Melville's Use of the Book of Job', *NCF* 25 (1970–71), pp. 69-83.

Straumann, H., *American Literature in the Twentieth Century* (London: Arrow Books, 1962).

Sunstein, E.W., *Mary Shelley: Romance and Reality* (Baltimore: The Johns Hopkins University Press, 1989).

Tannenbaum, L., 'From Filthy Type to Truth: Miltonic Myth in *Frankenstein*', *K-SJ* 26 (1977), pp. 101-13.

Thiselton, A.C., *New Horizons in Hermeneutics* (London: HarperCollins, 1992).

Thompson, L., *Melville's Quarrel with God* (Princeton, NJ: Princeton University Press, 1952).

Thornburg, M.K.P., *The Monster in the Mirror: Gender and the Sentimental/Gothic Myth in Frankenstein* (Ann Arbor, MI: UMI Research Press, 1987).

Tillotson, M., '"A Forced Solitude": Mary Shelley and the Creation of Frankenstein's Monster', in J.E. Fleenor (ed.), *Female Gothic* (London: Eden Press, 1983), pp. 167-75.

Timmerman, J.H., *John Steinbeck's Fiction: The Aesthetics of the Road Taken* (Norman: University of Oklahoma Press, 1986).

—'John Steinbeck's Use of the Bible: A Descriptive Bibliography of the Critical Tradition', *SQ* 21 (1988), pp. 24-39.

Tomalin, C., *The Life and Death of Mary Wollstonecraft* (London: Penguin Books, 1985).

Trible, P., *God and the Rhetoric of Sexuality* (Philadelphia: Fortress Press, 1978).

Veeder, W., *Mary Shelley and Frankenstein: The Fate of Androgyny* (Chicago: University of Chicago Press, 1986).

Wagner, L. (ed.), *Ernest Hemingway: Six Decades of Criticism* (East Lansing: Michigan State University Press, 1987).

Wallstein, R., with E. Steinbeck, *Steinbeck: A Life in Letters* (London: Heinemann, 1975).

Warren, R.P., 'Ernest Hemingway', in Bloom (ed.), *Modern Critical Views*, pp. 35-62.

Watters, R.E., 'The Meanings of the White Whale', in Stern (ed.), *Moby-Dick*, pp. 77-86.

—'Melville's "Isolatoes"', in Stern (ed.), *Moby-Dick*, pp. 107-14.

Wedeles, J., with B. Everest, 'The Neglected Rib: Women in *East of Eden*', *SQ* 21 (1988), pp. 13-23.

Weeks, R.P. (ed.), *Hemingway: A Collection of Critical Essays* (Englewood Cliffs, NJ: Prentice-Hall, 1962).

Wiesel, E., *Night* (London: Fontana Books, 1958).

Welles, O., *Moby Dick Rehearsed: A Drama in Two Acts* (London: Samuel French, 1965).

West, R.B., Jr, 'The Biological Trap', in Weeks (ed.), *Hemingway*, pp. 139-51.

Westermann, C., *Genesis 1–11: A Commentary* (London: SPCK, 1984).

Whitley, C.F., *Koheleth: His Language and Thought* (Berlin: de Gruyter, 1979).

Whitlow, R., *Cassandra's Daughters: The Women in Hemingway* (London: Greenwood Press, 1984).

Whybray, R.N., 'Qoheleth, Preacher of Joy', *JSOT* 23 (1982), pp. 87-98.

—'Ecclesiastes 1.5-7 and the Wonders of Nature', *JSOT* 41 (1988), pp. 105-12.

—*Ecclesiastes* (NCB; Grand Rapids: Eerdmans, 1989).

—'Ecclesiastes', in R.J. Coggins and J.L. Houlden (eds.), *A Dictionary of Biblical Interpretation* (London: SCM Press, 1990), pp. 183-84.

Williams, J.G., 'What Does it Profit a Man?: The Wisdom of Koheleth', in J.L Crenshaw (ed.), *Studies in Ancient Israelite Wisdom* (New York: Ktav, 1976), pp. 375-89.

Wilson, E., 'On Hemingway (1939)', in J. Meyers (ed.), *Hemingway: The Critical Heritage* (London: Routledge & Kegan Paul, 1982), pp. 297-303.

Wilson, J.V.K., 'A Return to the Problems of Behemoth and Leviathan', *VT* 25 (1975), pp. 1-14.

Wolde, E. van, 'The Story of Cain and Abel: A Narrative Study', *JSOT* 52 (1991), pp. 25-41.

Woodson, T., 'Ahab's Greatness: Prometheus as Narcissus', *ELH* 33 (1966), pp. 351-69.

Wright, A.G., 'The Riddle of the Sphinx: The Structure of the Book of Qoheleth', *CBQ* 30 (1968), pp. 313-34.

Wright, C.H.H., *The Book of Koheleth, Commonly Called Ecclesiastes, Considered in Relation to Modern Criticism and to the Doctrines of Modern Pessimism* (London: Hodder & Stoughton, 1883).

Wright, G., *Horrorshows: The A-to-Z of Horror in Film, TV, Radio and Theatre* (London: David & Charles, 1986).

Wright, N., *Melville's Use of the Bible* (Durham, NC: Duke University Press, 1949).

—'*Moby-Dick*: Jonah's or Job's Whale?', *AL* 37 (1965), pp. 190-95.

Wright, T.R., *Theology and Literature* (Signposts in Theology; Oxford: Basil Blackwell, 1988).

York, A.D., 'Adam', in D.L. Lyle (ed.), *A Dictionary of Biblical Tradition in English Literature* (Grand Rapids: Eerdmans, 1992), pp. 15-21.

Young, J.D., 'The Nine Gams of the *Pequod*', in Stern (ed.), *Moby-Dick*, pp. 98-106.

Young, P., *Ernest Hemingway: A Reconsideration* (University Park: Pennsylvania State University Press, 1966).

Young, W.A., 'Leviathan in the Book of Job and *Moby-Dick*', *Soundings* 25 (1982), pp. 388-401.

Yu, B., 'Ishmael's Equal Eye: The Source of Balance in *Moby-Dick*', *ELH* 32 (1965), pp. 110-25.

INDEXES

INDEX OF REFERENCES

INDEX OF NAMES